Study Guide and Workbook

for use with

Foundations of Financial Management

Tenth Edition

Stanley B. Block
Texas Christian University

Geoffrey A. Hirt
DePaul University

Prepared by
Dwight C. Anderson
Louisiana Tech University

Boston   Burr Ridge, IL   Dubuque, IA   Madison, WI   New York   San Francisco   St. Louis
Bangkok   Bogotá   Caracas   Kuala Lumpur   Lisbon   London   Madrid   Mexico City
Milan   Montreal   New Delhi   Santiago   Seoul   Singapore   Sydney   Taipei   Toronto

McGraw-Hill Higher Education

A Division of The McGraw·Hill Companies

Study Guide and Workbook for use with
FOUNDATIONS OF FINANCIAL MANAGEMENT
Stanley B. Block and Geoffrey A. Hirt

Published by McGraw-Hill/Irwin, an imprint of the McGraw-Hill Companies, Inc., 1221 Avenue of the Americas, New York, NY 10020. Copyright © 2002, 2000, 1996, 1994, 1992, 1989, 1987, 1984, 1981, 1978 by the McGraw-Hill Companies, Inc. All rights reserved.

4 5 6 7 8 9 0 CUS/CUS 0 9 8 7 6 5 4 3 2

ISBN 0-07-242280-7

www.mhhe.com

To the Student:

The purpose of this book is to assist you in your study of the *Foundations of Financial Management*. To maximize the assistance provided by the *Study Guide*, you should formulate a plan of study. A suggested plan follows:

1. Read the summary of the textbook chapter provided in the *Study Guide*. The summary is a succinct statement of the major issues covered in the corresponding chapter of the textbook.

2. Read through the outline of the text chapter that follows the summary in the *Study Guide*. The outline includes the most significant components of the chapter.

3. Carefully read the text chapter. Be especially attentive to the chapter components identified in the *Study Guide* outline.

4. Quickly review the textbook chapter by again reading the summary and outline in the *Study Guide*.

5. Test your knowledge of the chapter concepts by answering the multiple choice questions in the *Study Guide*. If you incorrectly answer several questions, the text chapter should be read again.

6. Work the problems in the *Study Guide*. It is suggested that you thoroughly attempt to solve the problems before referring to the solutions provided. If your answers differ from the solutions, study the solutions to detect the errors (yours or mine) and rework the problems correctly.

7. Work the end of chapter problems in *Foundations of Financial Management*. You should strive to solve the problems without referring to the author's examples. If you cannot do so, reread the applicable portion of the text.

A study guide can be a valuable learning aid when used properly. Remember--it should be used as a supplement to the textbook, not as a substitute.

Dwight C. Anderson

Contents

Chapter 1

Summary: This chapter traces the evolution and interrelationships of finance as a field of study and the role of the financial manager in a dynamic economy.

I.   The Field of Finance. [p. 6]

   A.   The field of finance is closely related to economics and accounting.
      1.   Economics provides a structure for decision-making in such areas as:
         a.   Risk analysis.
         b.   Price theory.
         c.   Comparative return analysis.
      2.   Economics provides the broad picture of the economic environment including the:
         a.   Institutional structure of the Federal Reserve System.
         b.   Commercial banking system.
         c.   Interrelationships between various economic sectors.
      3.   Accounting, sometimes said to be the language of finance, provides financial data through income statements, balance sheets, and the statement of cash flows.
      4.   Finance links economic theory with accounting data. All corporate managers must be familiar with such data in order to assess the financial performance of the firm.

   B.   The demand for financial management skills exists in many sectors of a global society including corporate management, financial institutions, and consulting.

II. Finance as a field of study has evolved over time in response to changing business management needs. [p. 6]

   A.   Finance achieved recognition as a separate field of study in response to the creation of giant corporations at the turn of the century.

   B.   The worst depression in United States' history caused a shift in emphasis from rapid merger growth to preservation of capital, liquidity, reorganization, and the bankruptcy process.

   C.   The most significant step in the evolution of contemporary financial management began in the mid-1950s. Emphasis was placed on the analytically determined employment of resources within the firm. The decision-making nature of financial management was manifested in the enthusiasm for the study of:
      1.   Allocation of **financial capital** for the purchase of **real capital** (plant and equipment).
      2.   Efficient utilization of current assets.
      3.   Capital structure theory.
      4.   Dividend policy.

   D.   The analytical orientation of financial management focused on risk-return relationships and the desire to maximize return at a given level of risk.

   E.   The rapid **inflation** experienced in the economy in the 1970s and early 1980s followed by a lengthy period of **disinflation** has impacted all areas of financial decision-making.

   F.   The technological changes in the 1990s rapidly impacted the financial management functions of business firms. E-commerce accelerated cash flows and significantly affected the management of inventory and accounts receivable. Financial managers must remain sensitive to the impacts of e-commerce and the Internet on finance functions in the 21st century.

III. Functions of Financial Management: A financial manager is responsible for financing an efficient level and composition of assets by obtaining financing through the most appropriate means.   [p. 8]

   A. Daily financial management activities.
      1. Credit management.
      2. Inventory control.
      3. Receipt and disbursement of funds.

   B. Less-routine activities.
      1. Sale of stocks and bonds.
      2. Capital budgeting.
      3. Dividend decisions.

   C. Forms of organization: The finance function may be carried out within a number of different forms of organizations. [p. 11]
      1. **Sole proprietorship**.
         a. Single ownership.
         b. Simplicity of decision making.
         c. Low organizational and operating costs.
         d. Unlimited liability.
         e. Earnings of the proprietorship are taxed as personal earnings of the individual owner.
      2. **Partnership**.
         a. Two or more partners.
         b. Usually formed by *articles of partnership* agreement.
         c. Unlimited liability for all partners unless a *limited partnership* is formed which provides limited liability for one or more partners. At least one partner must be a general partner.
         d. Earnings are taxed as personal earnings of partners.
      3. **Corporation**.
         a. Most important form of business in terms of revenue and profits.
         b. Legal entity.
         c. Formed by *articles of incorporation*.
         d. Stockholders (owners) have limited liability.
         e. Easy divisibility of ownership.
         f. Managed by the board of directors.
         g. Double taxation of earnings: Earnings of the corporation are subject to the corporate income tax; dividends (distributed net income) are subject to personal taxation. Small subchapter S corporations, however, avoid the double taxation disadvantage.

IV. Goals of Financial Management. [pp. 11-15]

   A. Are the goals of the three basic forms of business organizations the same? Does the management of a corporation make the same decision that a sole proprietor would make?

   B. **Agency theory**, a major area of financial research, focuses on the relationship between the owners of a firm and the managers of the firm.

   C. Because of their large percentage of ownership, mutual funds and pension funds can influence the decisions of major U.S. companies.

   D. Alternative goals.
      1. Profit maximization (or maximizing earnings per share) has several drawbacks.

        a.   Does not capture risk effects.
        b.   Fails to consider the timing of the benefits.
        c.   Variations in definitions of profit cause measurement problems.
        d.   Inflation and international currency transactions complicate the issue.

      2.   **Maximization of owner's wealth** or **shareholder wealth maximization** if the firm is a corporation is the goal of the firm. **Valuation** is the key concept of this goal. The valuation process captures the **timing** of the expected **cash flows** and the **risk** associated with the cash flows.

  E.   Incentives for management to act in the best interest of the owners (shareholders).
      1.   The only way for management to maintain its position over the long run is to be sensitive to shareholder concerns.
      2.   Stock option incentives.
      3.   Institutional influence.

V.   Social Responsibility and Ethical Behavior. [p. 15]

  A.   Is the goal of shareholder wealth maximization consistent with social responsibility?
      1.   In most cases the answer is "yes." Maximizing shareholder wealth attracts capital and provides employment and other benefits to the community (national, state, local, etc.).
      2.   Some socially desirable actions may be less compatible with shareholder wealth maximization. For example, pollution controls, equitable hiring practices, and fair pricing standards may be inconsistent with achieving maximum market value. Such actions may have to be mandatory.

  B.   Unethical and/or illegal financial practices may lessen confidence in U.S. securities markets and make it more difficult for managers to maximize shareholder wealth. During the 1980s and 1990s, illegal **insider trading** activities ~~have~~ made news headlines. Insider trading occurs when individuals seek to profit from trading using information that has not been made available to the public.

VI.   The Role of Financial Markets. [pp. 15-17]

  A.   **Financial markets** are the meeting places for people, corporations, and institutions that either need money or have money to lend or invest.
      1.   National, state, and local governments seek funds in **public financial markets**.
      2.   Corporations raise funds in corporate financial markets.

  B.   Financial markets may be classified in several ways.
      1.   Domestic.
      2.   International.
      3.   Corporate.
      4.   Government.
      5.   Money and capital.
         a.   Markets that focus on short-term securities that have a life of a year or less are called **money markets**.
         b.   **Capital markets** are defined as markets where securities have a life of more than one year. Capital markets are further classified as **intermediate** (1-10 years) and **long-term** (more than 10 years).

  C.   Financial markets allocate capital to the highest bidder within a risk-return framework. Individuals possessing capital seek to earn the highest rate of return at a given level of risk. Prices of securities in the market reflect the collective judgement of all participants. Securities price movements provide feedback to corporate managers indicating the market's evaluation of their activities. Corporations raise capital by selling new securities in the **primary market**. Securities previously sold by corporations trade in the **secondary market** between investors.

    D.   In addition to the pressure placed on corporate management through adjustment of securities prices, some investors seek to directly influence corporate boards of directors. Institutional investors have used their influence to bring about the **restructuring** of a number of firms. Restructuring may be manifested by a change in the capital structure of the firm, a merger or acquisition, selling off low-return divisions, reductions in the workforce, and even the removal of the existing management team.

    E.   The **internationalization of financial markets** is necessary for the support of expanding international product markets. Modern corporate financial managers must understand international capital flows, electronic funds transfer, foreign currency hedging strategies, and many other global trading factors.

    F.   The Internet and changes in the capital markets: Technology has significantly impacted capital markets. [p. 18]
        1.   Cost reduction for trading securities which has led to consolidations of markets and brokerage firms.
        2.   Creation of new electronic markets.
        3.   Internet trading provided by discount brokerage firms has forced full-service brokers to offer less profitable Internet trading to their clients.

VII.   Format of the Text. [pp. 18-19]

    A.   Introduction: An examination of the goals of financial management within an analytical framework.

    B.   Financial analysis and planning.
        1.   Review of accounting relationships with finance.
        2.   Ratio analysis.
        3.   Construction of budgets and pro forma statements.
        4.   Operating and financial leverage.

    C.   Working capital management: Techniques for managing the levels of current assets and short-term financing in a risk-return context.

    D.   Capital budgeting and related valuation concepts.
        1.   Time value of money.
        2.   Cost of capital.
        3.   Capital budgeting techniques.

    E.   Long-term financing: An analysis of the characteristics of the structure, participants, and instruments of the capital markets.

    F.   Corporate growth through mergers: An integration of financial management concepts within the framework of corporate growth strategy.

    G.   International financial management: An examination of the complex, risky environment of international finance.

Chapter 1 - Multiple Choice Questions

1. Profits of a sole proprietorship are: [p. 9]
    a. Taxed as income of the individual owner.
    b. Taxed as business income and again as personal income of the proprietor.
    c. Not taxed if retained in the business.
    d. Taxed at the same rates as earnings of corporations.
    e. None of the above are correct.

2. Corporate managers: [pp. 11-13]
    a. Ignore the desires of stockholders.
    b. May make decisions that are contrary to the interests of stockholders.
    c. Are sensitive to investors risk-return preferences when pursuing the goals of financial management.
    d. Are insensitive to the desires of stockholders.
    e. Both *b* and *c* are correct.

3. The goal of financial management is: [p. 12]
    a. To maximize profit.
    b. To maximize cash flow.
    c. To maximize revenues (sales).
    d. To maximize owners' wealth.
    e. To maximize earnings per share.

4. Which of the following business forms exposes all owners to unlimited liability? [p. 9]
    a. Partnerships
    b. Proprietorships
    c. Corporations
    d. Limited partnerships
    e. Both *a* and *b* are correct.

5. Which of the following changes are related to the development of the Internet and e-commerce. [pp. 8, 18]
    a. Creation of new electronic markets
    b. An increase in the speed of cash flows through business firms
    c. A decrease in the cost of trading securities
    d. Consolidation of securities markets
    e. All of the above are correct.

6. Daily activities of the financial manager include: [p. 8]
    a. Credit management.
    b. Inventory control.
    c. Capital budgeting.
    d. Receipt of funds.
    e. Answers *a, b,* and *d* are correct.

7. Insider trading: [p. 14]
    a. Contributes to market efficiency because all information is reflected in the price of securities.
    b. Is illegal.
    c. Is protected against by the FDIC.
    d. Has no negative impact on stockholders.
    e. None of the above are correct.

8. Which of the following has been the result of institutional investors influencing the decisions of corporate boards of directors? [pp. 16-17]
   a. Incorporation
   b. Globalization
   c. Registration with the Securities Exchange Commission
   d. Allocation of capital
   e. Restructuring

9. New common stock is sold by corporations in the _____ market and individuals trade securities in the _____ market. [p. 16]
   a. Money; primary
   b. Secondary; capital
   c. Primary; secondary
   d. International; domestic
   e. Government; corporate

10. Select the pair of terms that indicates a correct match. [pp. 9-10]
    a. Corporation; limited partnership
    b. Partnership; articles of incorporation
    c. Proprietorship; limited liability
    d. Subchapter S corporation; personal taxation only
    e. Partnership; double taxation

Multiple Choice Answer Key - Chapter 1

1. a	2. e	3. d	4. e	5. e
6. e	7. b	8. e	9. c	10. d

Summary: An understanding of financial statements is a prerequisite for financial management decision making. In this chapter the characteristics of three basic financial statements--**income statement**, **balance sheet**, and **statement of cash flows**--are presented. The impact of income tax provisions on financial decisions is also examined.

I.   Financial Statements

    A.   The income statement. [p. 28]
        1.   The income statement begins with the aggregate amount of sales (revenues) that are generated within a specific period of time.
        2.   The various expenses that occur in generating the sales are subtracted in stair-step fashion to arrive at the net income for the defined period.
        3.   The separation of the expense categories such as cost of goods sold, selling and administrative expenses, depreciation, interest and taxes enables the management to assess the relative importance and appropriateness of the expenditures in producing each level of sales.
        4.   The "bottom line" value, net income, is the aggregate amount available to the owners.
        5.   Net income is converted from an aggregate value to an **earnings per share (EPS)** value by dividing net income by the number of shares of outstanding stock.
        6.   The EPS is a measurement of the return available to providers of equity capital to the firm. The return to the providers of debt capital, interest, appears earlier in the income statement as a tax-deductible expense.
        7.   The earnings per share may be converted to a measure of current value through application of the price/earnings (P/E) ratio.
        8.   The P/E ratio is best used as a *relative* measure of value because the numerator, price, is based on the future and the denominator, earnings, is a current measure.
        9.   The income statement reflects only income occurring to the individual or the business firm from verifiable transactions as opposed to the economist's definition of income.

    B.   Balance sheet. [p. 31]
        1.   Whereas the income statement provides a summary of financial transactions for a *period* of time, the balance sheet portrays the cumulative results of transactions at a *point* in time. The balance sheet may present the position of the firm as a result of transactions for 6 months, 25 years, or other periods.
        2.   The balance sheet is divided into two broad categories. The assets employed in the operations of the firm compose one category while the other, liabilities and net worth, is composed of the sources of financing for the employed assets.
        3.   Within the asset category, the assets are listed in their order of liquidity.
            a.   Cash (including demand deposits).
            b.   Marketable securities: Investments of temporarily excess cash in highly liquid securities.
            c.   Accounts receivable.
            d.   Inventory.
            e.   Prepaid expenses: Future expense items that have already been paid.
            f.   Investments: Investments in securities and other assets for longer than one operating cycle.
            g.   Plant and equipment adjusted for accumulated depreciation.

4. The various sources of financing of a firm are listed in their order of maturity. Those sources that mature within the defined period, current liabilities, are listed first. The more permanent debt and equity sources follow.
    a. Accounts payable.
    b. Notes payable.
    c. Accrued expenses: An obligation to pay is incurred but payment has not been made.
    d. Long-term debt: All or a majority of the principal will be paid beyond the current period.
    e. Preferred stock.
    f. Common stock accounts:
        (1) Common stock (par value).
        (2) Capital paid in excess of par.
        (3) Retained earnings.
5. Confusing balance-sheet-related terms.
    a. Retained earnings: All of the assets of a firm are listed on the *asset* side of the balance sheet, yet many individuals envision a pile of money when the term **retained earnings** is used. Retained earnings is simply a cumulative total of the earnings of the firm since its beginning until the date of the balance sheet that have not been paid to the owners. Earnings that are retained are used to purchase assets, pay liabilities, throw a big party for the management, etc. Regardless, there is no money available from a "container" labeled retained earnings.
    b. Net worth or book value of the firm is composed of the various common equity accounts and represents the net contributions of the owners to the business. **Book value** is a historical value and does not necessarily coincide with the **market value** of the owners' equity.
6. Limitations of the balance sheet: Values are recorded at cost; replacement cost of some assets, particularly plant and equipment, may greatly exceed their recorded value. The Financial Accounting Standards Board (FASB) issued a ruling in October 1979 that required many large companies to disclose inflation-adjusted accounting data in their annual reports. However, the standard is no longer in force, and the inclusion of inflation-adjusted data in financial reports is purely a voluntary act.

C. Statement of cash flows. [p. 34]
    1. In November 1987 the accounting profession replaced the statement of changes in financial position with the Statement of Cash Flows as a required financial statement.
    2. The new statement emphasizes the critical nature of cash flow to operations of the firm.
    3. The three primary sections of the statement of cash flows are:
        a. Cash flows from operating activities.
        b. Cash flows from investing activities.
        c. Cash flows from financing activities.
    4. Income from operations may be translated from an accrual basis to a cash basis in two ways to obtain **cash flow from operations**.
        a. Direct method: Each and every item on the income statement is adjusted from accrual accounting to cash accounting.
        b. Indirect method: A less tedious process than the direct method is usually preferred. Net income is used as the starting point and adjustments are made to convert net income to cash flows from operations. Beginning with net income:
            (1) *Add* depreciation for the current period, decreases in individual current asset accounts (other than cash), and increases in current liabilities;
            (2) *Subtract* increases in current asset accounts (other than cash) and decreases in current liabilities.

8

      c.   Students should note that depreciation for the period is treated as a source of cash only because of the deduction of depreciation expense in calculating net income. Depreciation, a noncash expense, reduces net income but not cash balances. In order to accurately determine cash flow from operations, depreciation for the period must be added to net income.

  5.   **Cash flow from investing** is found by summing the changes of investment in securities and plant and equipment. Increases are uses of funds; decreases are sources of funds.

  6.   **Cash flow from financing activities** is found by summing the sale or retirement of corporate securities and dividends. The sale of securities is a source of funds, and the retirement of securities and payment of dividends are uses of funds.

  7.   Cash flows from operations, cash flows from investing, and cash flows from financing are combined to arrive at the statement of cash flows. The net increase or decrease shown in the statement of cash flows will be equal to the change in the cash balance on the balance sheet.

D.   Free cash flow. [p. 42]

  1.   **Free cash flow** is available for **special financial activities** such as leveraged buy-outs.

  2.   Free cash flow = cash flow from operating activities - capital expenditures required to maintain the productive capacity of the firm - dividends necessary to maintain the necessary payout on common stock and to cover any preferred stock obligation.

E.   Income tax considerations. [pp. 42-44]

  1.   Most financial decisions are influenced by federal income tax considerations.

      a.   Personal taxes at varying rates apply to earnings of proprietors and partners.

      b.   Corporate earnings are subject to taxation at two levels--at the corporate level and at the personal level when received as dividends.

  2.   The aftertax cost of a tax-deductible business expense is equal to the (expense) X (1 - tax rate).

  3.   Although depreciation is a noncash expense, it does affect cash flow by reducing taxes. The reduction in cash outflow for taxes resulting from depreciation charges may be computed by multiplying the (depreciation expense) x (tax rate).

Chapter 2 - Multiple Choice Questions

1.   The financial statement that reflects the profitability of a firm over a period of time is the: [p. 28]
    a.   Balance sheet.
    b.   Income statement.
    c.   Statement of cash flows.
    d.   Income tax return.
    e.   None of the above are correct.

2.   Assuming a tax rate of 30%, the aftertax cost of $1,000,000 in interest and $1,000,000 in dividends respectively is: [p. 43]
    a. $1,000,000; $1,000,000.
    b. $700,000; $1,000,000.
    c. $700,000; $700,000.
    d. $1,000,000; $700,000.
    e.   None of the above are correct.

3.   If a firm has retained earnings of $1,500,000 on its balance sheet, which of the following statements is correct? [p. 33]
   a.   The firm may get $1,500,000 in cash from retained earnings.
   b.   The firm has a market value of at least $1,500,000.
   c.   The firm has retained $1,500,000 of earnings since the firm's beginning until the date of the balance sheet.
   d.   The assets of the firm are worth at least $1,500,000.
   e.   All of the above are correct.

4.   Temporarily, excess cash will often be invested in: [p. 32]
   a.   Inventory.
   b.   Accounts receivable.
   c.   Common stock.
   d.   Accounts payable.
   e.   Marketable securities.

5.   The depreciation expense shown on the income statement: [pp. 40-42]
   a.   Is equal to the accumulated depreciation on the balance sheet.
   b.   Will reduce the tax liability of the firm.
   c.   Is a noncash expense.
   d.   Both *b* and *c* are correct.
   e.   Answers *a*, *b*, and *c* are correct.

6.   Assets on the balance sheet are listed in order of: [p. 32]
   a.   Age.
   b.   Amount.
   c.   Importance.
   d.   Liquidity.
   e.   Market value.

7.   The Statement of Cash Flows is composed of cash flow from operations, cash flow from financing activities, and: [p. 35]
   a.   Free cash flow.
   b.   Cash flow from changes in working capital.
   c.   Cash flow from depreciation.
   d.   Cash flow from investing activities.
   e.   All of the above are correct.

8.   Which of the following appropriately describe the correct relationship between the book value and market value of a firm's assets? [p. 33]
   a.   Market value will be greater than book value.
   b.   Book value will be greater than market value.
   c.   Market value will equal book value.
   d.   Market value may be more or less than book value.
   e.   None of the above are correct.

9.   Free cash flow is equal to cash flow from operations: [p. 42]
   a.   Plus capital expenditures to maintain productive capacity and dividends.
   b.   Minus dividends.
   c.   Minus capital expenditures to maintain productive capacity and dividends.
   d.   Minus depreciation.
   e.   Plus depreciation and dividends.

10. The price earnings ratio of a firm is found by: [pp. 28-29]
    a. Dividing the market price per share of stock by the earnings per share.
    b. Multiplying the market price per share of stock by the payout ratio.
    c. Dividing the earnings per share by the market price per share of stock.
    d. Dividing the market price per share of stock by the book value per share.
    e. Multiplying the P/E times E.

Multiple Choice Answer Key - Chapter 2

1. b	2. b	3. c	4. e	5. d
6. d	7. d	8. d	9. c	10. a

Chapter 2 - Problems

2-1. Given the information below, complete the income statement for DALIA Corporation.

Shares outstanding	100,000
Earnings per share	$6
Taxes	40%

DALIA CORPORATION
Income Statement
For the Year Ended December 31, 2002

Sales	$
Cost of goods sold	8,000,000
Gross profit	$
Selling and administrative expense	1,150,000
Depreciation expense	250,000
Operating profit	$
Interest expense	200,000
Earnings before taxes	$
Taxes	
Net profit	$

2-2. DALIA Corporation (2-1) has 12,000 shares of preferred stock outstanding with an annual dividend of $4 per share. The firm also has 100,000 shares of common stock outstanding and follows a 50% payout policy.

(a) Calculate the earnings per share and dividends per share for common stockholders of Dalia Corporation.
(b) What was the increase in retained earnings for the year?

2-3. **(a)** Using the Sources (S) and Uses (U) information provided below, construct the year-end 2002 balance sheet for the Kroll Corporation.

Assets	Year-End 2001	Year-End 2002	Change	Source (S) or Use (U)
Current Assets:				
Cash	$ 200,000		$ 20,000	S
Marketable securities	30,000		10,000	S
Accounts receivable (net)	440,000		50,000	U
Inventory	520,000		70,000	U
Prepaid expenses	35,000		5,000	S
Total Current Assets	$1,225,000			
Investments	$ 45,000		10,000	S
Plant and equipment	1,600,000			
Less: Accumulated depreciation	600,000			
Net plant and equipment	1,000,000		200,000	U
Total Assets	$2,270,000			
Liabilities and Stockholders' Equity				
Current Liabilities:				
Accounts payable	$ 352,000		$ 68,000	S
Notes payable	44,000		6,000	U
Accrued expenses	80,000		10,000	S
Total Current Liabilities	$ 476,000			
Long-Term Liabilities:				
Bonds payable, 2019	330,000		---	
Total Liabilities	$ 806,000			
Stockholders' Equity:				
Preferred stock, $100 par value	$ 100,000		---	S
Common stock, $1 par value	400,000		$100,000	S
Capital paid in excess of par	175,000		50,000	S
Retained earnings	789,000		53,000	S
Total Stockholders' Equity	$1,464,000			
Total Liabilities and Stockholders' Equity	$2,270,000			

(b) Prepare a Statement of Cash Flows for the Kroll Corporation that reflects the following:

(1) Net income = $114,000
(2) Dividends = $61,000
(3) Gross additions to plant and equipment = $500,000
(4) Depreciation expense = $300,000

2-4. Given the information below, prepare a balance sheet for Zhong Manufacturing as of December 31, 2002.

Total current assets = $11,800,000
Cash = ____?____
Inventory = $5,800,000

12

Accounts payable = $4,200,000
Gross fixed assets = $15,000,000
Stockholders' equity = $6,450,000
Accrued expenses = $600,000
Notes payable = $3,800,000
Taxes payable = $200,000
Retained earnings = ___?___
Accrued depreciation = $6,800,000
Long-term debt = $4,750,000
Accounts receivable = $3,600,000
Common stock $1 par value = $2,000,000
Marketable securities = $2,000,000
Capital paid in excess of par = $1,000,000

2-5.   Using the information in 2-4 above, compute the following values for Zhong Manufacturing.

(a)   Book value per share.
(b)   Market value per share if the P/E ratio is 12 and Zhong's total earnings are $5,000,000.
(c)   The ratio of market value per share to book value per share.

2-6.   Suppose the earnings of Zhong Manufacturing (*2-5* above) rise to $6,000,000 but their P/E ratio declines to 10.

(a)   What is the market value per share of common stock?
(b)   What is the total market value of the common stock of Zhong Manufacturing?

2-7.   The FMA Corporation ended 2000 operations with the following balance sheet.

FMA CORPORATION
Balance Sheet
December 31, 2000

Current Assets			Current Liabilities		
Cash	$ 15,000		Accounts payable	$ 60,000	
Marketable securities	20,000		Notes payable	50,000	
Accounts receivable	50,000		Total current liabilities	$110,000	
Inventory	80,000				
Total current assets	$165,000		Long-term bonds	$ 75,000	
Fixed Assets			Stockholders' Equity		
Gross plant & equipment . . $250,000			Common stock	$ 60,000	
Less: accum. depr. 75,000			Paid-in-capital	40,000	
Net plant & equipment	$175,000		Retained earnings	55,000	
Total assets	$340,000		Total liabilities & equity	$340,000	

FMA's sales in 2001 were $360,000 with cost of goods sold averaging 65% of sales. Selling and administrative expenses were $36,000 and depreciation expense for the year was $50,000. On December 31, 2001, the firm paid the interest (10%) on its bank loan (notes

13

payable) for the year and also renewed the loan after paying $10,000 on the principal balance. Interest at a 12% rate was paid to the firm's bondholders. During 2001, accounts receivable declined by 5%, but inventory increased by 10%. A rise of 12% in accounts payable provided financing for much of the added inventory. The firm purchased a new machine for $65,000 in October and paid a total cash dividend of $10,805 at the end of the year. The management elected not to raise any additional external capital in 2001, but all of the marketable securities were converted to cash and used for business operations. The firm is in a 15% tax bracket.

(a)   Prepare an income statement for 2001.
(b)   Prepare a balance sheet as of December 31, 2001.
(c)   Prepare a statement of cash flows for 2001.

Chapter 2 - Solutions

2-1.

DALIA CORPORATION
Income Statement
For the Year Ended December 31, 2002

Sales	$10,600,000
Cost of goods sold	8,000,000
Gross profit	$ 2,600,000
Selling and administrative expense	1,150,000
Depreciation expense	250,000
Operating profit	$ 1,200,000
Interest expense	200,000
Earnings before taxes	$ 1,000,000
Taxes	400,000
Net profit	$ 600,000

Steps:
(1)   Net profit = ($6)(100,000) = $600,000
(2)   Earnings before taxes = (NPAT/1 - tax rate) = $1,000,000
(3)   Taxes = EBT - NPAT = $1,000,000 - $600,000 = $400,000
(4)   Operating profit = EBT + Interest expense = $1,000,000 + $200,000 = $1,200,000
(5)   Gross profit = Operating profit + Selling and administrative expense + Depreciation expense = $1,200,000 + $1,150,000 + $250,000 = $2,600,000
(6)   Sales = Gross profit + COGS = $2,600,000 + $8,000,000 = $10,600,000

2-2.   (a)   Preferred dividends = 12,000 X $4 = $48,000

Earnings available to common stockholders = net income minus preferred dividends
$600,000 - $48,000 = $552,000

Earnings per share =

$$\frac{\$552,000}{100,000} = \mathbf{\$5.52}$$

Total dividends = payout ratio times earnings available = .50 x $552,000 = $276,000

Dividends per share =

$$\frac{\$276,000}{100,000} = \$2.76$$

(b)   Addition to retained earnings = earnings available to common stockholders minus dividends

$552,000 - $276,000 = **$276,000**

2-3. (a)   Using the Sources (S) and Uses (U) information provided below, construct the year-end 2002 balance sheet for the Krtoll Corporation.

Assets	Year-End 2001	Year-End 2002	Change	Source (S) or Use (U)
Current Assets:				
Cash	$ 200,000	$ 180,000	$ 20,000	S
Marketable securities	30,000	20,000	10,000	S
Accounts receivable (net)	440,000	490,000	50,000	U
Inventory	520,000	590,000	70,000	U
Prepaid expenses	35,000	30,000	5,000	S
Total Current Assets	$1,225,000	$1,310,000		
Investments	$ 45,000	35,000	10,000	S
Plant and equipment	1,600,000			
Less: Accumulated depreciation	600,000			
Net plant and equipment	1,000,000	1,200,000	200,000	U
Total Assets	$2,270,000	$2,545,000		

Liabilities & Stockholders' Equity

	Year-End 2001	Year-End 2002	Change	Source (S) or Use (U)
Current Liabilities:				
Accounts payable	$ 352,000	$ 420,000	$ 68,000	S
Notes payable	44,000	38,000	6,000	U
Accrued expenses	80,000	90,000	10,000	S
Total Current Liabilities	$ 476,000	$ 548,000		
Long-Term Liabilities:				
Bonds payable, 2019	330,000	330,000	---	
Total Liabilities	$ 806,000	$ 878,000		
Stockholders' Equity:				
Preferred stock, $100 par value	$ 100,000	$ 100,000	---	
Common stock, $1 par value	400,000	500,000	$100,000	S
Capital paid in excess of par	175,000	225,000	50,000	S
Retained earnings	789,000	842,000	53,000	S
Total Stockholders' Equity	$1,464,000	$1,667,000		
Total Liab. & Stock Equity	$2,270,000	$2,545,000		

(b)

KROLL CORPORATION
Statement of Cash Flows
For the Year Ended December 31, 2002

Cash flows from operating activities:

Net income		$114,000
Adjustments to determine cash flow from operating activities:		
Add back depreciation	$300,000	
Decrease in marketable securities	10,000	
Increase in accounts receivable	(50,000)	
Increase in inventory	(70,000)	
Decrease in prepaid expense	5,000	
Increase in accounts payable	68,000	
Decrease in notes payable	(6,000)	
Increase in accrued expenses	10,000	
Total adjustments		267,000
Net cash flows from operating activities		381,000
Cash flows from investing activities:		
Decrease in investments	10,000	
Increase in plant and equipment	(500,000)	
Net cash flow from investing activities		(490,000)
Cash flows from financing activities:		
Increase in common stock	150,000	
Dividends paid	(61,000)	
Net cash flows from financing activities		89,000
Net increase (decrease) in cash flows		($ 20,000)

2-4

ZHONG MANUFACTURING
Balance Sheet
For the Year Ended December 31, 2002

Assets

Current Assets:

Cash		$ 400,000
Marketable securities		2,000,000
Accounts receivable (net)		3,600,000
Inventory		5,800,000
Total Current Assets		$11,800,000
Fixed Assets:		
Gross fixed assets	$15,000,000	
Less: accumulated depreciation	6,800,000	
Net fixed assets		8,200,000
Total Assets		$20,000,000

Liabilities and Stockholders' Equity

Current Liabilities:

Accounts payable	$ 4,200,000
Taxes payable	200,000
Notes payable	3,800,000
Accrued expenses	600,000
Total Current Liabilities	$ 8,800,000
Long-Term Debt	4,750,000
Total Liabilities	$13,550,000

Stockholders' Equity:

Common stock, $1 par value	$ 2,000,000
Capital paid in excess of par	1,000,000
Retained earnings	3,450,000
Total Stockholders' Equity	$ 6,450,000
Total Liabilities and Stockholders' Equity	$20,000,000

NOTE: The cash and retained earnings balances are "plug" figures.

2-5. (a) Zhong Manufacturing

$$Number\ of\ shares = \frac{common\ stock}{par\ value\ per\ share} = \frac{\$2,000,000}{\$1} = 2,000,000$$

$$Book\ value\ per\ share = \frac{stockholders'\ equity}{number\ shares\ of\ common\ stock} = \frac{\$6,450,000}{2,000,000} = \mathbf{\$3.225}$$

(b)

$$EPS = \frac{net\ income}{number\ shares\ of\ common\ stock} = \frac{\$5,000,000}{2,000,000} = \$2.50$$

$$Market\ value\ per\ value = P/E \times E$$

$$Market\ value\ per\ share = 12 \times \$2.50 = \mathbf{\$30}$$

(c)

$$\frac{Market\ value\ per\ share}{Book\ value\ per\ share} = \frac{\$30}{\$3.225} = \mathbf{9.3}$$

2-6. (a) The new EPS of Zhong would be:

$$\frac{\$6,000,000}{2,000,000} = \mathbf{\$3}$$

The market value per share at the lower P/E ratio = 10 would be 10 x $3 = **$30**. The increase in EPS is offset by the decline in the P/E ratio.

(b)   The total market value of Zhong's common stock = 2,000,000 x $30 = **$60,000,000**.

2-7.   (a)

FMA CCORPORATION
Income Statement
For the Year Ended December 31, 2001

Sales	$ 360,000
Cost of goods sold	234,000
Gross profit	$ 126,000
Selling and administrative expense	36,000
Depreciation expense	50,000
Earnings before interest and taxes	$ 40,000
Interest expense	14,000
Earnings before taxes	$ 26,000
Taxes	3,900
Net income	$ 22,100

(1)   Cost of goods sold = ($360,000)(.65) = $234,000
(2)   Interest expense = ($50,000)(.10) + ($75,000)(.12) = $5,000 + $9,000 = $14,000
(3)   Taxes = ($26,000)(.15) = $3,900

(b)

FMA CORPORATION
Balance Sheet
December 31, 2001

Current Assets			*Current Liabilities*	
Cash		$ 22,995	Accounts payable	$ 67,200
Accounts receivable		47,500	Notes payable	40,000
Inventory		88,000	Total current liabilities . . .	$107,200
Total current assets		$158,495		
			Long-term bonds	$ 75,000
Fixed Assets				
Gross plant & equipment . . .	$315,000		*Stockholders' Equity*	
Less: accum. depreciation . .	125,000		Common stock	$ 60,000
Net plant & equipment		$190,000	Paid-in-capital	40,000
Total Assets		$348,495	Retained earnings	66,295
			Total liabilities & equity . .	$348,495

(1)   Accounts receivable = $50,000 - (.05)($50,000) = $47,500
(2)   Inventory = $80,000 + (.10)($80,000) = $88,000
(3)   Gross plant and equipment = $250,000 + $65,000 = $315,000
(4)   Accumulated depreciation = $75,000 + $50,000 = $125,000
(5)   Accounts payable = $60,000 + (.12)($60,000) = $67,200
(6)   Notes payable = $50,000 - $10,000 = $40,000
(7)   Retained earnings = previous retained earnings + addition to retained earnings
         [addition to retained earnings = net income - dividends]
         Retained earnings = $55,000 + ($22,100 - $10,805) = $55,000 + $11,295 = $66,295
(8)   Cash = "plug" figure = $348,495 - $325,500 = $22,995

(c)

FMA CORPORATION
Statement of Cash Flows
For the Year Ended December 31, 2001

Cash flows from operating activities:

Net income		$ 22,100
Adjustments to determine cash flow from operating activities:		
Add back depreciation	$ 50,000	
Decrease in marketable securities	20,000	
Decrease in accounts receivable	2,500	
Increase in inventory	(8,000)	
Increase in accounts payable	7,200	
Decrease in notes payable	(10,000)	
Total adjustments		61,700
Net cash flows from operating activities		$83,800
Cash flows from investing activities:		
Increase in plant and equipment	($65,000)	
Net cash flow from investing activities		($65,000)
Cash flows from financing activities:		
Common stock dividends paid	(10,805)	
Net cash flows from financing activities		($10,805)
Net increase (decrease) in cash flows		$ 7,995

(1) Net income from income statement
(2) Depreciation given
(3) Dividends given
(4) All other sources and uses were determined by comparing balance sheets of December 31, 2000, and December 31, 2001.

Summary: The thrust of this chapter is twofold. First, the use of financial ratios to evaluate the success of a firm is examined. Second, the impact of inflation and disinflation on business operations is assessed and explored.

I. **Ratio Analysis** [p. 55]

    A.   Uses of ratios.
        1.   Provide a basis for evaluating the operating performance of a firm.
        2.   Facilitate comparison with other firms.

    B.   Sources of comparative ratios. [p. 55]
        1.   Dun & Bradstreet.
        2.   Robert Morris Associates.
        3.   Trade organizations.
        4.   Standard & Poor's Industry Surveys
        5.   Value Line Investment Survey.
        6.   Moody's Corporation.
        7.   Computer databases such as COMPUSTAT.

    C.   Classification and computation. [pp. 56-64]
        1.   **Profitability**: Measures of returns on sales, total assets, and invested capital.
            a.   Profit Margin = Net Income/Sales
            b.   Return on Assets (Investment) = Net Income/Total Assets
            c.   Return on Equity = Net Income/Stockholders' Equity = Return on Assets/(1 - Debt/Assets)
        2.   **Asset utilization**: Measures of the speed at which the firm is turning over accounts receivable, inventories, and the productivity of longer-term assets.
            a.   Receivables Turnover = Sales/Receivables
            b.   Average Collection Period = Accounts Receivable/Average Daily Credit Sales
            c.   Inventory Turnover = Sales/Inventory or COGS/Inventory
            d.   Fixed Asset Turnover = Sales/Fixed Assets
            e.   Total Asset Turnover = Sales/Total Assets
        3.   **Liquidity ratios**: Measures of the firm's ability to pay off short-term obligations as they come due.
            a.   Current Ratio = Current Assets/Current Liabilities
            b.   Quick Ratio = Current Assets minus Inventory/Current Liabilities
        4.   **Debt-utilization ratios**: Measures of the firm's debt position evaluated in light of its asset base and earning power.
            a.   Debt to total assets = Total Debt/Total Assets
            b.   Times Interest Earned = Earnings Before Interest and Taxes/Interest
            c.   Fixed Charge Coverage = Earnings Before Fixed Charges and Taxes/ Fixed Charges

    D.   Interpreting financial ratios.
        1.   Individually, financial ratios convey little meaning.
        2.   Collectively, financial ratios provide an evaluation for the firms' investors, creditors, and management.

    E.   **Du Pont system**. [pp. 58-60]

        1.   The Du Pont Company was one of the first firms to stress the relationship of profitability and asset turnover in determining return on investment.

2. The profitability of a firm is determined by its ability to utilize its assets efficiently by generating profitable sales.

Return on Assets (Investment) = Profit Margin x Asset Turnover

$$\frac{Net\ income}{Total\ assets} = \frac{net\ income}{sales} \times \frac{sales}{total\ assets}$$

3. Profit margin is the profit-per-dollar of sales.
4. Asset turnover indicates the dollar sales generated per dollar of assets employed.
5. The return on equity is a function of a firm's return on assets and its financing plan.

$$Return\ on\ equity = \frac{Return\ on\ assets}{(1 - Debt/Assets)}$$

F. **Trend analysis** consists of computing the financial ratios of a firm at various points in time to determine if it is improving or deteriorating. [p. 63]

G. **Comparative analysis** provides the management and external evaluators with information as to how successful the firm is relative to other firms in the industry. [p. 63]

II. Impact of **Inflation** and **Disinflation** on Financial Analysis [pp. 64-67]

A. Impact on profits.
1. First-in, first-out (**FIFO**) inventory valuation during inflation periods "understates" cost of goods sold and causes "inventory profits."
2. The use of replacement cost accounting reduces income and interest coverage during inflationary periods.
3. A leveling off of prices, referred to as disinflation, may cause a reduction in profits. Some areas of the world, such as Russia, have experienced **deflation**, a decline in prices that results in widespread bankruptcies and a severe negative impact on the economy.

B. Impact on asset value.
1. Assets on the balance sheet are recorded at cost.
2. In inflationary periods, the replacement cost of long-term assets may greatly exceed the reported values.
3. The use of replacement cost accounting increases asset values during inflationary periods. This increase lowers the debt-to-asset ratio but does not necessarily enhance the firm's ability to service its debt.

C. Raising capital.
1. Investors generally require higher rates of return during periods of inflation.
2. Although earnings may drop because of disinflation, the declining rate of return demanded by investors may cause the value of a firm's securities to increase.
3. The movement away from financial assets (stocks and bonds) into tangible assets (gold, silver, etc.) by investors during periods of inflation makes it difficult and more expensive for firms to raise capital. Likewise, the reverse trend during periods of disinflation enhances a firm's ability to issue securities.

III. Other Elements of Distortion in Reported Income [pp. 67-70]

A. Recognition of revenue.
1. A conservative firm may recognize long-term installment sales revenues when payments are received, whereas other firms report the full amount of the sale as soon as possible.
2. Firms that lease assets may report a long-term lease as a sale.

B.   Extraordinary losses are reported in total as deductions from operating income by some firms but shown as deductions (net of taxes) from net income by others.

Chapter 3 - Multiple Choice Questions

1. Stock prices: [pp. 64-67]
    a. Frequently rise during periods of rapid inflation.
    b. Are not affected by inflation.
    c. Frequently fall during periods of rapid inflation.
    d. Rise more than the price of tangible assets during periods of inflation.
    e. Answers *a* and *d* are correct.

2. Times interest earned is a: [p. 62]
    a. Profitability ratio.
    b. Debt utilization ratio.
    c. Asset utilization ratio.
    d. Liquidity ratio.
    e. Quick ratio.

3. A firm may use _____ inventory valuation to reduce "inventory profits" during _____ periods. [p. 68]
    a. LIFO; disinflation
    b. FIFO; inflation
    c. LIFO; stable cost/price periods
    d. LIFO; inflation
    e. LILO; inflation

4. Analyzing the financial condition of a firm over time is called: [pp. 63-64]
    a. Comparative analysis.
    b. Ratio analysis.
    c. Trend analysis.
    d. The Du Pont system.
    e. Profitability analysis.

5. A shift from investment in _____ assets into _____ assets such as gold and silver may occur during periods of inflation. [p. 67]
    a. Liquid; tangible
    b. Tangible; liquid
    c. Financial; tangible
    d. Fixed; current
    e. Tangible; financial

6. Employing the Du Pont system, the ROA is determined by: [p. 58]
    a. Multiplying ROE by the net profit margin.
    b. Multiplying the net profit margin by the asset turnover.
    c. Dividing the gross profit by net profit.
    d. Multiplying ROA by the debt ratio.
    e. None of the above are correct.

7. A firm that has a total asset turnover of 1.8: [pp. 58-60]
    a. Requires $1.80 in assets to produce $1 of sales.
    b. Is highly profitable.
    c. Will soon become bankrupt.
    d. Requires $1 in assets to produce $1.80 in sales.
    e. Should lower its investment in assets.

8. During periods of disinflation, investors may: [pp. 66-68]
   a. Require lower rates of return.
   b. Bid the prices of securities up.
   c. Require higher rates of return.
   d. Invest heavily in financial assets.
   e. Both a and b are correct.

9. A firm's return on equity (ROE) is calculated by: [pp. 58-59]
   a. Dividing net income by stockholders' equity.
   b. Multiplying net income by stockholders' equity.
   c. Dividing return on assets by (1 - debt/assets).
   d. Dividing net income by total assets.
   e. Answers *a* and *c* are correct; either approach may be used.

10. The ability of a firm to pay off short-term obligations as they come due is indicated by: [p. 56]
   a. Profitability ratios.
   b. Liquidity ratios.
   c. Debt utilization ratios.
   d. Asset utilization ratios.
   e. My grade point average.

Multiple Choice Answer Key - Chapter 3

1. c	2. b	3. d	4. c	5. c
6. b	7. d	8. e	9. e	10. b

Chapter 3 - Problems

3-1. Using the following information, construct the income statement of the Bulldog Corporation.

Times interest earned	5
Gross profit margin	20%
Tax rate	30%

THE BULLDOG CORPORATION
Income Statement 2002

Sales	$
Cost of goods sold	1,600,000
Gross profit	
Selling and administrative expense	
Operating profit (EBIT)	
Interest	50,000
Earnings before taxes	
Taxes	
Net income	$

3-2. Without referring to the text or the preceding outline, complete the following:

Ratio	Computation	Primary Ratio Group
(a) Current ratio	$\dfrac{\text{Current assets}}{\text{Current liabilities}}$	_____
(b) Inventory turnover	$\dfrac{\rule{2cm}{0.4pt}}{\text{Inventory}}$	Asset utilization
(c) _____	$\dfrac{\text{EBIT}}{\text{Interest}}$	_____
(d) Average collection period	_____	_____
(e) _____	$\dfrac{\text{Net income}}{\text{Sales}}$	_____
(f) _____	$\dfrac{\text{Net income}}{\rule{2cm}{0.4pt}}$	Profitability
(g) Quick ratio	$\dfrac{\rule{2cm}{0.4pt}}{\text{Current liabilities}}$	_____
(h) Fixed charge coverage	_____	_____
(i)* _____	_____	_____
(j)* _____	_____	_____

*In *i* and *j* indicate the name, computation, and grouping of two ratios not previously used.

3-3. The financial statements of the Salazar Company for 2000, 2001, and 2002 are given below.

THE SALAZAR COMPANY
Balance Sheets for Years 2000-2002

	2000	2001	2002
Assets			
Cash	$ 10,000	$ 8,000	$ 20,000
Accounts receivable	50,000	30,000	30,000
Inventories	44,000	68,000	50,000
Total Current Assets	$104,000	$106,000	$100,000
Net property	50,000	50,000	52,000
Other assets	4,000	4,000	4,000
Total Assets	$158,000	$160,000	$156,000
Liabilities and Stockholders' Equity			
Accounts payable	$ 20,000	$ 24,000	$ 24,000
Notes payable (6%)	14,000	14,000	14,000
Accrued expenses	4,000	2,000	4,000
Total Current Liabilities	$ 40,000	$ 40,000	$ 42,000
Long-term debt (8%)	30,000	30,000	30,000
Common stock (25,000 shares; $1 par value)	25,000	25,000	25,000
Retained earnings	63,000	65,000	59,000
Total Liabilities and Stockholders' Equity	$158,000	$160,000	$156,000

THE SALAZAR COMPANY
Income Statements for Years 2000-2002

	2000	2001	2002
Sales	$240,000	$220,000	$260,000
Cost of goods sold	192,000	173,000	201,000
Gross profit	$ 48,000	$ 47,000	$ 59,000
Selling and administrative expenses	39,000	38,500	27,500
Operating profit	$ 9,000	$ 8,500	$ 21,500
Interest expense	3,240	3,240	3,240
Net income before taxes	$ 5,760	$ 5,620	$ 18,260
Taxes (15%)	864	789	2,739
Net income	$ 4,896	$ 4,471	$ 15,521

Required: Fill in the blanks to show Salazar's financial position.

THE SALAZAR COMPANY
Financial Ratios

		2000	2001	2002
1.	Current Ratio = $\dfrac{\text{Current Assets}}{\text{Current Liabilities}}$	_____	_____	_____
2.	Quick Ratio = $\dfrac{\text{Current Assets - Inventory}}{\text{Current Liabilities}}$	_____	_____	_____
3.	(a) Inventory Turnover = $\dfrac{\text{Sales}}{\text{Inventory}}$	_____	_____	_____
3.	(b) Inventory Turnover = $\dfrac{\text{Cost of Goods Sold}}{\text{Inventory}}$	_____	_____	_____
4.	Average Collection Period = $\dfrac{\text{Accounts Receivable}}{\text{Average Daily Credit Sales}}$	_____	_____	_____
5.	Fixed Asset Turnover = $\dfrac{\text{Sales}}{\text{Fixed Assets}}$	_____	_____	_____
6.	Total Asset Turnover = $\dfrac{\text{Sales}}{\text{Total Assets}}$	_____	_____	_____
7.	Debt to Total Assets = $\dfrac{\text{Total Debt}}{\text{Total Assets}}$	_____	_____	_____
8.	Times Interest Earned = $\dfrac{\text{Earnings Before Interest \& Taxes}}{\text{Interest}}$	_____	_____	_____
9.	Profit Margin = $\dfrac{\text{Net Income}}{\text{Sales}}$	_____	_____	_____
10.	Return on Investment = $\dfrac{\text{Net Income}}{\text{Total Assets}}$	_____	_____	_____
11.	Return on Equity = $\dfrac{\text{Net Income}}{\text{Stockholders' Equity}}$	_____	_____	_____

3-4. Using the data below, complete the balance sheet (round to the nearest $) and sales data for the Bienville Corporation.

BIENVILLE CORPORATION
Balance Sheet, December 31, 2002

Assets		*Liabilities & Stockholders' Equity*	
Cash	$_____	Accounts payable	$_____
Accounts receivable	_____	Long-term debt	_____
Inventory	250,000	Common stock	150,000
Plant & equipment	_____	Retained earnings	260,000
Total assets	_____	Total L & SE	_____
Sales	_____		
Cost of goods sold	_____		

All sales are credit sales.
Average collection period = 75 days
Credit purchases = 60% of sales
Accounts payable period = 72 days
Total asset turnover = 2
Quick ratio = 2.1
Inventory turnover (Sales/Inventory) = 5
Gross Profit Margin = .2

3-5. The Kolari Corporation currently has the following ratios:

Total asset turnover = 1.6
Total debt to total assets = .5
Current ratio = 1.7
Current liabilities = $2,000,000

(a) If Kolari's sales are currently $16,000,000, what is the amount of total assets?

(b) Of the total in (a) above, what amount is current assets?

(c) What is the total debt of the firm?

(d) If Kolari's sales are expected to increase by $6,400,000 and existing ratios remain unchanged, what is the amount of additional assets required?

3-6. The Sharpe Corporation is planning a major expansion. As a recently employed financial "wizard," you are expected to provide some guidance regarding financing the expansion. Using the information given, answer the questions that would likely be asked by your supervisor. (Assume all ratios remain the same after expansion unless directed otherwise.)

2001 operating and financial characteristics:

Sales = $100,000,000
Total assets = $125,000,000
Fixed assets = $70,000,000
Total debt to total assets = .4
Long-term debt to equity = .5
Net profit margin = 5%

(a) If Sharpe expects sales to increase by 80%, what amount of assets must the firm add (assuming all relationships are maintained)?

(b) How much of the increase in assets will be financed by debt? How much will be financed by long-term debt?

3-7. In *3-6* above, Sharpe Corporation must finance 60% of the increase in assets with equity (TD/TA = .4).

(a) If Sharpe Corporation retains all earnings, will it be necessary to issue any new common stock?

(b) If Sharpe distributes 40% of earnings as dividends, what amount of new common stock must be issued?

3-8. Using the data below, complete the income statement and balance sheet for the Pennathur Corporation.

PENNATHUR CORPORATION
Income Statement
For the Year Ended December 31, 2002

Sales	$
Cost of goods sold	_____
Gross profit	
Selling & administrative expense	$2,000,000
Operating profit (EBIT)	
Interest	_____
Earnings before taxes	_____
Taxes	_____
Net Income	$_____

PENNATHUR CORPORATION
Balance Sheet
December 31, 2002

Assets			Liabilities & Stockholders' Equity	
Cash		$ 500,000	Accounts payable	$2,000,000
Accounts receivable			Notes payable	
Inventory			Long-term debt	
Gross plant & equipment	$		Preferred stock; $100 par	$1,000,000
Less: Accum. depr.	3,000,000		Common stock; $1 par	
Net plant & equipment		_____	Retained earnings	_____
Total assets		$10,000,000	Total L & SE	$_____

Total asset turnover = 2
Gross profit margin = 25%
Times interest earned = 5
Tax rate = 34%
Current ratio = 2
All sales are on credit.
Average collection period = 45 days
Size of parking lot = 600 cars
Inventory turnover (using sales) = 10
Total debt to assets = .5
2001 balance sheet, retained earnings = $3,000,000
Pennathur paid out 60% of 2002 earnings in dividends.

Chapter 3 - Solutions

3-1.
THE BULLDOG CORPORATION
Income Statement, 2002

Sales	$ 2,000,000
Cost of goods sold	1,600,000
Gross profit	$ 400,000
Selling and administrative expenses	150,000
EBIT	$ 250,000
Interest expense	50,000
Earnings before taxes	$ 200,000
Taxes	60,000
Net income	$ 140,000

(a)

$$Gross\ profit\ margin = \frac{gross\ profit}{sales} = .2$$

$$\frac{Cost\ of\ goods\ sold}{sales} + \frac{gross\ profit}{sales} = 1$$

$$\frac{\$1,600,000}{sales} + .2 = 1$$

$$\frac{\$1,600,000}{Sales} = .8$$

$$Sales = \frac{\$1,600,000}{.8} = \mathbf{\$2,000,000}$$

(b) Sales - Cost of goods sold = Gross profit
$2,000,000 - $1,600,000 = **$400,000**

(c)

$$Times\ interest\ earned = \frac{EBIT}{Interest}$$

$$5 = \frac{EBIT}{\$50,000}$$

$$EBIT = 5 \times \$50,000 = \mathbf{\$250,000}$$

(d) Gross profit - Selling and administrative expense = EBIT
$400,000 - Selling and administrative expense = $250,000
Selling and administrative expense = **$150,000**

(e) Earnings before taxes = EBIT - Interest
Earnings before taxes = $250,000 - $50,000 = **$200,000**

(f) Taxes = .30 x $200,000 = **$60,000**

(g) Net income = earnings before taxes - taxes
Net income = $200,000 - $60,000 = **$140,000**

3-2. Without referring to the text or preceding problems, complete the following:

	Ratio	Computation	Primary Ratio Group
(a)	Current ratio	Current assets / Current liabilities	**Liquidity**
(b)	Inventory turnover	**Sales** / Inventory	Asset utilization
(c)	**Times interest earned**	EBIT / Interest	**Debt utilization**
(d)	Average collection period	**Accounts receivable** / **Avg daily credit sales**	**Asset utilization**
(e)	**Profit margin**	Net income / Sales	**Profitability**
(f)	**Return on investment**	Net income / **Total assets**	Profitability
(g)	Quick ratio	**Current assets - inventory** / Current Liabilities	**Liquidity**

(h)	Fixed charge coverage	Earnings before fixed charges and taxes	Debt utilization
		Fixed charges	
(i)*	_____	_____	_____
(j)*	_____	_____	_____

_____

*In problems *i* and *j* indicate the name, computation, and grouping of two ratios not previously used.

3-3.
THE SALAZAR COMPANY
Financial Ratios

	2000	2001	2002
1. Current Ratio = Current Assets / Current Liabilities	2.60	2.65	2.38
2. Quick Ratio = Current Assets - Inventory / Current Liabilities	1.50	0.95	1.19
3. (a) Inventory Turnover = Sales / Inventory	5.45	3.23	5.20
(b) Inventory Turnover = Cost of Goods Sold / Inventory	4.36	2.54	4.02
4. Average Collection Period = Accounts Receivable / Average Daily Credit Sales	75 days	49 days	41 days
5. Fixed Asset Turnover = Sales / Fixed Assets	4.44	4.07	4.64
6. Total Asset Turnover = Sales / Total Assets	1.52	1.38	1.67
7. Debt to Total Assets = Total Debt / Total Assets	0.44	0.44	0.46
8. Times Interest Earned = Earnings Before Interest & Taxes / Interest	2.78	2.62	6.64
9. Profit Margin = Net Income / Sales	2.0%	2.0%	6.0%
10. Return on Investment = Net Income / Total Assets	3.1%	2.8%	9.9%
11. Return on Equity = Net Income / Stockholders' Equity	5.6%	5.0%	18.5%

3-4. Sales:

$$\frac{Sales}{Inventory} = 5$$

$$\frac{Sales}{\$250,000} = 5$$

$$Sales = \$250,000 \times 5 = \mathbf{\$1,250,000}$$

Cost of goods sold:

$$Sales - COGS = gross\ profit$$

$$Gross\ profit = .2 \times sales$$

$$Gross\ profit = .2 \times \$1,250,000 = \$250,000$$

$$Cost\ of\ goods\ sold = \$1,250,000 - \$250,000 = \mathbf{\$1,000,000}$$

Total assets:

$$Total\ asset\ turnover = \frac{sales}{total\ assets} = 2$$

$$Total\ asset\ turnover = \frac{\$1,250,000}{TA} = 2$$

$$TA = \frac{\$1,250,000}{2} = \mathbf{\$625,000}$$

Total liabilities & stockholders' equity: Plug figure

$$TA = Total\ Liabilities\ plus\ Stockholders\ Equity$$

$$\$625,000 = \mathbf{\$625,000}$$

Accounts receivable:

$$Average\ collection\ period = \frac{\frac{accounts\ receivable}{credit\ sales}}{360}$$

$$\frac{Credit\ sales}{360} = \frac{\$1,250,000}{360} = \$3,472.22 = daily\ credit\ sales$$

$$Average\ collection\ period = \frac{accounts\ receivable}{\$3,472.22} = 75$$

$$Accounts\ receivable = \$3,742.22 \times 75 = \mathbf{\$260,416}$$

Accounts payable: The accounts payable period is analogous to the average collection period

$$\text{Average payables period} = \frac{\frac{\text{accounts payable}}{\text{credit purchases}}}{360} = 72$$

$$\text{Credit purchases} = .6 \times \text{sales} = .6 \times \$1{,}250{,}000 = \$750{,}000$$

$$\frac{\text{Credit purchases}}{360} = \frac{\$750{,}000}{360} = \$2{,}083.33 = \text{daily credit purchases}$$

$$\text{Accounts payable} = \$2{,}083.33 \times 72 = \textbf{\$150{,}000}$$

Cash:

$$\text{Quick ratio} = \frac{\text{quick assets}}{\text{current liabilities}} = 2.1$$

The only quick assets that the Bienville Corp. has are cash and accounts receivable.

$$QR = \frac{C + AR}{CL} = 2.1$$

$$QR = \frac{C + \$260{,}416}{\$150{,}000} = 2.1$$

$$C + \$260{,}416 = 2.1 \times \$150{,}000 = \$315{,}000$$

$$C = \$315{,}000 - \$260{,}416 = \textbf{\$54{,}584}$$

Long-term debt: Plug figure

$$\$625{,}000 - \$150{,}000 - \$150{,}000 - \$260{,}000 = \textbf{\$65{,}000}$$

Plant & Equipment: Plug figure

$$\$625{,}000 - \$54{,}584 - \$260{,}416 - \$250{,}000 = \textbf{\$60{,}000}$$

BIENVILLE CORPORATION
Balance Sheet, December 31, 2002

Assets		Liabilities & Stockholders' Equity	
Cash	$ 54,584	Accounts payable	$ 150,000
Accounts receivable	260,416	Long-term debt	65,000
Inventory	250,000	Common stock	150,000
Plant & equipment	60,000	Retained earnings	260,000
Total Assets	$ 625,000	Total L & SE	$ 625,000
Sales	$1,250,000		
Cost of goods sold	$1,000,000		

3-5. Kolari Corporation

(a)

$$\text{Total asset turnover} = \frac{\text{sales}}{\text{total assets}} = \frac{\$16,000,000}{TA} = 1.6$$

$$\$16,000,000 = 1.6 \; TA$$

$$TA = \frac{\$16,000,000}{1.6} = \mathbf{\$10,000,000}$$

(b)

$$\text{Current ratio} = \frac{\text{current assets}}{\text{current liabilities}} = 1.7$$

$$\frac{\text{Current assets}}{\$2,000,000} = 1.7$$

$$\text{Current assets} = 1.7 \times \$2,000,000 = \mathbf{\$3,400,000}$$

(c)

$$\frac{\text{Total debt}}{\text{Total assets}} = .5$$

$$\frac{TD}{\$10,000,000} = .5$$

$$TD = .5 \times \$10,000,000 = \mathbf{\$5,000,000}$$

(d) The increase in total assets can be found by applying the total asset turnover ratio to the increase in sales.

$$\frac{\text{Additional sales}}{\text{Additional assets}} = 1.6$$

$$\frac{\$6,400,000}{\text{Additional assets}} = 1.6$$

$$\$6,400,000 = 1.6 \; \text{additional assets}$$

$$\text{Additional assets} = \frac{\$6,400,000}{1.6} = \mathbf{\$4,000,000}$$

3-6. Sharpe Corporation

(a)

$$Total\ asset\ turnover = \frac{\$100,000,000}{\$125,000,000} = .8$$

If ratios are maintained, additional assets can be found as follows:

$$Additional\ assets = \frac{additional\ sales}{total\ asset\ turnover}$$

$$Additional\ sales = .8(\$100,000,000) = \$80,000,000$$

$$Additional\ assets = \frac{\$80,000,000}{.8} = \mathbf{\$100,000,000}$$

(b)

$$\frac{Total\ debt}{Total\ assets} = .4$$

$$Additional\ debt = \frac{TD}{TA} \times additional\ assets$$

$$Additional\ debt = .4 \times \$100,000,000 = \$40,000,000$$

If $\frac{TD}{TA} = .4$, the $\frac{equity}{TA}$ must equal .6.

If $\frac{long-term\ debt}{equity} = .5$, then LTD is half as much as equity; $\frac{LTD}{assets}$ must be .3.

The additional amount of long-term debt = .3 × \$100,000,000 = **\$30,000,000**.

3-7. Sharpe Corporation

(a) Sixty percent of assets are financed with equity.
Additional equity financing needed is: .60 x \$100,000,000 = \$60,000,000.
New sales = 1.8 x \$100,000,000 = \$180,000,000
Net profit = net profit margin x sales = .05 x \$180,000,000 = \$9,000,000
If all earnings are retained, (\$60,000,000 - \$9,000,000) = **\$51,000,000** in new common stock must be issued.

(b) Dividends = .40 x \$9,000,000 = \$3,600,000
Addition to retained earnings = \$9,000,000 - \$3,600,000 = \$5,400,000
Amount of new common stock to be issued is: \$60,000,000 - \$5,400,000 = **\$54,600,000**

3-8.

PENNATHUR CORPORATION
Income Statement
For the Year Ended December 31, 2002

Sales	**$20,000,000**
Cost of goods sold	15,000,000
Gross profit	$ 5,000,000
Selling & administrative expense	2,000,000
Operating profit (EBIT)	$ 3,000,000
Interest	600,000
Earnings before taxes	$ 2,400,000
Taxes	816,000
Net income	$ 1,584,000

PENNATHUR CORPORATION
Balance Sheet
December 31, 2002

Assets			*Liabilities & Stockholders' Equity*	
Cash	$	500,000	Accounts payable	$ 2,000,000
Accounts receivable		2,500,000	Notes payable	500,000
Inventory		2,000,000	Long-term debt	2,500,000
Gross plant & equip. **$8,000,000**			Preferred stock; $100 par	1,000,000
Less: accum. depr. 3,000,000			Common stock; $1 par	366,400
Net plant & equipment		5,000,000	Retained earnings	3,633,600
Total Assets		$10,000,000	Total Liab. & St. Equity	$10,000,000

The solution to this problem requires a series of calculations that illustrate the relationships among ratios.

Sales = total asset turnover x total assets
    = 2 x $10,000,000
    = **$20,000,000**

COGS = sales - gross profit
     = $20,000,000 - (.25)($20,000,000)
     = $20,000,000 - $5,000,000 = **$15,000,000**

Operating profit (EBIT) = gross profit - selling and administrative expense
                        = $5,000,000 - $2,000,000 = **$3,000,000**

$$\textit{Times interest earned} = \frac{EBIT}{I} = 5$$

$$= \frac{\$3,000,000}{I} = 5$$

$$I = \textbf{\$600,000}$$

Earnings before taxes = EBIT - I

$$= \$3,000,000 - \$600,000 = \mathbf{\$2,400,000}$$

Taxes = .34 x \$2,400,000 = **\$816,000**

$$\textit{Average daily credit sales} = \frac{\textit{credit sales}}{360}$$

$$= \frac{\$20,000,000}{360} = \mathbf{\$55,555.55}$$

$$\textit{Average collection period} = \frac{\textit{accounts receivable}}{\textit{daily credit sales}} = 45$$

$$= \frac{AR}{\$55,555.55} = 45$$

$$AR = 45 \times \$55,555.55 = \mathbf{\$2,500,000} \ (\textit{rounded})$$

$$\textit{Inventory turnover} = \frac{\textit{sales}}{\textit{inventory}} = 10$$

$$= \frac{\$20,000,000}{\textit{inventory}} = 10$$

$$\textit{Inventory} = \mathbf{\$2,000,000}$$

Net plant and equipment is a "plug" figure.

Total assets - current assets = net fixed assets

\$10,000,000 - (\$500,000 + \$2,500,000 + \$2,000,000) = NFA

NFA = **\$5,000,000**

Gross plant and equipment = NFA + accumulated depreciation

$$= \$5,000,000 + \$3,000,000 = \mathbf{\$8,000,000}$$

$$\textit{Current ratio} = \frac{\textit{current asssets}}{\textit{current liabilities}} = 2$$

$$= \frac{\$5,000,000}{AP + NP} = 2$$

$$= \frac{\$5,000,000}{\$2,000,000 + NP} = 2$$

$$NP = \mathbf{\$500,000}$$

$$\text{Total debt to assets} = \frac{\text{current liabilities} + \text{long-term debt}}{\text{total assets}} = .5$$

$$= \frac{\$2,500,000 + LTD}{\$10,000,000} = .5$$

$$LTD = \mathbf{\$2,500,000}$$

Addition to retained earnings in 2002 = net income - dividends

dividends = .60 x $1,584,000
dividends = $950,400

Addition to retained earnings   = $1,584,000 - $950,400
                                = $633,600

Balance sheet retained earnings December 31, 2002:

BS retained earnings December 31, 2001 + addition to retained earnings during 2002 = $3,000,000 + $633,600 = **$3,633,600**

Common stock = "plug" figure

Total liabilities and stockholders' equity = $10,000,000

CS = $10,000,000 - $2,000,000 - $500,000 - $2,500,000 - $1,000,000 - $3,633,600
    = **$366,400**

Summary: Financial planning is essential for a successful business firm. In this chapter the construction and use of various pro forma financial statements for financial forecasting are explained.

I.   Need for Financial Planning [pp. 87-88]

   A.   Growth requires additions to assets; arrangements for financing such asset additions must be made in advance.

   B.   Financial planning is necessary, not only for success, but for survival as well.

   C.   Lenders frequently require evidence of planning prior to making funds available.

II.   *Pro Forma* Statements

   A.   ***Pro forma* income statement**: A projection of how much profit a firm will make over a specific time period. [p. 88]
      1.   Establish a sales projection.
         a.   Forecast economic conditions.
         b.   Survey sales personnel.
      2.   Determine a production schedule and required materials, labor, and expenses.
         a.   Determine units to be produced.

                     Projected unit sales
                  +Desired ending inventory
                   - Beginning inventory
                     Production requirements

         b.   Determine the cost of producing the units.
            (1)   Unit cost = materials + labor + overhead.
            (2)   Total product costs = number of units to be produced x unit cost.
         c.   Compute cost of goods sold.
            (1)   Estimate unit sales.
            (2)   Cost of goods sold = unit sales x unit cost (FIFO or LIFO).
         d.   Compute value of ending inventory.

                     Beginning inventory
                  +Total production costs
                     Total inventory available for sale
                   - Cost of goods sold
                     Ending inventory

      3.   Compute other expenses.
         a.   General and administrative.
         b.   Interest expense.
      4.   Construct the *pro forma* income statement.

                     Sales revenue
                   - Cost of goods sold
                     Gross profit
                   - General and administrative expenses
                     Operating profit
                   - Interest expense
                     Earnings before taxes
                   - Taxes
                     Earnings after taxes
                   - Common stock dividends
                     Increase in retained earnings

B. **Cash budget**: A summary of expected *cash* receipts and disbursements for a specific period of time. [p. 93]
1. Estimate cash sales and collection timing of credit sales.
2. Forecast cash payments.
    a. Payments for materials purchases according to credit terms.
    b. Wages.
    c. Capital expenditures.
    d. Principal payments.
    e. Interest payments.
    f. Taxes.
    g. Dividends.
3. Construct cash budget.

> Total receipts (for each month, week, etc.)
> - Total payments (for each month, week, etc.)
> Net cash flow (for the period)
> +Beginning cash balance
> Cumulative cash balance

Note: The beginning cash balance for each period of the cash budget is equal to the cumulative cash balance of the previous period in the absence of borrowing or investing of cash balances.
4. Determine cash excess or need for borrowing.

> Cumulative cash balance (at end of period).
> Loan required or cash excess (desired cash balance - cumulative cash balance)
> Ending cash balance

C. *Pro forma* **balance sheet**: An integrated projection of the firm's financial position based on its existing position, forecasted profitability (from *pro forma* income statement), anticipated cash flows (cash budget), asset requirements, and required financing. [p. 96]
1. Construction of *pro forma* balance sheet.
    a. Assets (source of information).
        (1) Cash - (cash budget).
        (2) Marketable securities - (previous balance sheet and cash budget)
        (3) Accounts receivable - (sales forecast, cash budget)
        (4) Inventory - (COGS computation for *pro forma* income statement)
        (5) Plant and equipment - (previous balance sheet + purchases - depreciation)
    b. Liabilities and net worth.
        (1) Accounts payable - (cash budget work sheet)
        (2) Notes payable - (previous balance sheet and cash budget)
        (3) Long-term debt - (previous balance sheet plus new issues minus principal payments)
        (4) Common stock - (previous balance sheet plus new issues)
        (5) Retained earnings - (previous balance sheet plus projected addition from *pro forma* income statement)

D. **Percent-of-sales method**: Shortcut, less exact, alternative for determining financial needs. [pp. 99-100]

1. Assume balance sheet accounts maintain a given relationship to sales:

$$\left(\frac{Assets}{Current\ sales} \right) = \%\ of\ sales$$

2. Project asset levels on basis of forecasted sales (percent of sales of each asset x forecasted sales).
3. Project spontaneous financing: Some financing is provided spontaneously when asset levels increase; for example, accounts payable increase when a firm buys additional inventory on credit.
4. Project internal financing from retention of earnings = profit margin x forecasted sales x retention percentage.
5. Determine external financing = required new assets to support sales - spontaneous financing - retained earnings. The relationship is expressed as follows:

$$\text{Required new funds} = \frac{A}{S}(\Delta S) - \frac{L}{S}(\Delta S) - PS_2(1 - D)$$

where A/S = percentage relationship of variable assets to sales, ΔS = change in sales, L/S = percentage relationship of variable liabilities to sales, P = profit margin, S_2 = new sales level, and D = payout ratio.

III. Key Formula

A. Required new funds [p. 101] =

$$\frac{A}{S}(\Delta S) - \frac{L}{S}(\Delta S) - PS_2(1 - D)$$

Chapter 4 - Multiple Choice Questions

1. The beginning step in financial forecasting is the projection of: [p. 90]
   a. Net profit.
   b. Sales.
   c. Cash flows.
   d. Liabilities.
   e. Equity.

2. A cash budget is a summary of _____ for some specific time period. [pp. 92-96]
   a. Revenues and expenses
   b. Asset and liabilities
   c. Expected cash receipts and disbursements
   d. Profit plus depreciation
   e. Credit and cash sales

3. On a *pro forma* balance sheet, the primary source of information for the cash balance is: [p. 97]
   a. Income statement.
   b. Cash budget.
   c. Previous balance sheet.
   d. *Pro forma* income statement.
   e. None of the above are correct.

4.   A substantial portion of the increase in assets necessitated by rising sales may be automatically financed through: [p. 100]
     a.   Accounts receivable.
     b.   Retained earnings.
     c.   Depreciation.
     d.   Spontaneous assets.
     e.   Accounts payable.

5.   Which of the following statements concerning the construction of a cash budget is (are) not true? [pp. 92-96]
     a.   Depreciation expense is a primary consideration.
     b.   A cash budget is a historical statement.
     c.   The beginning step is a forecast of sales.
     d.   Collection of receivables must be forecasted.   ·
     e.   Both *a* and *b* are not true.

6.   The percent-of-sales method is a shortcut approach to constructing a: [p. 99]
     a.   *Pro forma* income statement.
     b.   Cash budget.
     c.   Balance sheet.
     d.   *Pro forma* balance sheet.
     e.   Statement of cash flows.

7.   Which of the following is not a step in preparing a *pro forma* income statement? [pp. 88-92]
     a.   Projection of sales
     b.   Projection of cost of goods sold
     c.   Projection of debt principal payments
     d.   Projection of taxes
     e.   Projection of gross profit

8.   The forecasted addition to retained earnings is included in the required new funds formula as [p. 100]
     a. $P\Delta S(1-D)$.
     b. $PS_2(D)$.
     c. PS_2.
     d. $P\Delta S$.
     e. $PS_2(1-D)$.

9.   As an estimate of the financing required to support an asset expansion, the firm must: [p. 100]
     a.   Add spontaneous assets and retention of earnings.
     b.   Add variable assets and spontaneous financing.
     c.   Subtract variable assets from the addition to retained earnings.
     d.   Subtract spontaneous financing and projected retention of earnings from the projected increase in assets.
     e.   None of the above are correct.

10. The primary benefit(s) of a cash budget is (are): [pp. 95-96]
     a.   Enables a financial manager to forecast borrowing needs.
     b.   Guarantees the success of the firm.
     c.   Provides a forecast of temporarily excess cash balances.
     d.   Answers *a*, *b*, and *c* are correct.
     e.   Both *a* and *c* are correct.

Chapter 4 - Problems

4-1.   The marketing staff of Vallee Corporation has forecast a 20% increase in sales for 2002. Assist the firm's financial manager in projecting the required external financing to support the increase in sales. Use the relationships below to forecast needed funds.

Variable assets/sales = 40%
Net profit margin = 3%
Payout ratio = 40%
2001 sales = $60,000,000
Spontaneous liabilities/sales = 25%

(a)   Will Vallee Corporation need additional external financing to support the anticipated sales increase?

(b)   Will Vallee need to arrange external financing if the spontaneous liabilities/sales = 30%?

4-2.   Tough Stuff Manufacturing had credit sales of $1,000,000; $1,500,000; and $800,000 in October, November, and December 2001, respectively. The company's credit sales projections for January through March of 2002 are as follows: January - $3,000,000; February - $2,400,000; March - $2,000,000.

Tough Stuff has normally collected 60% of its credit sales in the month following the sale, 30% in the second following month and 10% in the third month. Assuming this collection pattern continues, prepare a schedule of cash receipts from receivables collection for the period January through March of 2002.

4-3.   Using the following information, prepare a *pro forma* income statement for 2002 for Middle Fork Lumber Company:

Projected sales	$10,000,000
Cost of goods sold	60% of sales
Selling and administrative expenses	$100,000/month
Depreciation expense	$140,000/month
Interest expense	$120,000
Tax rate	34%
Dividend payout rate	50%

4-4.   Using the income information from 4-3 and the December 31, 2001 balance sheet for the Middle Fork Lumber Company, prepare a *pro forma* balance sheet for December 31, 2002. You should use the percent-of-sales method and assume that all long-term financing will be achieved from retention of earnings and borrowing. Sales for 2001 were $8,000,000.

MIDDLE FORK LUMBER COMPANY
Balance Sheet
December 31, 2001

Assets		*Liabilities & Net Worth*	
Cash	$ 400,000	Accounts payable	$ 800,000
Accounts receivable	900,000	Long-term debt	1,500,000
Inventory	1,200,000	Common stock	1,800,000
Net plant & equipment	2,500,000	Retained earnings	900,000
Total Assets	$5,000,000	Total Liabilities & Net Worth ...	$5,000,000

4-5.   Using the following information, prepare a *pro forma* income statement for 2002 for Shongaloo, Inc.

Projected sales = $20,000,000
Cost of goods sold = 72% of sales
Selling and administrative expenses = estimated to be 15% of COGS
Depreciation expense = $100,000 per month for January through March, $108,000 per month April through November and $117,000 in December
Interest expense is projected on the basis of the following: 10.5% on $10,000,000 bonds outstanding throughout the year and 9% on a 3-month bank loan of $2,500,000
Tax rate = 40%

4-6.   One of your first jobs as a new employee of the Zero Corporation is to prepare a cash budget for the period January 1 through June 30, 2002. Use the data below.

(a)   Eighty percent (80%) of all sales are credit sales; 80% of credit sales are collected in the following month; 15% and 4% of credit sales are collected 60 days and 90 days after sale, respectively; 1% of sales become bad debts and are never collected.

(b)   Purchases during each month equal 65% of the following month's estimated sales. Payment for purchases is made in the month following the purchase.

(c)   The firm seeks to maintain a minimum cash balance of $300,000. The January 1 cash balance is $300,000.

(d)   The firm anticipates delivery of new equipment in April. A payment of $400,000 will be made upon delivery.

(e)   A quarterly tax payment of $500,000 is anticipated in March and June.

(f)   Rent is $100,000 per month. Other cash expenses average 3% of current month's sales.

(g)   Depreciation expense averages $150,000 monthly.

(h)   Labor costs paid monthly average 10% of the following month's sales.

(i)   The board of directors desires to maintain the firm's current dividend policy. A dividend payment of $450,000 is scheduled for June.

(j)   The company experienced sales of $3,000,000 in October 2001 and sales of $2,000,000 during each of the last two months of 2001.

(k)   The projected sales schedule for the first seven months of 2002 is given below:

Sales Projections for January-July of 2002

January	$3,000,000
February	5,000,000
March	5,000,000
April	6,000,000
May	3,000,000
June	2,000,000
July	2,000,000

(l)   The firm must make a semiannual interest payment of $310,000 in June 2002.

4-7.   Quasimoto Corporation has the following balance sheet/sales relationships.

Cash: 6%
Accounts receivable: 18%
Inventory: 22%
Net fixed assets: 35%
Accounts payable: 20%
Accruals: 13%

Quasimoto's financial manager must formulate a plan to finance a projected 20% increase in sales in 2002. The firm has a net profit margin of 6% and the board of directors voted to pay out 40% of the firm's $3,000,000 net income in 2001.

(a)   Assuming the firm was operating at full capacity to produce 2001 sales of $50,000,000, how much external capital will be needed to finance the sales expansion? The directors desire to maintain a 40% payout ratio, and no debt payments are due in 2002.

(b)   What amount of financing would be needed if the firm were operating considerably below capacity and no new fixed assets would be required?

(c)   What amount of external financing will Quasimoto need if the payout ratio is lowered to 35% and a $5,000,000 long-term debt is retired?   (Assume full-capacity operations in 2001.)

(d)   Under the conditions of (*a*) above and assuming that all external financing will be achieved through issuing long-term bonds, prepare a *pro forma* balance sheet for December 31, 2002. The firm's long-term debt at the end of 2001 was $9,000,000 and its common stock and retained earnings balances were $7,000,000 and $8,000,000 respectively.

Chapter 4 - Solutions

4-1. Vallee Corporation

(a)

$$\text{Required new funds} = \frac{A}{S}\,(\Delta S) - \frac{L}{S}\,(\Delta S) - PS_2\,(1 - D)$$

ΔS = .20 (60,000,000) = $12,000,000

RNF = .4 ($12,000,000) - .25 ($12,000,000) - .03 ($72,000,000) (1 - .4)

RNF = $4,800,000 - $3,000,000 - $1,296,000

RNF = **$504,000**

(b) RNF = .4 ($12,000,000) - .3 ($12,000,000) - .03 ($72,000,000) (1 - .4)

RNF = $4,800,000 - $3,600,000 - $1, 296,000

RNF = **-$96,000**.

No, spontaneous financing and retention of earnings is expected to provide more than sufficient financing.

4-2.

TOUGH STUFF MANUFACTURING
Schedule of Forecasted Cash Collections January-March 2002

	October	November	December	January	February	March
Credit Sales	$1,000,000	$1,500,000	$800,000	$3,000,000	$2,400,000	$2,000,000
Collections:						
60% of previous month's sales				480,000	1,800,000	1,440,000
30% of credit sales 2 months prior				450,000	240,000	900,000
10% of credit sales 3 months prior				100,000	150,000	80,000
Total forecasted cash collections				**$1,030,000**	**$2,190,000**	**$2,420,000**

4-3.

MIDDLE FORK LUMBER COMPANY
Pro Forma Income Statement
For the Year Ending December 31, 2002

Sales	$10,000,000
Cost of goods sold	6,000,000
Gross profit	$ 4,000,000
Depreciation expense	1,680,000
Selling and administrative expenses	1,200,000
Operating profit (EBIT)	$ 1,120,000
Interest expense	120,000
Profit before taxes	$ 1,000,000
Taxes (34%)	340,000
Net income	$ 660,000
Less dividends	330,000
Increase in Retained Earnings	$ 330,000

4-4.

PERECENT OF SALES (2001)

Assets as a percent of sales
 Cash/Sales = $400,000/$8,000,000 = .05
 Accounts receivable/sales = $900,000/$8,000,000 = .1125
 Inventory/sales = $1,200,000/$8,000,000 = .15
 Net plant and equipment/sales = $2,500,000/$8,000,000 = .3125
 Total assets/sales = $5,000,000/$8,000,000 = .625

Spontaneous financing
 Accounts payable/sales = $800,000/$8,000,000 = .10

Required assets to support projected sales of $10,000,000
 $10,000,000 x .625 = $6,250,000
 Present assets   5,000,000
 Addition to assets $1,250,000

Required financing

New assets to be financed		$1,250,000
Spontaneous financing from accounts payable:		
.10 x $10,000,000	= $1,000,000	
Less existing accounts payable	800,000	200,000
		$1,050,000
Less additions to retained earnings		330,000
External financing required		$ 720,000

MIDDLE FORK LUMBER COMPANY
Pro Forma Balance Sheet
For the Year Ending December 31, 2002

Assets		*Liabilities & Net Worth*	
Cash	$ 500,000	Accounts payable	$1,000,000
Accounts receivable	1,125,000	Long-term debt	2,220,000
Inventory	1,500,000	Common stock	1,800,000
Net plant & equipment	3,125,000	Retained earnings	1,230,000
	$6,250,000		$6,250,000

An alternative approach to determining needed external financing is:

$$\text{Required new funds} = \frac{A}{S}(\Delta S) - \frac{L}{S}(\Delta S) - PS_2 (1 - \text{dividend payout percentage})$$

$$\text{Required new funds} = \frac{\$5,000,000}{\$8,000,000}(\$2,000,000) - \frac{\$800,000}{\$8,000,000}(\$2,000,000)$$

$$- (.066)(\$10,000,000)(.5)$$

$$\text{Required new funds} = .625(\$2,000,000) - .10(\$2,000,000) - (.066)(\$10,000,000)(.5)$$

$$\text{Required new funds} = \$1,250,000 - \$200,000 - \$330,000$$

$$\text{Required new funds} = \mathbf{\$720,000}$$

4-5.

Shongaloo, Inc.
***Pro Forma* Income Statement**
For the Year Ended December 31, 2002

Sales	$20,000,000
Cost of goods sold	14,400,000
Gross profit	$ 5,600,000
Depreciation expense	1,281,000
Selling and administrative expenses	2,160,000
Operating profit (EBIT)	$ 2,159,000
Interest expense	1,106,250
Taxable income	$ 1,052,750
Taxes (40%)	421,100
Net income	$ 631,650

Calculations:

$$COGS = .72 \times \$20,000,000 = \$14,400,000$$

$$\text{Selling and Administrative expense} = .15 \times \$14,400,000 = \$2,160,000$$

$$\text{Depreciation expense} = (3 \times \$100,000) + (8 \times \$108,000) + \$117,000 = \$1,281,000$$

$$\text{Interest expense} = .105(\$10,000,000) + .09(\$2,500,000) \times .25$$

$$= \$1,050,000 + \$56,250 = \$1,106,250$$

4-6.

SCHEDULE OF FORECASTED CASH RECEIPTS

	October	November	December	January	February	March	April	May	June	July
Total Sales	$3,000,000	$2,000,000	$2,000,000	$3,000,000	$5,000,000	$5,000,000	$6,000,000	$3,000,000	$2,000,000	$2,000,000
Credit Sales	2,400,000	1,600,000	1,600,000	2,400,000	4,000,000	4,000,000	4,800,000	2,400,000	1,600,000	1,600,000
Cash Sales	$ 600,000	$ 400,000	$ 400,000	$ 600,000	$1,000,000	$1,000,000	$1,200,000	$ 600,000	$ 400,000	
Collections:										
80% of previous month's credit sales		1,920,000	1,280,000	1,280,000	1,920,000	3,200,000	3,200,000	3,840,000	1,920,000	
15% of credit sales two months prior			360,000	240,000	240,000	360,000	600,000	600,000	720,000	
4% of credit sales 3 months prior				96,000	64,000	64,000	96,000	160,000	160,000	
Total Cash Receipts				$2,216,000	$3,224,000	$4,624,000	$5,096,000	$5,200,000	$3,200,000	

SCHEDULE OF FORECASTED MONTHLY CASH PAYMENTS

	December	January	February	March	April	May	June
Monthly material purchase	$1,950,000	$3,250,000	$3,250,000	$3,900,000	$1,950,000	$1,300,000	$1,300,000
Payment for materials (prior month's purchases)		$1,950,000	$3,250,000	$3,250,000	$3,900,000	$1,950,000	$1,300,000
Monthly labor cost (10% of following month's sales)		500,000	500,000	600,000	300,000	200,000	200,000
Monthly rent		100,000	100,000	100,000	100,000	100,000	100,000
Other cash expenses (3% of current month's sales)		90,000	150,000	150,000	180,000	90,000	60,000
Interest expense							310,000
Capital purchases					400,000		
Taxes				500,000			500,000
Dividends							450,000
Total payments		$2,640,000	$4,000,000	$4,600,000	$4,880,000	$2,340,000	$2,920,000

MONTHLY CASH BUDGET
January 1 - June 30, 2002

	January	February	March	April	May	June
Total cash receipts.........	$2,216,000	$3,224,000	$4,624,000	$5,096,000	$5,200,000	$3,200,000
Total payments	2,640,000	4,000,000	4,600,000	4,880,000	2,340,000	2,920,000
Net cash flow	(424,000)	(776,000)	24,000	216,000	2,860,000	280,000
Beginning monthly cash balance ...	300,000	(124,000)	(900,000)	(876,000)	(660,000)	2,200,000
Cumulative cash balance	(124,000)	(900,000)	(876,000)	(660,000)	2,200,000	2,480,000

BORROWING AND REPAYMENT PLAN FOR CASH BUDGET

	January	February	March	April	May	June
Cumulative cash balance	$ (124,000)	$ (900,000)	$ (876,000)	$ (660,000)	$2,200,000	$2,480,000
Desired cash balance	$ 300,000	$ 300,000	$ 300,000	$ 300,000	$ 300,000	$ 300,000
Loans required (cumulative)	$ 424,000	$1,200,000	$1,176,000	$ 960,000	—	—
Additional loans required	$ 424,000	$ 776,000	$ (24,000)*	$ (216,000)*	$ (960,000)*	—
Ending cash balance	$ 300,000	$ 300,000	$ 300,000	$ 300,000	$1,240,000	$2,480,000
Available for investment	—	—	—	—	$ 940,000	$2,180,000

---

*The assumption is made that payments are made on the outstanding loan as soon as possible.

49

4-7. (a) Variable assets as a percent of sales = 6% + 18% + 22% + 35% = 81%
Variable liabilities as a percent of sales = 20% + 13% = 33%
Projected increase in sales = (.2) ($50,000,000) = $10,000,000

$$\text{Required new funds} = \frac{A}{S} (\Delta S) - \frac{L}{S} (\Delta S) - PS_2 (1 - D)$$

Required new funds = (.81)($10,000,000) − (.33)($10,000,000) − (.06)($60,000,000)(1 − .4)

Required new funds = $8,100,000 − $3,300,000 − $2,160,000 = **$2,640,000**

(b)

Required new funds = (.81−.35)($10,000,000) − (.33)($10,000,000) − (.06)($60,000,000)(1−.4)

Required new funds = $4,600,000 − $3,300,000 − $2,160,000 = **($860,000)**

No new external funds would be needed under these conditions. The firm would generate more than enough spontaneously and internally to finance the expansion.

(c)

Required new funds = (.81)($10,000,000) − (.33)($10,000,000)
− (.06)($60,000,000)(1 − .35) + $5,000,000

Required new funds = $8,100,000 − $3,300,000 − $2,340,000 + $5,000,000 = **$7,460,000**

(d)
QUASIMOTO CORPORATION
Pro Forma Balance Sheet
For the Year Ending December 31, 2002

Assets		*Liabilities & Net Worth*	
Cash	$ 3,600,000	Accounts payable	$12,000,000
Accounts receivable . . .	10,800,000	Accruals	7,800,000
Inventory	13,200,000	Long-term debt	11,640,000
Net fixed assets	21,000,000	Common stock	7,000,000
	$48,600,000	Retained earnings	10,160,000
			$48,600,000

(1) Cash = (.06)($60,000,000) = $3,600,000
(2) Accounts receivable = (.18)($60,000,000) = $10,800,000
(3) Inventory = (.22)($60,000,000) = $13,200,000
(4) Net fixed assets = (.35)($60,000,000) = $21,000,000
(5) Accounts payable = (.2)($60,000,000) = $12,000,000
(6) Accruals = (.13)($60,000,000) = $7,800,000
(7) Common stock = no change
(8) Retained earnings = $8,000,000 + (.06)($60,000,000)(1 - 4)
= $8,000,000 + $2,160,000 = $10,160,000
(9) Long-term debt = plug figure or $9,000,000 + additional required funds
= $9,000,000 + $2,640,000 = $11,640,000

Summary: This chapter examines the possible effects of a firm employing fixed cost factors for operating purposes or financing purposes. Operating leverage is associated with fixed production costs, and financial leverage results from using sources of financing to which a fixed return is paid.

I.   Leverage: The use of fixed charge obligations with the intent of magnifying the potential returns to the firm. [pp. 112-113]

    A.   Fixed operating costs: Those operating costs that remain relatively constant regardless of the volume of operations such as rent, depreciation, property taxes, and executive salaries.

    B.   Fixed financial costs: The interest costs arising from debt financing that must be paid regardless of the level of sales or profits.

II.   Break-Even Analysis and Operating Leverage [pp. 113-119]

    A.   Break-even analysis: A numerical and graphical technique used to determine at what point the firm will break even.

        1.   Break-even point: the unit sales where total revenue = total costs.

        2.   Break-even point formula:

$$BE = \frac{fixed\ costs}{contribution\ margin} = \frac{fixed\ costs}{price\ -\ variable\ cost\ per\ unit} = \frac{FC}{P\ -\ VC}$$

$$BE = \frac{\$60,000}{\$2.00\ -\ \$.80} = 50,000\ units$$

        3.   It may be desirable to calculate the break-even point in sales dollars rather than in units. (See problem 19 in text.) Break-even sales may be calculated as follows:

$$BES = \frac{fixed\ costs}{1\ -\ TVC/S}$$

where TVC/S = the percentage relationship of total variable costs to sales.

    B.   Cash break-even analysis. [p. 117]

        1.   Deducting noncash fixed expenses such as depreciation in the break-even analysis enables one to determine the break-even point on a cash basis.

        2.   Cash break-even point formula:

$$Cash\ BE = \frac{fixed\ costs\ -\ noncash\ fixed\ costs}{P\ -\ VC}$$

FIGURE 5-1
BREAK-EVEN CHART

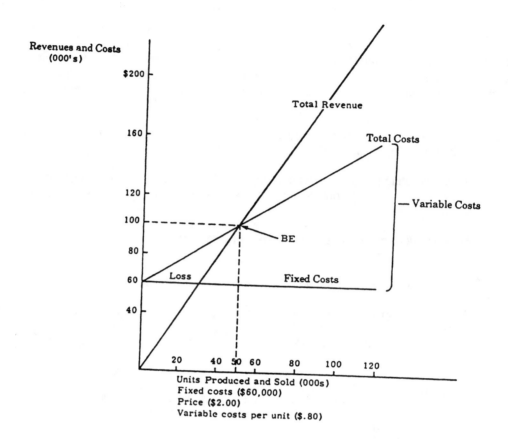

Units Produced and Sold (000s)
Fixed costs ($60,000)
Price ($2.00)
Variable costs per unit ($.80)

TABLE 5-1
VOLUME-COST-PROFIT-ANALYSIS
Leveraged Firm

	Units Sold	Total Variable Costs	Fixed Costs	Total Costs	Total Revenue	Operating Income (Loss)
1.	-0-	-0-	$60,000	$ 60,000	-0-	$(60,000)
2.	20,000	$16,000	60,000	76,000	$ 40,000	(36,000)
3.	40,000	32,000	60,000	92,000	80,000	(12,000)
4.	50,000	40,000	60,000	100,000	100,000	-0-
5.	60,000	48,000	60,000	108,000	120,000	12,000
6.	80,000	64,000	60,000	124,000	160,000	36,000
7.	100,000	80,000	60,000	140,000	200,000	60,000

C. **Operating Leverage**: A reflection of the extent fixed assets and fixed costs are utilized in the business firm. The employment of operating leverage causes operating profit to be more sensitive to changes in sales.

1. The use of operating leverage increases the potential return, but it also increases potential losses.

2. The amount of leverage employed depends on anticipated economic conditions, nature of the business (cyclical or noncyclical), and the risk aversion of management.

3. The sensitivity of a firm's operating profit to a change in sales as a result of the employment of operating leverage is reflected in its degree of operating leverage.

4. **Degree of operating leverage (DOL)** is defined as the ratio of percentage change in operating income in response to percentage change in volume. [pp. 117-118]

$$DOL = \frac{\% \ change \ of \ operating \ income}{\% \ change \ of \ volume}$$

Example: In Table 5-1, if the firm's sales increased by 25% from 80,000 units to 100,000 units, operating profit increases by 66.67%. The DOL is:

$$DOL = \frac{66.67\%}{25.0\%} = 2.67$$

5. The DOL may also be computed using the formulation:

$$DOL = \frac{Q(P - VC)}{Q(P - VC) - FC}$$

where Q= quantity at which DOL is computed
P= price per unit
VC = variable cost per unit
FC = fixed costs

Illustration: Applying the DOL formula to the previous example, DOL at 80,000 units is:

$$DOL = \frac{80,000(\$2.00 - \$.80)}{80,000(\$2.00 - \$.80) - \$60,000} = 2.67$$

Interpretation: The percentage *change* in operating profit will be 2.67 times as large as the percentage change in sales from 80,000 units *in either direction*.

6. The DOL is associated with a specific level of sales and changes as sales change. The DOL for the example firm at 60,000 units sales would be:

$$DOL = \frac{60,000(\$2.00 - \$.80)}{60,000(\$2.00 - \$.80) - \$60,000} = 6$$

7. The analysis of operating leverage is limited by the assumptions of linear variable costs and prices. The concept is applicable, however, over a reasonable operating range for most firms.

III. **Financial Leverage**: A measure of the amount of debt used in the capital structure of the firm. [pp. 119-124]

A. Two firms may have the same operating income but greatly different net incomes due to the magnification effect of financial leverage. The higher the financial leverage, the greater the profits or losses at high or low levels of operating profit, respectively.

TABLE 5-2
IMPACT OF FINANCING PLAN ON EARNINGS PER SHARE

	Plan A (leveraged)	Plan B (conservative)
(1) EBIT - 0		
Earnings before interest and taxes (EBIT)	$ -0-	$ -0-
- Interest (I)	12,000	4,000
Earnings before taxes (EBT)	(12,000)	(4,000)
- Taxes (T)*	(6,000)	(2,000)
Earnings after taxes (EAT)	(6,000)	(2,000)
Shares	8,000	24,000
Earnings per share (EPS)	($ 0 .75)	($ 0 .08)
(2) EBIT - $12,000		
Earnings before interest and taxes (EBIT)	$12,000	$12,000
- Interest (I)	12,000	4,000
Earnings before taxes (EBT)	-0-	8,000
- Taxes (T)	-0-	4,000
Earnings after taxes (EAT)	-0-	4,000
Shares	8,000	24,000
Earnings per share (EPS)	$ -0-	$ 0 .17
(3) EBIT - $36,000		
Earnings before interest and taxes (EBIT)	$36,000	$36,000
- Interest (I)	12,000	4,000
Earnings before taxes (EBT)	24,000	32,000
- Taxes (T)	12,000	16,000
Earnings after taxes (EAT)	12,000	16,000
Shares	8,000	24,000
Earnings per share (EPS)	$ 1.50	$ 0 .67
(4) EBIT - $60,000		
Earnings before interest and taxes (EBIT)	$60,000	$60,000
- Interest (I)	12,000	4,000
Earnings before taxes (EBT)	48,000	56,000
- Taxes (T)	24,000	28,000
Earnings after taxes (EAT)	24,000	28,000
Shares	8,000	24,000
Earnings per share (EPS)	$ 3.00	$ 1.17

---

*The assumption is made that large losses can be written off against other income, perhaps in other years, thus providing the firm with a tax savings benefit.

B.   Financial leverage is beneficial only if the firm can employ the borrowed funds to earn a higher rate of return than the interest rate on the borrowed amount.

C.   The extent of a firm's use of financial leverage may be measured by computing its **degree of financial leverage (DFL)**. The DFL is the ratio of the percentage change in net income (or earnings per share) in response to a percentage change in EBIT. [p. 123]

$$DFL = \frac{\% \text{ change of EPS}}{\% \text{ change of EBIT}}$$

In Table 5-2 the DFL for the conservative firm at an EBIT level of $12,000 is:

$$DFL = \frac{\frac{\Delta EPS}{EPS}}{\frac{\Delta EBIT}{EBIT}} = \frac{\frac{.67 - .17}{.17}}{\frac{36,000 - 12,000}{12,000}} = \frac{300\%}{200\%} = 1.5$$

D. The DFL may also be computed utilizing the following formula:

$$DFL = \frac{EBIT}{EBIT - I}$$

$$DFL = \frac{12,000}{12,000 - 4,000} = \frac{12,000}{8,000} = 1.5$$

Interpretation: Earnings per share will increase or decrease by a factor 1½ times the *percentage* increase or decrease of EBIT.

E. The DFL is associated with a specific level of EBIT and changes as EBIT changes.

F. The purpose of employing financial leverage is to increase return to the owners, but its use also increases their risk.

G. The use of financial leverage is not unlimited.
   1. Interest rates that a firm must pay for debt financing rise as it becomes more highly leveraged.
   2. As the risk to the stockholders increases with leverage, their required rate of return increases and stock prices may decline.

IV. **Combined Leverage** [pp. 124-127]

A. Combining operating and financial leverage provides maximum magnification of returns-- it also magnifies the risk.

B. The combined leverage effect can be illustrated through the income statement.

    Sales ⎫
    EBIT ⎭   DOL ⎫
                   ⎬   DCL
    EBIT ⎫   DFL ⎭
    Net Income ⎭

C. The **degree of combined leverage (DCL)** is a measure of the effect on net income as a result of a change in sales. The DCL is computed similar to DOL or DFL: [pp. 125-126]

$$DCL = \frac{\% \text{ change EPS}}{\% \text{ change sales}}$$

TABLE 5-3

OPERATING AND FINANCIAL LEVERAGE

	80,000 Units	100,000 Units
Sales: $2 per unit	$160,000	$200,000
Fixed costs	-60,000	-60,000
Variable costs ($.80 per unit)	-64,000	-80,000
Operating income (EBIT)	$ 36,000	$ 60,000
Interest	12,000	12,000
Earnings before taxes	$ 24,000	$ 48,000
Taxes	12,000	24,000
Earnings after taxes	$ 12,000	$ 24,000
Shares	8,000	8,000
Earnings per share	$ 1.50	$ 3.00

D.   In Table 5-3 an increase in sales of 25% ($200,000-$160,000)/$160,000 generates a 100% ($3.00-$1.50)/$1.50 increase in EPS.

$$DCL = \frac{100\%}{25\%} = 4$$

E.   The DCL may also be computed as follows: [p. 126]

$$DCL = \frac{Q(P - VC)}{Q(P - VC) - FC - I}$$

$$DCL = \frac{80,000(\$2.00 - \$.80)}{80,000(\$2.00 - \$.80) - \$60,000 - \$12,000}$$

$$= \frac{\$96,000}{\$96,000 - \$60,000 - \$12,000} = 4$$

Interpretation: Earnings per share will increase by 4% with each 1% increase in sales. Likewise, EPS will decrease by 4% with each 1% decline in sales.

F.   DCL may also be found by multiplying DOL times DFL. Using the information in Table 5-3

$$DOL = \frac{80,000(\$2.00 - \$.80)}{80,000(\$2.00 - \$.80) - \$60,000} = 2.67$$

$$DFL = \frac{\$36,000}{\$36,000 - \$12,000} = 1.5$$

$$DCL = DOL \times DFL$$

$$DCL = 2.67 \times 1.5 = 4$$

IV.   Key Formulas

A.   Break-even point [p. 115]

$$BE = \frac{FC}{P - VC}$$

B. Break-even sales [*Study Guide* p. 51]

$$BES = \frac{FC}{1 - TVC/S}$$

C. Cash break-even [p. 117]

$$BE = \frac{FC - depreciation}{P - VC}$$

D. Degree of operating leverage [pp. 117-119]

$$DOL = \frac{Q(P - VC)}{Q(P - VC) - FC}$$

or

$$DOL = \frac{S - TVC}{S - TVC - FC}$$

E. Degree of financial leverage [p. 123]

$$DFL = \frac{EBIT}{EBIT - I}$$

F. Degree of combined leverage [p. 126, *Study Guide* p. 56]

$$DCL = \frac{Q(P - VC)}{Q(P - VC) - FC - I}$$

or

$$DCL = \frac{S - TVC}{S - TVC - FC - I}$$

or

$$DCL = DOL \times DFL$$

Chapter 5 - Multiple Choice Questions

1. At a firm's break-even point: [pp. 113-117]
    a. Total costs = total revenues.
    b. Total contribution = total fixed costs.
    c. Contribution per unit = variable cost per unit.
    d. Both *a* and *b* are correct.
    e. Answers *a*, *b*, and *c* are correct.

2. A firm that has a DOL = 3 will experience what change in operating earnings if sales decrease from $100,000 to $80,000? [p. 118]
    a.   25%
    b.   20%
    c.   75%
    d.   60%
    e.   8.33%

3. Financial leverage is the result of having: [p. 119-120]
    a.   Fixed financial costs.
    b.   Depreciation.
    c.   Fixed operating costs.
    d.   A low break-even point.
    e.   None of the above are correct.

4. Assuming no change in financing strategy, the substitution of machinery for labor: [pp. 112-113]
    a.   Decreases a firm's operating leverage.
    b.   Increases a firm's financial leverage.
    c.   Decreases operating and financial leverage.
    d.   Increases operating leverage.
    e.   Increases operating and combined leverage.

5. A firms break-even point in sales dollars may be computed by which of the following? [SG, p. 51]
    a.   DOL x DFL
    b.   Fixed Costs/(1 - TVC/S)
    c.   DOL/DFL
    d.   EBIT/(EBIT - I)
    e.   Q(P - VC)

6. Which of the following influence a firm's use of operating leverage? [Chpt. 5]
    a.   Nature of the business
    b.   Anticipated economic conditions
    c.   The desire to increase returns
    d.   The risk aversion of management
    e.   All of the above are correct.

7. The DCL of a firm with a DOL = 1.5 and DFL = 1.2 is: [SG, p. 56]
    a.   1.8
    b.   1.25
    c.   2.7
    d.   0.8
    e.   Answer cannot be computed from the information given.

8. A firm currently has earnings per share of $2.72. If its DFL is 2.1 and operating earnings increase by 20%, what will be its new EPS? (Assume no change in the number of shares of stock.) [p. 123]
    a. $3.26
    b. $2.72
    c. $3.86
    d. $1.58
    e. $6.58

9. The DFL of a firm: [pp. 119-124]
    a.   Is invariant with the level of operations of the firm.
    b.   Varies with the level of EBIT.
    c.   Can easily be determined from the balance sheet.
    d.   Is equal to the break-even point in units.
    e.   All of the above are correct.

10. Beyond the break-even point: [pp. 113-117]
   a. All of the contribution per unit is profit.
   b. All of the contribution per unit is absorbed by fixed cost.
   c. All of the contribution per unit is absorbed by variable cost.
   d. There is no contribution per unit.
   e. None of the above are correct.

Multiple Choice Answer Key - Chapter 5

1. d	2. d	3. a	4. e	5. b
6. e	7. a	8. c	9. b	10. a

Chapter 5 - Problems

5-1.   A recently retired professor, Hy Dollar, plans to establish the Hot-Air Fan Company and manufacture circulating fans. He estimates the fixed costs of operations to be $250,000 annually. The variable cost of producing the fans is forecasted to be $75 per unit.

   (a) If the fans are priced at $100, how many must be sold to break even?

   (b) What is the cash break-even point if $100,000 depreciation expense is included in fixed costs?

   (c) If Mr. Dollar seeks to earn $50,000 in profits, how many fans must be sold?

   (d) What would Hot-Air's degree of operating leverage be:
       (1) At a sales level of 11,000 units?
       (2) At 15,000 units?

   (e) What would be the percentage loss of operating profit if Hot-Air's sales tumbled to 12,000 from a high of 20,000 units?
       (1) Answer by computing the operating profit at each level of sales.
       (2) Answer by using the DOL measure.

   (f) Construct a break-even chart on Figure 5-1. On the chart indicate the following:
       (1) Total revenue.
       (2) Total cost.
       (3) Total fixed cost.
       (4) Profit area.
       (5) Loss area.
       (6) Break-even point.

FIGURE 5-1

$

Units

5-2.   Rock Industries has recently begun operations. The firm has estimated that 100,000 units can be sold by the third year of operation if their product can be reasonably priced. The firm has estimated that fixed operating costs will be $1,300,000 and the variable cost per unit will be approximately $6.

   (a)   At what price must the units be sold if Rock is to break even in the third year?

   (b)   If Rock sells 90,000 units, how much will its profit be?

   (c)   How much profit will Rock have if 150,000 units are sold?

5-3.   Using the information in 5-2 above, answer the following questions.

   (a)   Assuming that $195,000 of the fixed costs is depreciation expense, what is the cash break-even point?

   (b)   What is Rock's DOL at a sales level of 90,000 units?

   (c)   What is Rock's DOL at a sales level of 200,000 units?

   (d)   What is Rock's DOL at a sales level of 100,000 units?

5-4.

	A	B	C
Sales	$10,000,000	$10,000,000	$10,000,000
Fixed costs	1,000,000	1,300,000	405,000
Variable costs	6,000,000	6,875,000	9,000,000
Interest	1,000,000	525,000	193,000
Price/Unit	5.00	4.00	2.50

   (a)   Which of the three companies above has the highest degree of operating leverage?

   (b)   Which has the highest degree of financial leverage?

   (c)   Which has the highest degree of combined leverage?

   (d)   If Company C should experience a 20% decline in sales, how would its net income be affected?

5-5.   Professional Supply sells bags of manure to retail nurseries. The retired professors who own and manage the firm must decide whether to further mechanize their operation or continue on a labor intensive basis. The variable cost is currently $.50 per bag and fixed costs are $100,000. By employing more machinery, the firm can reduce variable costs to $.35 per bag although new fixed costs are estimated to be $126,000. The wholesale price of manure is expected to be $2 per bag regardless of the decision.

   (a)   What is the current break-even point in units?

(b)   What will the break-even point be if the firm increases mechanization?

(c)   If the firm anticipates sales of 85,000 bags per year, should the firm increase mechanization?

(d)   How many bags must be sold for increased mechanization to be preferable?

(e)   If Professional Supply has annual interest payments of $15,000, calculate its degree of financial leverage at 75,000 and 90,000 units under current conditions?

5-6.   The officers of the Jekyl and Hyde Corporation are debating the merits of alternative capital structures. The more conservative officers prefer capital structure A, whereas other officers would prefer that capital structure B be established.

A		B	
Long-term debt (6%)	$ 3,500,000	Long-term debt (6%)	$ 5,000,000
Common stockholders' equity ...	6,500,000	Common stockholders' equity ..	5,000,000
	$10,000,000		$10,000,000

(a)   Compute the degree of financial leverage under each capital structure at the following levels of operating earnings:
(1) $1,000,000
(2) $500,000
(3) $350,000

(b)   Compute the earnings per share under each structure for an EBIT of:
(1) $2,000,000 and
(2) $300,000.
Assume 650,000 and 500,000 shares outstanding under structures A and B, respectively, and a 40% tax rate.

5-7.

BRET-MARK CORPORATION
Balance Sheet

Assets		Liabilities & Stockholders' Equity	
Current assets	$ 8,750,000	Current liabilities	$ 4,375,000
Fixed assets	13,125,000	Long-term debt	5,000,000
Total	$21,875,000	Common equity	12,500,000
			$21,875,000

The Bret-Mark Corporation currently produces and sells 1,750,000 zippets per year at an average price of $50 per unit. The variable cost per unit is $35, and the firm's total fixed cost is $7,000,000.

The marketing and financial managers are considering a change in pricing strategy and capital structure. The two managers estimate that unit sales would increase by 20% if the price of a zippet is lowered to $45. Although variable cost per unit would not change, total fixed cost would rise to $8,000,000. The firm is operating at capacity, and an increase in assets would be necessary to support the additional sales.

The financial manager has suggested that additional long-term debt be used to finance the expansion of sales if the pricing change is made. Although using more long-term debt would cause the debt/equity ratio to rise, the financial manager thinks that the new long-term debt can be raised at a cost of 12%, only 2% above the cost of existing debt.

Using the abbreviated balance sheet and the information above, compute the following for B-M on a before and after expansion basis.

(a)   Break-even point.

(b)   Degree of operating leverage.

(c)   Degree of financial leverage.

(d)   Earnings per share (assume a 34% tax rate, a constant asset turnover ratio, and 2,000,000 shares of common stock outstanding).

Chapter 5 - Solutions

5-1.

(a)

$$BEP = \frac{FC}{P - VC} = \frac{\$250,000}{\$100 - \$75} = \frac{\$250,000}{\$25} = \mathbf{10,000\ units}$$

(b)

$$Cash\ BEP = \frac{FC - depreciation}{P - VC}$$

$$Cash\ BEP = \frac{\$250,000 - \$100,000}{\$100 - \$75} = \frac{\$150,000}{\$25} = \mathbf{6,000\ units}$$

(c)   Units that must be sold to provide $50,000 profit =

$$\frac{FC + \$50,000}{P - VC} = \frac{\$250,000 + \$50,000}{\$100 - \$75} = \frac{\$300,000}{\$25} = \mathbf{12,000\ units}$$

(d)   (1)

$$DOL = \frac{Q(P - VC)}{Q(P - VC) - FC} = \frac{11,000(\$100 - \$75)}{11,000(\$100 - \$75) - \$250,000} = \frac{\$275,000}{\$275,000 - \$250,000}$$

$$= \frac{\$275,000}{\$25,000} = \mathbf{11}$$

(2)

$$DOL = \frac{15,000(\$100 - \$75)}{15,000(\$100 - \$75) - \$250,000} = \mathbf{3}$$

(e) (1)

Sales (20,000 units)	=	$2,000,000	
Total variable costs	=	1,500,000	
Total contribution	=	$ 500,000	
Fixed costs	=	250,000	
Operating profit	=	$ 250,000	
Sales (12,000 units)	=	$1,200,000	
Total variable costs	=	900,000	
Total contribution	=	$ 300,000	
Fixed costs	=	250,000	
Operating profit	=	$ 50,000	

$$\text{Percentage decline of profits} = \frac{\$200,000}{\$250,000} = \mathbf{80\%}$$

(2)

$$DOL(20,000 \ units) = \frac{20,000(\$100 - \$75)}{20,000(\$100 - \$75) - \$250,000} = \frac{\$500,000}{\$500,000 - \$250,000} = 2$$

$$\text{Percentage decline of sales} = \frac{\$800,000}{\$2,000,000} = 40\%$$

$$\text{Percentage decline of profit} = DOL \times \text{percentage decline of sales} = 2 \times 40\% = \mathbf{80\%}$$

(f)

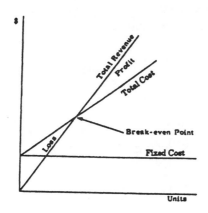

5-2. Rock Industries

(a) $BE = \dfrac{FC}{P - VC}$

$100,000 = \dfrac{\$1,300,000}{P - \$6}$

$100,000(P - \$6) = \$1,300,000$

$100,000P = \$1,900,000$

$P = \$1,900,000/100,000 = \mathbf{\$19}$

(b)   TR - TVC - FC = profit

90,000($19) - 90,000($6) - $1,300,000 = profit

$1,710,000 - $540,000 - $1,300,000 = **-$130,000**

(c)   Since all contributions beyond break-even goes to profits and 100,000 units is estimated to be the break-even point, profits at 150,000 units of sales would be:

50,000($19 - $6) = **$650,000**

5-3.   (a)

$$Cash\ break\ even = \frac{\$1,300,000 - \$195,000}{\$19 - \$6} = \mathbf{85,000}$$

(b)

$$DOL = \frac{90,000(\$19 - \$6)}{90,000(\$19 - \$6) - \$1,300,000} = \frac{\$1,170,000}{\$1,170,000 - \$1,300,000} = \mathbf{-9}$$

(c)

$$DOL = \frac{200,000(\$19 - \$6)}{200,000(\$19 - \$6) - \$1,300,000} = \mathbf{2}$$

(d)

$$DOL = \frac{100,000(\$19 - \$6)}{100,000(\$19 - \$6) - \$1,300,000} = \frac{\$1,300,000}{0} = \mathbf{undefined}$$

The break-even point for Rock Industries is 100,000 units. At break-even, profit equals zero. The percentage change from zero is not defined.

5-4.   (a)

$$Company\ A\ unit\ sales = \frac{\$10,000,000}{\$5} = 2,000,000$$

$$Company\ B\ unit\ sales = \frac{\$10,000,000}{\$4} = 2,500,000$$

$$Company\ C\ unit\ sales = \frac{\$10,000,000}{\$2.50} = 4,000,000$$

$$A\ variable\ cost/unit = \frac{\$6,000,000}{2,000,000} = \$3$$

$$B\ variable\ cost/unit = \frac{\$6,875,000}{2,500,000} = \$2.75$$

$$C\ variable\ cost/unit = \frac{\$9,000,000}{4,000,000} = \$2.25$$

$$DOL(A) = \frac{2,000,000(\$5 - \$3)}{2,000,000(\$5 - \$3) - \$1,000,000} = \frac{\$4,000,000}{\$4,000,000 - \$1,000,000} = \mathbf{1.33}$$

$$DOL(B) = \frac{2,500,000(\$4 - \$2.75)}{2,500,000(\$4 - \$2.75) - \$1,300,000} = \frac{\$3,125,000}{\$3,125,000 - \$1,300,000} = \mathbf{1.712}$$

$$DOL(C) = \frac{4,000,000(\$2.50 - \$2.25)}{4,000,000(\$2.50 - \$2.25) - \$405,000} = \frac{\$1,000,000}{\$1,000,000 - \$405,000} = \mathbf{1.68}$$

(b) $EBIT(A) = \$10,000,000 - \$1,000,000 - \$6,000,000 = \$3,000,000$
  $EBIT(B) = \$10,000,000 - \$1,300,000 - \$6,875,000 = \$1,825,000$
  $EBIT(C) = \$10,000,000 - \$405,000 - \$9,000,000 = \$595,000$

$$DFL(A) = \frac{\$3,000,000}{\$3,000,000 - \$1,000,000} = \frac{\$3,000,000}{\$2,000,000} = \mathbf{1.5}$$

$$DFL(B) = \frac{\$1,825,000}{\$1,825,000 - \$525,000} = \frac{\$1,825,000}{\$1,300,000} = \mathbf{1.40}$$

$$DFL(C) = \frac{\$595,000}{\$595,000 - \$193,000} = \frac{\$595,000}{\$402,000} = \mathbf{1.48}$$

(c)

$$DCL(A) = \frac{2,000,000(\$5 - \$3)}{2,000,000(\$5 - \$3) - \$1,000,000 - \$1,000,000} = \frac{\$4,000,000}{\$2,000,000} = \mathbf{2}$$

$$DCL(B) = \frac{2,500,000(\$4 - \$2.75)}{2,500,000(\$4 - \$2.75) - \$1,300,000 - \$525,000} = \frac{\$3,125,000}{\$1,300,000} = \mathbf{2.4} \ (rounded)$$

$$DCL(C) = \frac{4,000,000(\$2.50 - \$2.25)}{4,000,000(\$2.50 - \$2.25) - \$405,000 - \$193,000} = \frac{\$1,000,000}{\$402,000} = \mathbf{2.5} \ (rounded)$$

(d) Percentage change in income
  DCL x % change in sales
  2.5 x 20% = 50%
  Net income would decline by 50%.
  An alternative approach to the solution would be as follows (assume a 34% tax rate):

	Present	20% Decline in Sales
Sales	$10,000,000	$8,000,000
Variable costs	9,000,000	7,200,000
	$ 1,000,000	$ 800,000
Fixed costs	405,000	405,000
EBIT	$ 595,000	$ 395,000
Interest	193,000	193,000
Taxable income	$ 402,000	$ 202,000
Taxes (34%)	136,680	68,680
Net Income	$ 265,320	$ 133,320

$132,000

$$\% \, \Delta \text{ of net income } = \frac{\$132,000}{\$265,000} = \textbf{50\%} \text{ (rounded)}$$

5-5. Professional Supply

(a)

$$BEP = \frac{\$100,000}{\$2.00 - \$.50} = \frac{\$100,000}{\$1.50} = \textbf{66,667} \text{ (rounded)}$$

(b)

$$BEP = \frac{\$126,000}{\$2.00 - \$.35} = \textbf{76,364} \text{ (rounded)}$$

(c) All contribution beyond the break-even point is profit. Under current operations the profit at 85,000 units of sales would be:

(85,000 - 66,667) x ($1.50) = **$27,499.50**

Under increased mechanization, profit at 85,000 units would be:

(85,000 - 76,364) x ($1.65) = **$14,249**

The firm should continue current operations.

(d) There are several approaches to this question. The easiest approach is to use the break even formula. Since the contribution per unit is .15 more per bag and the fixed costs are $26,000 more under mechanization,

$$BEP = \frac{\$26,000}{\$.15} = \textbf{173,333}$$

Under current operations, profit at 173,333 bags would be:

Profit = 173,333($2 - $.50) - $100,000 = $159,999.50

Under mechanization profit would be:

Profit = 173,333($2 - $.35) - $126,000 = $159,999.45

Beyond 173,333 bags in sales, mechanization will provide greater profits.

(e) *EBIT* @ 75,000 units

EBIT = 75,000($2 - $.50) - $100,000 = $12,500

$$DFL = \frac{\$12,500}{\$12,500 - \$15,000} = \frac{\$12,500}{-\$2,500} = \textbf{-5}$$

EBIT @ 90,000 units

EBIT = 90,000($2 - $.50) - $100,000 = $35,000

$$DFL = \frac{\$35,000}{\$35,000 - \$15,000} = \textbf{1.75}$$

5-6. (a)

$$DFL = \frac{EBIT}{EBIT - I}$$

	A	B

(1) $DFL = \dfrac{\$1,000,000}{\$1,000,000 - \$210,000} = \mathbf{1.27}$ $DFL = \dfrac{\$1,000,000}{\$1,000,000 - \$300,000} = \mathbf{1.43}$

(2) $DFL = \dfrac{\$500,000}{\$500,000 - \$210,000} = \mathbf{1.72}$ $DFL = \dfrac{\$500,000}{\$500,000 - \$300,000} = \mathbf{2.5}$

(3) $DFL = \dfrac{\$350,000}{\$350,000 - \$210,000} = \mathbf{2.5}$ $DFL = \dfrac{\$350,000}{\$350,000 - \$300,000} = \mathbf{7}$

(b) (1)

A			B		
EBIT	=	$2,000,000	EBIT	=	$2,000,000
Interest	=	210,000	Interest	=	300,000
Taxable income	=	1,790,000	Taxable income	=	1,700,000
Taxes (40%)	=	716,000	Taxes (40%)	=	680,000
Net income	=	$1,074,000	Net income	=	$1,020,000

$$EPS = \frac{\$1,074,000}{650,000} = \mathbf{\$1.65} \qquad EPS = \frac{\$1,020,000}{500,000} = \mathbf{\$2.04}$$

(2)

A			B		
EBIT	=	$300,000	EBIT	=	$300,000
Interest	=	210,000	Interest	=	300,000
Taxable income	=	90,000	Taxable income	=	0
Taxes (40%)	=	36,600	Taxes (40%)	=	0
Net income	=	$ 54,000	Net income	=	$ 0

$$EPS = \frac{\$54,000}{650,000} = \mathbf{\$.083} \qquad EPS = \frac{\$0}{500,000} = \mathbf{\$0}$$

5-7. (a)

Before: $BEP = \dfrac{FC}{P - VC} = \dfrac{\$7,000,000}{\$50 - \$35} = \dfrac{\$7,000,000}{\$15} = \mathbf{466,667\ units}$

After: $BEP = \dfrac{\$8,000,000}{\$45 - \$35} = \mathbf{800,000\ units}$

(b)

$$\text{Before: } DOL = \frac{Q(P - VC)}{Q(P - VC) - FC} = \frac{1,750,000(\$50 - \$35}{1,750,000(\$50 - \$35) - \$7,000,000}$$

$$DOL = \frac{\$26,250,000}{\$26,250,000 - \$7,000,000} = \frac{\$26,250,000}{\$19,250,000} = \textbf{1.36}$$

After: *Unit sales* = 1,750,000 + 1,750,000(.2) = 2,100,000

$$DOL = \frac{2,100,000(\$45 - \$35)}{2,100,000(\$45 - \$35) - \$8,000,000} = \frac{\$21,000,000}{\$13,000,000} = \textbf{1.62}$$

(c)

Before: Annual interest = .10(\$5,000,000) = \$500,000

EBIT = sales - variable operating costs - fixed operating costs
EBIT = \$87,500,000 - \$61,250,000 - \$7,000,000
EBIT = \$19,250,000

$$DFL = \frac{EBIT}{EBIT - I} = \frac{\$19,250,000}{\$19,250,000 - \$500,000} = \frac{\$19,250,000}{\$18,750,000} = \textbf{1.03}$$

After: New sales = 2,100,000(\$45) = \$94,500,000

If the total asset turnover ratio remains the same (this would depend upon the interrelationships of price, sales volume, and production characteristics), \$87,500,000/\$21,875,000 = 4, then the new required asset level will be \$94,500,000/4 = \$23,625,000.

Additional assets required = \$23,625,000 - \$21,875,000 = \$1,750,000

New long-term debt level = \$5,000,000 + \$1,750,000 = \$6,750,000

Annual interest = \$5,000,000(.10) + \$1,750,000(.12) = \$500,000 + \$210,000 = \$710,000

EBIT = \$94,500,000 - \$2,100,000(\$35) - \$8,000,000

    = \$94,500,000 - \$73,500,000 - \$8,000,000 = \$13,000,000

$$DFL = \frac{\$13,000,000}{\$13,000,000 - \$710,000} = \textbf{1.06}$$

(d)   Before: EPS = net income/number of shares outstanding

Taxable income = EBIT - I = \$19,250,000 - \$500,000 = \$18,750,000

Taxes = .34(\$18,750,000) = \$6,375,000

Net income = \$18,750,000 - \$6,375,000 = \$12,375,000

$$EPS = \frac{\$12,375,000}{2,000,000} = \textbf{\$6.19}$$

After: Taxable income = $13,000,000 - $710,000 = $12,290,000

Taxes = .34($12,290,000) = $4,178,600

Net income = $12,290,000 - $4,178,600 = $8,111,400

$$EPS = \frac{\$8,111,400}{2,000,000} = \mathbf{\$4.06}$$

The change in pricing strategy of the firm would probably have a negative impact on the firm and should not be undertaken.

Summary: **Working capital management** is concerned with the financing and management of the current assets of the firm. This chapter emphasizes the factors that the financial manager must consider in determining the mix between **temporary and permanent current assets** and the nature of the financing arrangement.

I.   Working Capital Management [p. 144]

  A.   Management of working capital is the financial manager's most time-consuming function.

  B.   Success in managing current assets in the short run is critical for the firm's long-run existence.

  C.   Nature of asset growth. [p. 144]
    1.   Changes in current assets may be temporary (seasonal) or "permanent."
      a.   Current assets by definition are those expected to become cash in one operating cycle, but the *level* of the current assets may be "permanent" or increasing.
      b.   Businesses subject to cyclical sales may have temporary fluctuations in the level of current assets.

FIGURE 6-1
USING LONG-TERM FINANCING FOR PART OF SHORT-TERM NEEDS

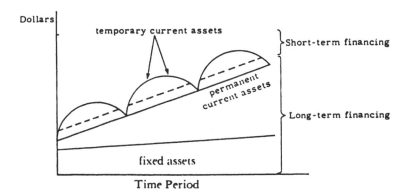

Study Note: An illustration should clarify the concept of seasonal and permanent working capital. A department store that expands its selling area by 10,000 square feet must stock the shelves with additional merchandise. Although the individual items are not expected to remain on the shelf, the shelves must always be stocked. The company's *level* of inventory has risen. There is a minimum or permanent level of inventory that the firm must always maintain. As the firm grows, this permanent level of inventory also grows. Likewise, other current asset levels increase with growth. If the department store sells on credit, its level of accounts receivable should rise as a result of the expansion due to the added sales. Cash requirements are likely to increase also as cash registers are added to the new sales area, and additional bank balances are needed.

Seasonal fluctuations also occur. During the Christmas shopping season, for example, the department store will place more merchandise than usual on its shelves. This temporary increase will not be replaced, however, at the end of the holiday season.

2. Matching sales and production.
   a. Both accounts receivable and inventory rise when sales increase as production increases. When sales rise faster than production, inventory declines and receivables rise.
   b. Level production may cause large buildups in current assets when sales are slack. These buildups drop rapidly during peak demand periods since sales exceed the level production output.

D. Both seasonal and permanent increases in working capital must be financed. [pp. 151-155]]
   1. Ideally, temporary increases in current assets are financed by short-term funds and permanent current assets are financed with long-term sources.
   2. The inability to precisely forecast temporary increases in working capital and the coinciding availability of short-term financing, constrains many firms to finance some temporary current assets with long-term capital.

II. The Term Structure of Interest Rates [pp. 156-159]

A. The relationship of interest rates at a specific point in time for securities of equal risk but different maturity dates is referred to as the term structure of interest rates.

B. The **term structure of interest rates** is depicted by yield curves. Generally, U.S. government securities are used to construct yield curves because they are free of default risk.

C. There are three theories describing the shape of the yield curve:
   1. **Liquidity premium theory**: the theory states that long-term rates should be higher than short-term rates because long-term securities are less liquid and more price sensitive. [p. 157]
   2. **Segmentation theory**: the yield curve is "shaped" by the relative demand for securities of various maturities. Some institutions such as commercial banks are primarily interested in short-term securities. Others such as insurance companies manifest a preference for much longer-term securities. [p. 157]
   3. **Expectations hypothesis**: the expectations hypothesis says that long-term rates reflect the average of expected short-term rates over the time period that the long-term security is outstanding. [p. 157]

D. Types of yield curves. [pp. 158-159]
   1. Normal: upward sloping; shorter maturities have lower required yields.
   2. Humped: intermediate interest rates are higher than both the short-term and long-term rates.
   3. Inverted, downward sloping: short-term rates are higher than intermediate or long-term rates.

E. Yield curves shift upward and downward in response to changes in anticipated inflation rates and other conditions of uncertainty.

III. A Decision Process [pp. 159-161]

A. The composition of a firm's financing of working capital is made within the risk-return framework.
   1. Short-term financing is generally less costly but more risky than long-term financing.
   2. During tight money periods, short-term financing may be unavailable or very expensive.

B.   Applying probabilities of occurrence of various economic conditions, an expected value of alternative forms of financing may be computed and used as a decision basis.

IV.   Shifts in Asset Structure [p. 162]

A.   Risk versus return considerations also affect the composition of the left-hand side of the balance sheet.

B.   A firm may compensate for high risk on the financing side with high liquidity on the asset side or vice versa.

C.   Since the early 1960s, business firms have reduced their liquidity as a result of:
1.   More efficient inventory management.
2.   More efficient transfer of cash and better utilization of cash balances.
3.   Ability to sell accounts receivable through securitization of assets.
4.   Willingness to take more liquidity risk.

D.   The ultimate current asset composition and financing decision should be consistent with the firm's **goal of maximizing owners' wealth**.
1.   An aggressive firm will borrow short term and carry high levels of inventory and longer term receivables. The firm's position is represented by panel 1 of Table 6-1.
2.   The conservative firm (panel 4) will maintain high liquidity and utilize more long-term financing.
3.   Moderate firms compensate for short-term financing with highly liquid assets (panel 2) or balance low liquidity with long-term financing (panel 3).

TABLE 6-1
ASSET LIQUIDITY AND FINANCING ASSETS

Financing Plan	Low Liquidity	High Liquidity
Short term	1 High Profit High Risk	2 Moderate Profit Moderate Risk
Long term	3 Moderate Profit Moderate Risk	4 Low Profit Low Risk

Chapter 6 - Multiple Choice Questions

1.   Working capital management is concerned with: [p. 144]
a.   Management of current assets.
b.   Management of fixed assets.
c.   Financing current assets.
d.   Management of seasonal assets.
e.   Both *a* and *c* are correct.

2. An aggressive firm will utilize more _____ and maintain _____ liquidity than a conservative firm. [pp. 162-163]
    a. Short-term debt; higher
    b. Long-term debt; lower
    c. Long-term debt; higher
    d. Short-term debt; lower
    e. None of the above are correct.

3. Usually yield curves are _____ _____, but in other periods (e.g., peak periods of economic expansion) yield curves may be _____ _____. [pp. 158-159]
    a. Upward sloping; downward sloping
    b. Downward sloping; sharply peaked
    c. Downward sloping; upward sloping
    d. Upward sloping; normally humped
    e. None of the above are correct.

4. The theory that the yield curve is "shaped" by the relative demand for securities of various maturities is the: [p. 157]
    a. Liquidity premium theory.
    b. Segmentation theory.
    c. Risk-return tradeoff.
    d. Block and Hirt theory.
    e. Expectations hypothesis.

5. The "term structure of interest rates" is depicted by: [p. 156]
    a. The level of permanent current assets.
    b. The level of seasonal current assets.
    c. The yield curve.
    d. The ratio of current assets to fixed assets.
    e. None of the above are correct.

6. A firm may compensate for _____ risk on the financing side with _____ liquidity on the asset side. [pp. 162-163]
    a. Low; high
    b. High; low
    c. Low; low
    d. High; high
    e. All of the above are acceptable answers.

7. The concept of "permanent" current assets refers to: [p. 144]
    a. Plant and equipment.
    b. Inventory.
    c. The minimum level of current assets.
    d. Accounts receivable plus cash.
    e. Total assets.

8. Since the mid-1960s, corporate liquidity has generally been: [p. 162]
    a. Falling.
    b. Rising.
    c. Unchanged.
    d. Sharply rising.
    e. Rising and falling.

9. A yield curve which depicts long-term interest rates to be higher than short-term interest rates is said to be: [p. 158]
   a. Inverted.
   b. Complex.
   c. Humped.
   d. Normal.
   e. Skewed.

10. Retail-oriented firms have been more successful in matching sales and orders in recent years as a result of: [p. 148]
    a. Hand-held calculators.
    b. Point-of-sales terminals.
    c. Level production.
    d. Reduction of liquidity.
    e. Using permanent current assets.

Multiple Choice Answer Key - Chapter 6

1. e	2. d	3. a	4. b	5. c
6. d	7. c	8. a	9. d	10. b

Chapter 6 - Problems

6-1. Digital Video requires $1 in current assets for each $4 of sales that it generates. If the firm has a net profit margin of 8% and the level of fixed assets does not change, what amount of external financing will the company require if sales increase from $2,000,000 to $3,600,000 (assume all earnings are retained and disregard depreciation)?

6-2. Holly Bofinger, owner of Bofinger Sporting Goods anticipates sales next year to be $780,000 if the economy is in recession as predicted by many analysts. Sales in the recently completed year were $975,000. Prior to the forecast of recession, Holly had hoped that sales would reach $1,100,000. Although it seems likely that the forecasted recession will occur, she feels that the probabilities of equaling last year's sales and reaching the $1,100,000 are 20% and 10%, respectively. What is the expected level of sales next year?

6-3. Broussard's U-Rent-It is rapidly expanding and needs to acquire several new items including two hydraulic log splitters, a ditching machine, two cement mixers, several lawn mowers of various sizes, five party tents, and three Santa Claus suits. Mr. Broussard needs $120,000 to acquire the new items and is contemplating two loan arrangements. National Bank will extend the $120,000 to be paid off over three years at the prime rate plus 2%. State bank will extend the loan at a fixed rate of 12% per year. Mr. Broussard expects the prime rate to be 11%, 9%, and 8%, respectively over the next three years.

(a) Assuming that under each loan, Mr. Broussard will pay $40,000 on the principal at the end of the year, what is the total amount of interest on each loan?

(b) Which of the borrowing arrangements is the more risky to Mr. Broussard?

6-4. The Opti-Mist Sprinkler Company is analyzing two financing plans to support an anticipated increase in sales. Officials of the firm anticipate that the firm will be able to maintain its operating profit margin of 20% regardless of the level of sales.

Using the probability estimates of the sales levels and associated financial characteristics, determine which financing plan will provide the highest expected net income. The firm is in the 40% tax bracket.

	Plan A		
Conditions	Below Normal	Normal	Above Normal
Probability of occurrence	.3	.4	.3
Sales	$8,000,000	$10,000,000	$12,000,000
Interest on long-term debt	180,000	180,000	180,000
Interest on short-term debt	40,000	50,000	60,000

	Plan B		
Conditions	Below Normal	Normal	Above Normal
Probability of occurrence	.3	.4	.3
Sales	$8,000,000	$10,000,000	$11,000,000*
Interest on long-term debt	100,000	100,000	100,000
Interest on short-term debt	60,000	100,000	130,000

*Sales are assumed to be less under above-normal conditions for Plan B than for Plan A due to lack of available short-term financing.

Chapter 6 - Solutions

6-1. $1,600,000 + 4 = $400,000 additional current assets required

$3,600,000
.08
$ 288,000 profit

$ 400,000
288,000
$112,000 external financing required

6-2. Bofinger Sporting Goods
Expected sales = $780,000(.70) + $975,000(.20) + $1,100,000(.10) = **$851,000**

6-3. Broussard's U-Rent-It

(a) National Bank
Total interest = .13($120,000) + .11($80,000) + .10($40,000) = **$28,400**
State Bank
Total interest = .12($120,000) + .12($80,000) + .12($40,000) = **$28,800**

(b)   Although the predicted total interest on the National Bank loan is less, the actual interest may be much more if interest rates rise. Of course, interest rates may be less than predicted. Mr. Broussard must weigh the expected savings against the potentially higher interest costs. (Timing, a very important consideration, is ignored in this analysis. The concept will be fully explored in chapter 9.)

6-4.

Plan A

Sales	$8,000,000	$10,000,000	$12,000,000
EBIT (20%)	$1,600,000	$ 2,000,000	$ 2,400,000
Interest:			
Long-term debt	180,000	180,000	180,000
Short-term debt	40,000	50,000	60,000
Taxable income . . .	$1,380,000	$ 1,770,000	$ 2,160,000
Taxes	552,000	708,000	864,000
Net income	$ 828,000	$ 1,062,000	$ 1,296,000

Expected net income from Plan A   = $828,000(.3) + $1,062,000(.4) + $1,296,000(.3)
                                     = $248,400 + $424,800 + $388,800
                                     =   **$1,062,000**

Plan B

Sales	$8,000,000	$10,000,000	$11,000,000
EBIT (20%)	$1,600,000	$ 2,000,000	$ 2,200,000
Interest:			
Long-term debt	100,000	100,000	100,000
Short-term debt	60,000	100,000	130,000
Taxable income . . .	$1,440,000	$ 1,800,000	$ 1,970,000
Taxes	576,000	720,000	788,000
Net Income	$ 864,000	$ 1,080,000	$ 1,182,000

Expected net income from Plan B   = $864,000(.3) + $1,080,000(.4) + $1,182,000(.3)
                                     = $259,200 + $432,000 + $354,600
                                     =   **$1,045,800**

Summary: This chapter examines the characteristics of cash, marketable securities, accounts receivable, and inventory and the processes utilized in determining the appropriate level of cash.

I.   Cash Management [p. 173]

    A.   Cash is a necessary but low-earning asset.

    B.   Financial managers attempt to minimize cash balances and yet maintain sufficient amounts to meet obligations in a timely manner.

    C.   Reasons for holding cash balances: [p. 173]
        1.   **Transactions balances** are needed for recurring expenses such as payrolls and taxes. The acquisition of long-term assets, though less frequent, also requires such balances.
        2.   Banks are compensated for services by maintaining cash balances on deposit. Such amounts are called **compensating balances**.
        3.   **Precautionary balances** are held as a hedge against unprojected negative cash flows.

    D.   The level of cash balances in a firm is largely determined by the pattern of its cash inflows and outflows. A firm's cash flow pattern is affected by many factors including:
        1.   Payment pattern of customers.
        2.   The mix of cash sales and credit sales.
        3.   Credit terms; 30 days, 60 days, etc.
        4.   Clearing time of disbursed checks.
        5.   Efficiency of the banking system.
        6.   The shelf life of inventory and/or production cycle of the firm.

    E.   Temporarily, excess cash balances are transferred into interest-earning marketable securities.

    F.   The financial manager attempts to get maximum use of minimum balances by speeding up inflows and slowing outflows.
        1.   Playing the **float**: using the difference in cash balances shown on the bank's records and those shown on the firm's records. [pp. 176-177]
        2.   Improving collections.
            a.   Decentralized collection centers speed collection of accounts receivable by reducing mailing time.
            b.   Wire transfer of funds--excess cash balances are transferred from collection points to a centralized location for use.
            c.   **Lock-box system**--customers mail payments to a post office box serviced by a local bank in their geographical area. Checks are cleared locally and balances transferred by wire to a central location. [p. 178]
        3.   Extended disbursement float to take advantage of slower clearing of checks.

    G.   Cost-benefit analysis. [pp. 178-179]
        1.   The primary benefits of speeding up inflows or slowing outflows is the earnings generated from the freed-up balances. If a firm can reduce its cash balances from $3,000,000 to $2,000,000 through the use of a lock-box system, the $1,000,000 that is freed up may be put to work.

2. The benefits must be weighed against the cost when employing cash management techniques. If, in the example above, the $1,000,000 could be employed to earn a 10% return ($100,000), the firm would not want to expend more than $100,000 for the services of the bank and other charges.

H. The use of **electronic funds transfer**, a system in which funds are moved between computer terminals without the use of a check, has reduced need for delaying payment and other float-creating processes. [pp. 179-181]
    1. Automated clearinghouse (ACH) transfers between financial institutions and from account to account via computer tape are an important element of electronic funds transfer. One of the most popular uses is direct deposit of payroll and pension checks. [p. 180]
    2. International electronic funds transfer is mainly carried out by the Society for Worldwide Interbank Financial Telecommunications (**SWIFT**).
        a. Over 6,500 financial institutions in 175 countries use SWIFT's services.
        b. Around-the-clock automated international message processing and transmission services for financial transactions.
        c. Messages are encrypted for security and SWIFT assumes financial liability for the accuracy, completeness, and confidentiality of transactions.
        d. With an estimated $2 trillion daily value of SWIFT messages, electronic fraud is a growing concern.

I. International cash management. [pp. 181-182]
    1. Multinational firms shift cash balances among countries in order to benefit from differing interest rates on marketable securities and/or to take advantage of currency exchange rates.
    2. The same techniques of cash management used domestically are utilized in the expanding international money markets. International cash management, however, is more complex due to differences in time zones, fluctuations in currency exchange rates and interest rates, differences in banking systems, and numerous other factors.

II. Marketable Securities [pp. 182-186]

A. Cash balances temporarily held for dividends, debt payments, or other purposes can frequently be utilized to purchase interest-earning **marketable securities** (see Table 7-1).

B. Many factors influence the choice of marketable securities:
    1. Yield.
    2. Maturity (interest rate risk).
    3. Minimum investment required.
    4. Safety.
    5. Marketability.

III. Management of Accounts Receivable [pp. 186-192]

A. Accounts receivable as a percentage of total assets almost doubled between 1960 and the year 2000 for the typical U.S. corporation. The primary reasons for the increases have been:
    1. Increasing sales.
    2. Inflation.
    3. Extended credit terms during recessions.

B. Accounts receivable are an investment. Investment in accounts receivable should generate a return equal to or in excess of the return available on alternative investments. [p. 187]

TABLE 7-1
TYPES OF SHORT-TERM INVESTMENTS

Investment	Maturity*	Minimum Amount	Safety	Market-ability	Yield 3/22/80	Yield 7/14/00
Federal government securities:						
Treasury bills	3 months	$ 1,000	Excellent	Excellent	14.76	6.06
Treasury bills	1 year	1,000	Excellent	Excellent	13.89	6.34
Treasury notes	1-10 years	5,000	Excellent	Excellent	13.86	6.29
Inflation-indexed Treasury securities	10 years	1,000	Excellent	Excellent	--	4.03
Federal agency securities:						
Federal Home Loan Bank	1 year	5,000	Excellent	Excellent	14.40	6.78
Student Loan Marketing Assoc.	1 year	5,000	Excellent	Excellent	--	6.12
Nongovernment securities:						
Certificates of deposit (large)	3 months	100,000	Good	Good	16.97	6.65
Certificates of deposit (small)	3 months	500	Good	Poor	15.90	6.00
Commercial paper	3 months	25,000	Good	Fair	17.40	6.50
Banker's acceptances	3 months	None	Good	Good	17.22	6.51
Eurodollar deposits	3 months	25,000	Good	Excellent	18.98	6.75
Savings accounts	Open	None	Excellent	None**	5.25	3.00
Money market funds	Open	500	Good	None**	14.50	6.00
Money market deposit accounts (financial institutions)	Open	1,000	Excellent	None**	--	5.50

*Several of the above securities can be purchased with maturities longer than indicated. The above are the most commonly quoted.

**Though not marketable, these investments are highly liquid in that funds may be withdrawn without penalty.

C.　There are three primary variables of credit policy. [pp. 186-191]
　　1.　Credit standards.
　　　　a.　The firm screens credit applicants on the basis of prior record of payment, financial stability, current net worth, and other factors.
　　　　b.　Bankers often refer to the **5 C's of credit** as an indication of whether a loan will be repaid. These characteristics are equally important to business firms which sell on credit. The C's of credit are: [p. 189]
　　　　　　(1)　**Character** - moral and ethical quality of those responsible for repayment.
　　　　　　(2)　**Capital** - the level of resources available to the company.
　　　　　　(3)　**Capacity** - sufficiency of firm's cash flow to repay debt.
　　　　　　(4)　**Conditions** - sensitivity of the firm's cash flow to changes in the economy and operating environment.
　　　　　　(5)　**Collateral** - quantity and quality of assets that can be pledged against the loan.
　　　　c.　Many sources such as Dun & Bradstreet Information Services, serve as a basis for credit evaluation.
　　2.　Terms of trade.
　　3.　Collection policy: Some of the measures used to assess collection efficiency are:
　　　　a.　Average collection period.
　　　　b.　Ratio of bad debts to sales.
　　　　c.　Aging of accounts receivable.

D.　An actual credit decision is based on the expected return on investment compared to the firm's required rate of return. [pp. 191-192]
　　1.　First, the expected after-tax return (in dollars) is calculated.
　　2.　The investment required to support the additional credit sales must also be

calculated. Additional credit sales will cause the investment in accounts receivable to rise and may increase the inventory required as well as other assets.

    3.   The expected return on investment (%) is projected by dividing the expected dollar returns by the additional investment.

    4.   If the expected return on investment exceeds the required return, the firm may make the credit sale.

IV.   Inventory Management [pp. 192-198]

    A.   Inventory is the least liquid of current assets.

    B.   A firm's level of inventory is largely determined by the cyclicality of sales and whether it follows a seasonal or level production schedule. The production decision is based on the trade-off of cost savings of level production versus the additional inventory carrying costs.

    C.   Rapid price movements complicate the inventory level decision.

    D.   There are two basic costs associated with inventory:
        1.   **Carrying costs**: [p. 193]
            a.   Interest on funds tied up in inventory.
            b.   Warehouse space costs.
            c.   Insurance.
            d.   Material handling expenses.
            e.   Risk of obsolescence (implicit cost).
        2.   **Ordering costs**. [p. 194]

    E.   Carrying costs vary directly with average inventory levels.

    F.   Total carrying costs increase as the order size increases.

    G.   Total ordering costs decrease as the order size increases.

    H.   The first step toward achieving minimum inventory costs is determination of the optimal order quantity. This quantity may be derived by use of the **economic order quantity formula**: [p. 195]

$$EOQ = \sqrt{\frac{2SO}{C}}$$

where EOQ = economic ordering quantity
               S = total sales in units
               O = ordering cost for each order
               C = carrying cost per unit in dollars

FIGURE 7-1
DETERMINING THE OPTIMUM INVENTORY LEVEL

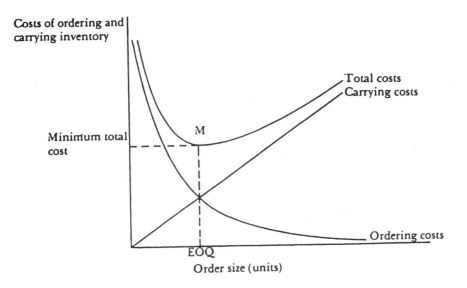

I.   Assumptions of the basic EOQ model:
      1.   Inventory usage is at a constant rate.
      2.   Order costs per order are constant.
      3.   Delivery time of orders is consistent and order arrives as inventory reaches zero.

J.   Minimum total inventory costs will result if the assumptions of the model are applicable
      and the firm's order size equals the economic ordering quantity.

K.   The EOQ model has also been applied to the management of cash balances. The
      opportunity cost (lost interest on marketable securities) of having cash is analogous to
      the carrying costs of inventory. Likewise, the transactions cost of shifting in and out of
      marketable securities is very similar to inventory order costs.

L.   Stock outs and safety stock. [pp. 195-196]
      1.   A **stock out** occurs when a firm misses sales because it is out of an inventory
           item.
      2.   A firm may hold **safety stock**, inventory beyond the level determined by the EOQ
           model, to reduce the risk of losing sales. Safety stock hedges against stock outs
           caused by delayed deliveries, production delays, equipment breakdown,
           unexpected surges in sales, etc.
      3.   Safety stock will increase a firm's average inventory and carrying costs.

        Average inventory = $\dfrac{EOQ}{2}$ + *safety stock*

        Carrying costs = *average inventory units* × *carrying cost per unit*

      4.   Ideally, the additional carrying costs from having safety stock is offset by
           eliminating lost profits on missed sales and/or maintenance of good customer
           relations.

M. Just-in-time inventory management (JIT). [pp. 197-198]
    1. **Just-in-time inventory management (JIT)** seeks to minimize the level of inventory within a highly effective quality control program.
    2. Manufacturers seek to utilize suppliers located nearby who are able to deliver small lot sizes quickly.
    3. The JIT process has enabled firms to reduce their number of suppliers, reduce ordering complexity, and enhance quality control.
    4. Computerized ordering-inventory tracking systems are necessary for JIT to be effective.
    5. JIT has resulted in various cost savings.
        a. Lower carrying costs.
        b. Lower investment in space and, therefore, lower costs of construction, utilities, and manpower.
        c. Lower clerical costs.
        d. Lower defects and waste-related costs.

Chapter 7 - Multiple Choice Questions

1. The primary purpose of a lock-box system is to: [p. 178]
    a. Increase float.
    b. Delay disbursement.
    c. Speed up inflows.
    d. Reduce excess cash balances.
    e. Reduce marketable securities.

2. Which of the following short-term securities is the least liquid? [p. 184]
    a. Treasury bills
    b. Eurodollar deposits
    c. Banker's acceptances
    d. Large certificates of deposit
    e. Commercial paper

3. If other costs remain the same, an increase in the ordering cost per order will: [pp. 193-195]
    a. Decrease the EOQ.
    b. Have no impact on the EOQ.
    c. Increase the number of orders each period.
    d. Increase the EOQ.
    e. Increase the level of accounts receivable.

4. An organization that facilitates the transmission of international transactions and messages is called: [p. 181]
    a. SPEEDO.
    b. NASDAQ.
    c. SWIFT.
    d. ZIFFLE.
    e. CASHCO.

5. Maintaining safety stock will usually: [pp. 195-196]
    a. Reduce the risk of stock outs.
    b. Increase a firm's carrying cost.
    c. Increase a firm's ordering cost.
    d. Decrease the EOQ.
    e. Both *a* and *b* are correct.

6. An increase in the average collection period will: [pp. 190-191]
    a. Decrease the account receivable balances.
    b. Reduce the ratio of bad debts to sales.
    c. Reduce the average age of accounts receivable.
    d. Increase the accounts receivable balance.
    e. None of the above are correct.

7. If a firm's order quantity is the EOQ: [p. 194]
    a. Total carrying costs are minimized.
    b. Total ordering costs are minimized.
    c. Total inventory costs are minimized.
    d. The inventory level is minimized.
    e. All of the above are correct.

8. Just-in-time inventory management, JIT, has: [p. 197]
    a. Lowered inventory levels.
    b. Reduced the number of a firm's suppliers.
    c. Reduced the amount of space a firm requires.
    d. Reduced overhead expenses for utilities and manpower.
    e. All of the above are correct.

9. The yields on short-term marketable securities in 2000 were _____ relative to the yields in 1980. [p. 184]
    a. Lower
    b. Higher
    c. Unchanged
    d. Some higher, some lower
    e. Much higher

10. Which of the following is an incorrect statement? [Chpt. 7]
    a. The management of marketable securities involves choosing between various short-term investments.
    b. Cash management focuses on controlling the receipt and payment of cash in order to maximize cash balances.
    c. The less liquid an asset, the higher the required rate of return.
    d. Total carrying costs vary directly with average inventory levels.
    e. Credit decisions are made within a risk-return framework.

Multiple Choice Answer Key - Chapter 7

1. c	2. e	3. d	4. c	5. e
6. d	7. c	8. e	9. a	10. b

Chapter 7 - Problems

7-1. The New Century Oil Company uses a continuous billing system that results in average daily receipts of $600,000. The company treasurer estimates that a proposed lock-box system could reduce its collection time by 2 days.

(a) How much cash would the lock-box system free up for the company?

(b) What is the maximum amount that New Century would be willing to pay for the lock-box system if it can earn 6% on available short-term funds?

(c) If the lock-box system could be arranged at an annual cost of $40,000, what would be the net gain from instituting the system?

7-2. Delcoure Industries has annual credit sales of $3,020,400 and an average collection period of 45 days. The firm uses about 40,000 units of raw materials each year. The firm estimates its cost per order to be $500 and the carrying cost per unit to be $8.

(a) What is the firm's average receivables balance? (360-day year)

(b) What is the firms EOQ?

7-3. The owner of Delcoure Industries, Natalya Delcoure, is evaluating the current credit and inventory policies of the firm (7-2 above). As her assistant, she has requested that you bring the following information to her office--in 15 minutes.

(a) What is the total inventory cost associated with the EOQ of the firm?

(b) If the average collection period could be reduced to 30 days with no loss of sales, what would be the annual savings (before-tax adjustment) to the firm assuming the freed-up balance could be invested to earn 12%?

7-4. In an effort to lower its receivables balances, Apex Manufacturing is considering switching from its no-discount policy to a 2% discount for payment by the 15th day. It is estimated that 60% of Apex's customers would take the discount and the average collection period is expected to decline from 60 days to 45 days. Company officials project a 2,000-unit increase in sales to 22,000 units at the existing price of $25 per unit. The variable cost per unit is $21 and the average cost per unit is $23. If the firm requires a 15% return on investment, should the discount be offered?

7-5. The EOQ of QOE Plastics is 4,000 units. The firm's ordering cost per order is $200 and its carrying cost per unit is $2.

(a) How many units does QOE purchase per year?

(b) If QOE increases the annual purchase of units to 96,000, what will its new EOQ be?

(c) How much will the firm's total inventory cost increase when its EOQ changes?

(d) How much would the maintenance of a safety stock of 4,000 units add to total inventory costs?

7-6. The new credit manager of Kay's Department Store plans to liberalize the firm's credit policy. The firm currently generates credit sales of $575,000 annually. The more lenient credit policy is expected to produce credit sales of $750,000. The bad debt losses on additional sales are projected to be 5% despite an additional $15,000 collection expenditure. The new manager anticipates production and selling costs other than additional bad debt and collection expenses will remain at the 85% level. The firm is in the 34% tax bracket.

(a) If the firm maintains its receivables turnover of 10 times, how much will the receivables balance increase?

(b) What would be Kay's incremental after-tax return on investment?

(c) Assuming additional inventory of $35,000 is required to support the additional sales, compute the after-tax return on investment.

7-7. The Hy-Voltage Electric Car Company purchases 20,000 units of a major component part each year. The firm's order costs are $200 per order, and the carrying cost per unit is $2 per year.

(a) Compute the total inventory costs associated with placing orders of 20,000; 10,000; 5,000; 2,000; and 1,000 units.

(b) Determine the EOQ for the component part. Is the answer consistent with calculations in (*a*)?

(c) Assuming the firm places orders of EOQ amount, how many orders will be required during the year?

(d) Assuming a 50-week year, how often will orders be placed?

7-8. Evergreen Company is considering switching from level production to seasonal production in order to lower very high inventory costs. Average inventory levels would decline by $300,000 but production costs would rise about $40,000 because of additional startups and other inefficiencies. The firm's cost of financing inventory balances is 15%.

(a) Should the firm switch to seasonal production? (Ignore tax effects.)

(b) At what interest rate would the cost of financing additional inventory under level production be equal to the added production costs of seasonal production? (Ignore tax effects.)

(c) Answer (*a*) and (*b*) if the applicable tax rate is 40%.

Chapter 7 - Solutions

7-1. (a) Cash freed up = 2 x $600,000
    = **$1,200,000**

(b) Savings = .06 x $1,200,000
    = **$72,000** = amount of savings

(c) Savings $72,000
    Cost   40,000
    Net gain $32,000

7-2. Delcoure Industries

(a)

$$ACP = \frac{accounts \; receivable}{daily \; credit \; sales}$$

$$45 = \frac{AR}{\$3,020,400/360} = \frac{AR}{\$8,390}$$

$$AR = \$8,390 \times 45 = \textbf{\$377,550}$$

(b)

$$EOQ = \sqrt{\frac{2SO}{C}} = \sqrt{\frac{2 \times 40,000 \times \$500}{\$8}}$$

$$EOQ = \sqrt{\frac{\$40,000,000}{\$8}} = \sqrt{5,000,000} = \textbf{2236} \; (rounded)$$

7-3. Delcoure Industries

(a) Total inventory cost = total carrying cost + total ordering cost

$$TIC = C\left(\frac{Q}{2}\right) + O\left(\frac{S}{Q}\right)$$

$$TIC = \$8\left(\frac{2236}{2}\right) + \$500\left(\frac{40,000}{2236}\right)$$

$$TIC = \$8,944 + \$9,000 = \textbf{\$17,944}$$

Note: Total ordering cost differs slightly from total carrying cost because of the need to round up on the number of orders.

(b)

$$ACP = 30 = \frac{AR}{\$3,020,400/360}$$

$$ACP = 30 = \frac{AR}{\$8,390}$$

$AR = 30 \times \$8,390 = \$251,700$

$Reduction \; in \; AR = \$377,550 - \$251,700 = \$125,850$

$Annual \; savings = .12 \times \$125,850 = \textbf{\$15,102}$

7-4.

Existing AR turnover $= \dfrac{360\ days}{60\ days} = 6$

Expected AR turnover $= \dfrac{360\ days}{45\ days} = 8$

Marginal revenue $= 2,000(\$25 - 21) = \$8,000$

Present AR investment $= \dfrac{20,000(\$23)}{6} = \$76,666.66$

Proposed AR investment $= \dfrac{20,000(\$23) + 2,000(\$21)*}{8} = \$62,750$

Reduction in investment in AR = $76,666.66 - $62,750 = $13,916.66

Savings on reduction in investment = .15($13,916.66) = $ 2,087.50

Benefits of offering discount:

Marginal revenue	$ 8,000.00
Savings	2,087.50
	$10,087.50

Discount cost = .02(.6)(22,000)($25) = $6,600

Since the benefits, $10,087.50, exceed the additional cost, $6,600, **the discount should be offered**.

---

*Only variable costs increase.

7-5. QOE Plastics

(a)

$$EOQ = \sqrt{\dfrac{2SO}{C}}$$

$$4,000 = \sqrt{\dfrac{2 \times S \times \$200}{\$2}} = \sqrt{200S}$$

$16,000,000 = 200S$

$S = \textbf{80,000}$

(b)

$$EQQ = \sqrt{\dfrac{2 \times 96,000 \times \$200}{\$2}} = \textbf{4,382}\ (rounded)$$

(c)

$$\text{Original TIC} = \$2\left(\frac{4,000}{2}\right) + \$200\left(\frac{80,000}{4,000}\right)$$

$$\text{Original TIC} = \$4,000 + \$4,000 = \$8,000$$

$$\text{New TIC} = \$2\left(\frac{4,382}{2}\right) + \$200\left(\frac{96,000}{4,382}\right)$$

$$\text{New TIC} = \$4,382 + \$4,382 = \$8,764$$

$$\text{Increase in TIC} = \$8,764 - \$8,000 = \mathbf{\$764}$$

(d) Safety stock of 4,000 units would increase total inventory cost by 4,000 x the carrying cost per unit = 4,000 x $2 = **$8,000**.

7-6.   (a)   *Additional sales = $750,000 - $575,000 = $175,000*

$$\text{Additional receivables balances} = \frac{175,000}{10} = \mathbf{\$17,500}$$

(b)

Additional sales ($750,000 - $575,000)	=	$175,000
Production and selling cost (85%)	=	148,750
		$ 26,250
Bad debt losses (5%)		8,750
		$ 17,500
Additional collection expenses		15,000
Additional income before taxes		$ 2,500
Taxes (34%)		850
Additional Net Income		$ 1,650

$$\text{After tax return on investment} = \frac{\$1,650}{\$17,500} = \mathbf{9.4\%}$$

(c)

$$\text{Aftertax return on investment} = \frac{\$1,650}{\$17,500 + \$35,000} = \mathbf{3.14\%}$$

7-7.   (a)

Quantity Ordered	Number of Orders	Order Costs	Average Inventory	Annual Carrying Costs	Total Costs
20,000	20K/20K = 1	$200(1) = $ 200	20K/2 = 10K	10,000($2) = $20,000	$20,200
10,000	20K/10K = 2	$200(2) = $ 400	10K/2 = 5K	5,000($2) = $10,000	$10,400
5,000	20K/5K = 4	$200(4) = $ 800	5K/2 = 2.5K	2,500($2) = $ 5,000	$ 5,800
2,000	20K/2K = 10	$200(10) = $2,000	2K/2 = 1K	1,000($2) = $ 2,000	$ 4,000 minimum
1,000	20K/1K = 20	$200(20) = $4,000	1K/2 = .5K	500($2) = $ 1,000	$ 5,000

(b)

$$EOQ = \sqrt{\frac{2SO}{C}}$$

S = 20,000
O = $200
C = $2

$$EOQ = \sqrt{\frac{2 \times 20,000 \times \$200}{\$2}}$$

$$= \sqrt{4,000,000}$$

$$= \mathbf{2,000 \textit{ units}}$$

(c)

$$\frac{20,000}{2,000} = \mathbf{10 \textit{ orders per year}}$$

(d)

$$\frac{50}{10} = 5, \textit{ every 5 weeks}$$

7-8.   (a)   *Reduction in inventory costs* = .15($300,000) = $45,000

               Savings from seasonal production = $45,000 - $40,000 = $5,000

               Based solely on the information given, **the switch should be made**.

       (b) $40,000/$300,000 = 13.33%

               If the firm's financing costs were below 13.33%, it would be preferable to continue level production.

               Example: Suppose the firm's financing cost was 12%.
                               Reduction in inventory cost = .12($300,000) = $36,000
                               Additional production costs = $40,000
                               Net benefit = $36,000 - $40,000 = ($4,000)

               At **13.33%**, additional production costs equal the reduction in inventory financing costs (.1333 x $300,000 = $40,000).

       (c)   Reduction in aftertax inventory costs = (.15)($300,000)(1 - .4) = $27,000
               Additional production costs = ($40,000)(1 - .4) = $24,000
               Savings from seasonal production = $27,000 - $24,000 = **$3,000**

               The aftertax interest rate that would yield equal costs of financing and production costs would be:

$$\frac{(\$40,000)(1 - .4)}{\$300,000} = \frac{\$24,000}{\$300,000} = 8\%$$

               The beforetax rate that would yield equivalent costs is .08/.6 = .1333 or 13.33% the same as when taxes were ignored.

Summary: The cost and availability of various sources of short-term funds are examined. Emphasis is given to trade credit, bank loans, corporate promissory notes, and loans against receivables and inventory.

I.   **Trade Credit** [p. 209]

    A.   Usually the largest source of short-term financing.

    B.   A spontaneous source of financing that increases or decreases as sales expand or contract.

    C.   Credit period is set by terms of credit but firms may be able to "stretch" the payment period.

    D.   Cash discount policy. [p. 209]
        1.   Suppliers may provide a **cash discount** for early payment. For example, a 3/15, net 60 policy would allow a buyer to deduct 3% from the billed charges if payment is made within 15 days. If not, the purchaser is expected to pay by the 60th day.

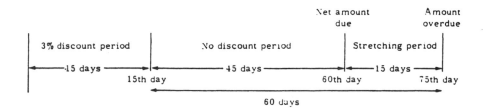

        2.   Forgoing discounts can be very expensive. The cost of failing to take a discount is computed as follows: [p. 209]

Cost of failing to take a discount =

$$\frac{discount\%}{100\% - discount\%} \times \frac{360}{final\ due\ date\ -\ discount\ period}$$

In the example above, the cost would be:

Cost of failing to take a discount =

$$\frac{3}{100 - 3} \times \frac{360}{60 - 15} = \frac{3}{97} \times \frac{360}{45} = 24.7\%$$

The buyer obtains the use of the amount not paid (billed charges - discount) for 45 days and agrees to forgo the discount for such use. The cost, 24.7% on an annual basis, is rather expensive. If, however, the supplier "permits" stretching payment of the account by 15 days, the buyer gains use of the funds for 60 days and the cost of foregoing the discount is reduced.

Cost of failing to take a discount =

$$\frac{3}{100 - 3} \times \frac{360}{75 - 15} = 18.6\%$$

3. Whether a firm should take a discount depends on the relative costs of alternative sources of financing.

E. Net credit position.
    1. The relationship between a firm's level of accounts receivable and its accounts payable determines its **net credit position**. [p. 210]
    2. If the firm's average receivables exceed average payables, it is a net provider of credit. If payables exceed receivables, the firm is a net user of trade credit.

II. Bank Credit

A. Banks prefer short-term, **self-liquidating loans**. [p. 210]

B. Bank lending is impacted by a continuously changing banking environment. Some of the notable changes that have occurred are:
    1. "Full-service banking" -- banking services that range from accepting deposits to pension fund management.
    2. The development of bank holding companies -- a legal entity where one key bank owns a number of affiliate banks.
    3. The internationalization of banking in order to support increased world trade and meet the competition of foreign banks.
    4. Bank deregulation which has fostered greater competition with financial institutions such as savings and loans, credit unions, brokerage houses, and new companies offering financial services.
    5. Widespread failure of banks in the 1980s.
    6. The economic recovery after 1991 accompanied by record bank profits.
    7. The merger of banks to create huge banking complexes capable of making loans nationwide.
    8. Competition from nonbanking companies such as General Electric Capital Services.

C. Bank loan terms and concepts.
    1. Prime rate: The interest rate charged the most credit-worthy borrowers. The **prime rate** serves as a base in determining the interest rate for various risk classes of borrowers. [p. 211]
    2. The accumulation of U.S. dollars in European financial centers such as London enables U.S. companies to borrow dollars internationally. Often, interest rates on loans are tied to the **London Interbank Offered Rate (LIBOR)** instead of the prime rate.
    3. Compensating balances.
        a. As a loan condition, a borrower may be required to maintain an average minimum account balance in the bank equal to a percentage of loans outstanding or a percentage of future commitments and/or pay a fee for services.
        b. **Compensating balances** raise the cost of a loan and compensate the bank for its services. [p. 213]
        c. If a compensating balance is required, the borrower must borrow more than the amount needed. [p. 213]

$$\textit{Amount borrowed} = \frac{\textit{amount needed}}{(1 - C)}$$

        where C = compensating balance in percent.
    4. Maturity provisions.
        a. Most bank loans are short-term and mature within a year.
        b. In the last decade more banks have extended intermediate term-loans (one to seven years) that are paid in installments.

5. Costs of commercial bank financing.
   a. The effective interest rate depends on the loan amount, interest paid, length of the loan, and method of repayment.
   b. The formula for determining the **effective rate of interest** of single payment loans is:

   $$\textit{Effective rate} = \frac{\textit{interest}}{\textit{principal}} \times \frac{\textit{days of the year (360)}}{\textit{days loan is outstanding}}$$

   c. If the loan is discounted (interest paid in advance): [p. 215]

   Effective rate on discounted loan =

   $$\frac{\textit{interest}}{\textit{principal} - \textit{interest}} \times \frac{\textit{days of the year (360)}}{\textit{days loan is outstanding}}$$

   d. If the loan requires compensating balances, the effective interest rate is found by dividing the stated interest rate by (1-c).

   $$\textit{Effective rate with compensating balances} = \frac{\textit{interest rate}}{(1-c)}$$

   If the stated rate is unknown, the following calculation may be used.

   $$\textit{Effective rate with compensating balances} = \frac{\textit{interest}}{\textit{principal} - \substack{\textit{compensating} \\ \textit{balance (dollars)}}} \times \frac{\textit{days of the year (360)}}{\textit{days loan is outstanding}}$$

   e. The interest rate computation of an installment loan is somewhat more complex. [p. 216]

   $$\textit{Rate on installment loan} = \frac{2 \times \textit{annual number of payments} \times \textit{interest}}{(\textit{total number of payments} + 1) \times \textit{principal}}$$

D. Annual percentage rate.
   1. The Truth in Lending Act enacted by Congress in 1968 requires that the **annual percentage rate (APR)** be given to a borrower. The thrust of the legislation was to protect unwary individuals from paying more than the stated rate without his or her knowledge. [p. 216]
   2. The APR requires the use of the actuarial method of compounded interest and corresponds to the effective rate used throughout the text.

E. Bank credit availability tends to cycle.
   1. Credit crunches seem to appear every few years with the most recent in 1969-1970, 1973-1974, and 1979-1981.
   2. The pattern of the credit crunch has been as follows:
      a. The Federal Reserve tightens the money supply to fight inflation.
      b. Lendable funds shrink, interest rates rise.
      c. Business loan demand increases due to cost-inflated inventories and receivables.
      d. Depositors withdraw savings from banks seeking higher return elsewhere, further reducing bank credit availability.
   3. A different type of credit crunch occurred in the 1990s. Bad loans by members of the U.S. financial system resulted in the partial collapse of the savings and loan industry and the severe weakening of many banks and insurance companies.

III. **Commercial Paper** [p. 217]

A. Short-term, unsecured promissory notes issued to the public in minimum units of $25,000.

B. Issuers.
1. Finance companies such as General Motors Acceptance Corporation (GMAC) that issue paper directly. Such issues are referred to as **finance paper** or **direct paper**
2. Industrial or utility firms that issue paper indirectly through dealers. This type of issue is called **dealer paper**. [p. 217]

C. Traditionally, commercial paper has been a paper certificate issued to the lender to signify the lender's claim to be repaid. There is a growing trend among companies that sell and buy commercial paper to handle the transaction electronically. Actual paper certificates are not created. Documentation of the transaction is provided by computerized book-entry transactions and transfers of money are accomplished by wiring cash between lenders and commercial paper issuers.

D. Advantages. [p. 218]
1. Commercial paper may be issued at below the prime rate at commercial banks.
2. No compensating balances are required, though lines of credit are necessary.
3. Prestige.

E. The primary limitation is the possibility that the commercial paper market might "dry up" unexpectedly as it did when Penn Central defaulted in 1970.

IV. Foreign Borrowing [p. 220]

A. Loans from foreign banks are an increasing source of funds for U.S. firms.

B. Foreign loans denominated in U.S. dollars are called Euro-dollar loans. These loans are usually short to intermediate term in maturity.

C. A possibly cheaper alternative to borrowing Euro-dollars is the borrowing of foreign currencies which are converted to dollars and forwarded to the United States parent company.

V. The Use of Collateral in Short-Term Financing [p. 220]

A. The lending institution may require collateral to be pledged when granting a loan.

B. Lenders lend on the basis of the cash-flow capacity of the borrower. Collateral is an additional but secondary consideration.

C. Accounts receivable financing.
1. **Pledging accounts receivable** as collateral. [pp. 220-221]
   a. Convenient means of financing. Receivables levels are rising as the need for financing is increasing.
   b. May be relatively expensive and preclude use of alternative financing sources.
   c. Lender screens accounts and loans a percentage (60% to 80%) of the acceptable amount.
   d. Lender has full recourse against borrower.
   e. The interest rate is usually well in excess of the prime rate. Interest is based on the frequently changing loan balance outstanding.
2. **Factoring** receivables. [p. 221]

a. Receivables are sold, usually without recourse, to a factoring firm.
b. A factor provides a credit-screening function by accepting or rejecting accounts and typically requires:
    (1) Commission of 1% to 3% of factored invoices.
    (2) Interest on advances.
3. **Asset-backed public offerings**. [p. 222]
a. *Public offerings* of securities backed by receivables as collateral is a recently employed means of short-term financing.
b. In 1990, IBM sold an asset-backed issue on which the interest is not taxable by the Federal government. The issue consisted of receivables due from state and municipal governments. The nontaxability status of the securities allowed IBM to issue them at below market rates.
c. Problems must be resolved:
    (1) Computer upgrading to service securities.
    (2) Potentially significant default effects.
d. The creation of asset-backed securities is referred to as **securitization of assets**. [p. 223]

VI. Inventory Financing [p. 224]

A. The collateral value of inventory is based on several factors.
1. Marketability.
    a. Raw materials and finished goods are more marketable than goods-in-process inventories.
    b. Standardized products or widely traded commodities qualify for higher percentage loans.
2. Price stability.
3. Perishability.
4. Physical control.
    a. **Blanket inventory liens**: Lender has general claim against inventory of borrower; no physical control. [p. 224]
    b. **Trust receipts**: Also known as floor planning; the borrower holds specifically identified inventory and proceeds from sale in trust for the lender.
    c. Warehousing: Goods are physically identified, segregated, and stored under the direction of an independent warehousing company. Inventory is released from warehouse only upon presentation of warehouse receipt controlled by the lender. [p. 224]
        (1) **Public warehouse**--facility on the premises of the warehousing firm.
        (2) **Field warehouse**--independently controlled facility on the premises of borrower.

B. Inventory financing and the associated control methods are standard procedures in many industries.

VII. Hedging to Reduce Borrowing Risk [pp. 225-228]

A. Firms that continually borrow to finance operations are exposed to the risk of interest rate changes.

B. **Hedging** activities in the financial futures market reduce the risk of interest rate changes. Hedging is also used by international firms to offset the risk of increased cost caused by changes in foreign exchange rates.

VIII. Key Formulas

A. *Cost of failing to take a cash discount* [p. 209] =

$$\frac{discount \ percent}{100\% - discount \ percent} \times \frac{360}{final \ due \ date - discount \ period}$$

B. *Amount of funds to be borrowed to meet needs under compensating balances* [p. 213] =

$$\frac{amount \ needed}{(1 - C)}$$

C. *Effective rate on a loan* [p. 214] =

$$\frac{interest}{principal} \times \frac{days \ of \ the \ year \ (360)}{days \ loan \ is \ outstanding}$$

D. *Effective rate on a discounted loan* [p. 215] =

$$\frac{interest}{principal - interest} \times \frac{days \ of \ the \ year \ (360)}{days \ loan \ is \ outstanding}$$

E. *Effective loan rate with compensating balances* [p. 215] =

$$\frac{interest \ rate}{(1 - C)}$$

F. *Effective loan rate with compensating balances (based on dollar values)* [p. 215] =

$$\frac{interest}{principal - compensating \ balance \ dollars} \times \frac{days \ of \ the \ year \ (360)}{days \ loan \ is \ outstanding}$$

G. *Effective loan rate on an installment loan* [p. 216] =

$$\frac{2 \times annual \ number \ of \ payments \times interest}{(total \ number \ of \ payments + 1) \times principal}$$

Chapter 8 - Multiple Choice

1. Many of the services of modern banks have been made possible by the development of the _____--a legal entity in which one key bank owns a number of affiliate banks. [p. 210]
   a. Bank holding company
   b. Investment bank
   c. Commercial bank
   d. International bank
   e. J. P. Morgan bank

2. The interest rate charged to the most creditworthy customers of a bank--usually tied to rates at New York banks--is referred to as: [p. 211]
    a. APR.
    b. Prime rate.
    c. Discount rate.
    d. Compensating rate.
    e. Asset-backed securities rate.

3. The difference between a firm's accounts receivable and its accounts payable is called its: [p. 210]
    a. Net working capital.
    b. Working capital.
    c. Trade credit.
    d. Net credit position.
    e. Compensating balance.

4. Which of the following is typically the largest source of short-term credit for a firm? [p. 209]
    a. Bank loans
    b. Commercial paper
    c. Factoring
    d. Asset-backed public offerings
    e. Trade credit

5. Trust receipt financing is also called: [p. 225]
    a. Warehousing.
    b. Pledging.
    c. Floor planning.
    d. Trade credit.
    e. Commercial paper.

6. Instead of issuing the traditional paper certificates when financing with commercial paper, there is a trend towards documenting the transaction by: [p. 218]
    a. Direct paper.
    b. Computerized book entry.
    c. Factoring.
    d. Securitization.
    e. Stretching.

7. Which of the following usually has the lowest interest rate? [Chpt. 8; p. 219]
    a. Prime rate bank loans
    b. Inventory loans
    c. Directly-placed commercial paper
    d. Dealer-placed commercial paper
    e. Secured loans

8. A firm that buys on credit terms of 2/10, net 30: [pp. 209-210]
    a. May take a 2% discount if the amount is paid by the 10th day.
    b. Will normally wait until the 30th day to pay if the discount is not taken.
    c. Will experience a cost of more than 36% if the discount is forgone.
    d. Should normally take the discount if the funds can be obtained at a cost of 14%.
    e. All of the above are correct.

9. A general claim against the inventory of a borrower is a: [p. 225]
    a. Trust receipt.
    b. Blanket lien.
    c. Pledge.
    d. Warehouse receipt.
    e. All of the above are correct.

10. Which of the following inventory financing arrangements provides the lender with the greatest control of the inventory? [p. 225]
    a. Trade credit
    b. Blanket liens
    c. Floor planning
    d. Public warehousing
    e. Trust receipts

Multiple Choice Answer Key - Chapter 8

1. a	2. b	3. d	4. e	5. c
6. b	7. c	8. e	9. b	10. d

Chapter 8 - Problems

8-1. Friendly Bank will lend you $5,000 for a year for $600 in interest.

    (a) What is the effective rate of interest?

    (b) If you are required to repay the principal and interest in 12 monthly installments, what is the rate of interest?

8-2. Katz Supply currently purchases on terms of 3/20, net 60.

    (a) What is the cost to Katz if the discount is not taken?

    (b) If Ms. Katz can stretch her payment to 75 days if the discount is not taken, what is the cost?

    (c) Suppose that Katz purchases $1,000,000 annually on the 3/20, net 60 terms. Ignoring other financing costs, what is the impact on before-tax profits of not taking the discount?

8-3. Myopic Optical is seeking to borrow $75,000 from National Bank.

    (a) If the bank requires a 20% minimum compensating balance, how much will Myopic Optical be able to effectively use?

    (b) If the bank quotes a rate of 12%, what will the interest rate be after considering the compensating balance requirement?

    (c) If Myopic must gain the use of $75,000, how much must be borrowed?

(d)   If Myopic normally maintains a balance in National Bank of $20,000, would your answers to (a), (b), and (c) be the same?

8-4.   Your banker indicates that she will lend you $5,000 at 10% interest. What is the effective rate under each of the following conditions?

(a)   The principal and interest are to be repaid at the end of one year.

(b)   The loan is discounted and the principal is repaid at the end of the year.

(c)   The loan is to be repaid in 12 monthly installments.

8-5.   Pfc. Bisping is considering borrowing $100 from a loan company advertised in a service newspaper. The advertisement indicates that he may repay the principal plus "only $3.50 interest" at the end of the 30-day period. What rate of interest would he be paying?

8-6.   Hammer and Nail Hardware can buy equivalent materials from two distributors. Supplier A offers terms 1/10, net 30 whereas Supplier B provides terms of 2/15, net 60.

(a)   If Hammer and Nail foregoes the discount, from which of the two suppliers should it purchase if supply prices are comparable.

(b)   If Hammer and Nail can borrow from Lendzit State Bank at a 16% rate, should it forego the discount?

(c)   If in (b) above the bank requires a 20% compensating balance for the loan, should the firm forego the discount?

8-7.   The High Fashion Dress Shop can borrow from a local bank at 12% interest if it maintains a 20% compensating balance. Alternatively, it may finance its operations by factoring its accounts receivable. The factor charges a commission of 1% of the monthly accounts factored and 1% per month for advances. Which of the two sources of financing is the least expensive?

8-8.   Meyer Appliance needs $100,000 to take advantage of a trade discount based on terms of 3/10, net 60. State Bank has agreed to lend the money at a 12% rate with a 15% compensating balance requirement. National Bank will lend at a 13% interest rate on a discounted loan for three months.

(a)   What is the effective rate of interest charged by each bank?

(b)   What is the cost of foregoing the discount?

(c)   How much would Meyer have to borrow from each bank in order to take the discount?

(d)   Suppose that Meyer normally banks with State bank and maintains deposit balances of $15,000, what amount would have to be borrowed, and what would the effective interest rate be?

Chapter 8 - Solutions

8-1. Friendly Bank

(a)

$$Effective\ rate = \frac{\$600}{\$5,000} \times \frac{360}{360} = \mathbf{12\%}$$

(b)

$$Rate\ on\ installment\ loan = \frac{2 \times 12 \times \$600}{(12 + 1) \times \$5,000} = \frac{\$14,400}{\$65,000} = \mathbf{22.15\%}$$

8-2. Katz Supply

(a) *Cost of failing to take discount =*

$$\frac{3\%}{100\% - 3\%} \times \frac{360}{60 - 20} = \frac{3\%}{97\%} \times 9 = \mathbf{27.84\%}$$

(b) *Cost of failing to take discount =*

$$\frac{3\%}{97\%} \times \frac{360}{75 - 20} = \frac{3\%}{97\%} \times 6.55 = \mathbf{20.26\%}$$

(c) *Cost of failing to take the discount (in dollars) =*

$1,000,000 \times .03 = \mathbf{\$30,000}$

8-3. Myopic Optical

(a)

Amount that can be effectively used = (1 - .20)($75,000) = **$60,000**

(b)

$$Effective\ rate\ with\ compensating\ balances = \frac{.12}{1 - .2} = \mathbf{.15}$$

(c)

$$Amount\ of\ funds\ borrowed = \frac{\$75,000}{1 - .2} = \mathbf{\$93,750}$$

(d) If Myopic maintains a balance of $20,000 in National Bank, the compensating balance requirement will not impact the loan. The answers for (a), (b), and (c) would be **$75,000** **.12**; and **$75,000**; respectively.

8-4. (a)

$$Effective\ rate = \frac{interest}{principal} \times \frac{days\ of\ the\ year\ (360)}{days\ loan\ is\ outstanding}$$

$$\text{Effective rate} = \frac{\$5,000 \times .10}{\$5,000} \times \frac{360}{360} = \frac{\$500}{\$5,000} \times 1 = \mathbf{10\%}$$

(b)

$$\text{Effective rate on discounted loan} = \frac{\text{interest}}{\text{principal} - \text{interest}} \times \frac{\text{days of the year}}{\text{days loan is outstanding}}$$

$$\text{Effective rate on discounted loan} = \frac{\$500}{\$5,000 - \$500} \times \frac{360}{360}$$

$$\text{Effective rate on discounted loan} = \frac{\$500}{\$4,500} \times 1 = \mathbf{11.1\%}$$

(c)

$$\text{Rate on installment loan} = \frac{2 \times \text{annual number of payments} \times \text{interest}}{(\text{total number of payments} + 1) \times \text{principal}}$$

$$= \frac{2 \times 12 \times \$500}{(12 + 1) \times \$5,000} = \frac{\$12,000}{\$65,000} = \mathbf{18.46\%}$$

8-5.

$$\text{Effective rate} = \frac{\text{interest}}{\text{principal}} \times \frac{\text{days of the year (360)}}{\text{days loan is outstanding}}$$

$$\text{Effective rate} = \frac{\$3.50}{\$100} \times \frac{360}{30} = .035 \times 12 = .42 = \mathbf{42\%}$$

8-6. (a) Cost of failing to take a cash discount =

$$\frac{\text{discount\%}}{100\% - \text{discount\%}} \times \frac{360}{\text{final due date} - \text{discount period}}$$

$$\text{Cost (Supplier A)} = \frac{1\%}{100\% - 1\%} \times \frac{360}{30 - 10} = \mathbf{18.18\%}$$

$$\text{Cost (Supplier B)} = \frac{2\%}{100\% - 2\%} \times \frac{360}{60 - 15} = \mathbf{16.33\%}$$

Supplier B

(b) No, H&N should borrow from the bank at 16% and take the discount.

(c)

$$\text{Effective rate on the bank loan} = \frac{.16}{1 - .2} = \frac{.16}{.8} = \mathbf{.20}$$

H&N should forgo the discount rather than borrow from the bank since the bank loan would cost 20% and the cost of forgoing the discount would be less.

8-7.

$$Cost \ of \ borrowing \ from \ bank = \frac{.12}{.8} = \textbf{15\%}$$

Cost of factoring: 1% Commission

<u>1%</u> Interest/month for advances

2%

<u>x 12</u>

24% Annual rate

Bank borrowing is the least expensive.

8-8.   (a)   Cost of borrowing from State Bank = .12/.85 = **14.12%**

Cost of borrowing from National Bank:

$$Effective \ rate \ on \ discounted \ loan = \frac{interest}{principal \ - \ interest} \times \frac{days \ of \ the \ year}{days \ loan \ is \ outstanding}$$

$$Interest = (.13)(\$100,000)(90/360) = \$3,250$$

$$Effective \ rate = \frac{\$3,250}{\$100,000 \ - \ \$3,250} \times \frac{360}{90} = \frac{\$3,250}{\$96,750} \times 4 = \textbf{13.44\%}$$

(b)

$$Cost \ of \ foregoing \ discount = \frac{3\%}{100\% \ - \ 3\%} \times \frac{360}{60 \ - \ 10} = \textbf{22.27\%}$$

(c)   Meyer needs $100,000 in order to take the discount. The amount to be borrowed from:

$$State \ Bank = \frac{\$100,000}{.85} = \textbf{\$117,647.06}$$

$$National \ Bank = \frac{\$100,000}{.9675} = \textbf{\$103,359.17}$$

(d)   The compensating balance would not impact the loan since Meyer's normal balances would satisfy the compensating balance requirement. Meyer would need to borrow $100,000; and the effective rate of interest would be 12%.

Summary: Money has time value because it can be put to work to earn a return. The sooner dollars are received the sooner they can begin working. This **time value of money** concept is an integral part of business decisions because cash inflows and outflows often take place at different points in time. To make appropriate business decisions, the cash inflows and outflows must be expressed in value units at the same point in time. In this chapter, the mathematical tools of the time value of money concept are developed and related to capital allocation decisions.

I.   Future Value--Single Amount [pp. 240-241]

     A.   The value of a beginning amount if that amount grows at a given rate (the interest rate) over a period of time is called the **future value.**

          Suppose an individual deposits $2,000 in a savings account paying 6% annual interest. At the end of one year, the account balance will be $2,120 = [$2,000 the original amount + the interest earned ($2,000 x .06)]. If the new amount is left on deposit during year two, interest will be paid on $2,120. The amount at the end of each of the following two years will be:

Year	Beginning Amount		Interest		Future Value
2nd Year	$2,120.00	+	[($2,120)(.06) = $127.20]	=	$2,247.20
3rd Year	$2,247.20	+	[($2,247.20)(.06) = $134.83]	=	$2,382.03

     B.   The relationships may be expressed in the following formula:

$$FV = PV(1 + i)^n$$

          where FV = future value
                   PV = present value
                     I = interest rate
                    n = number of periods

          Applying the formula to the example above:

$$FV = 2,000(1 + .06)^3$$
$$FV = 2,000(1.191) = \$2,382$$

     C.   The future value formula may be shortened by designating $(1 + i)^n$ as the **interest factor** (FV_{IF}). Then $FV = PV(FV_{IF})$.

     D.   The interest factor (FV_{IF}) can be quickly found by using a future value table. The FV_{IF} value of 1.191 is found in row three (3 periods) of the 6% column of Table 9-1.

     E.   The FV_{IF} = 1.191 is equal to $(1.06)^3$ or $(1.06)(1.06)(1.06)$.

TABLE 9-1
FUTURE VALUE OF $1

Periods	1%	2%	3%	4%	6%	8%	10%
1	1.010	1.020	1.030	1.040	1.060	1.080	1.100
2	1.020	1.040	1.061	1.082	1.124	1.166	1.210
3	1.030	1.061	1.093	1.125	1.191	1.260	1.331
4	1.041	1.082	1.126	1.170	1.262	1.360	1.464
5	1.051	1.104	1.159	1.217	1.338	1.469	1.611
10	1.105	1.219	1.344	1.480	1.791	2.159	2.594
20	1.220	1.486	1.806	2.191	3.207	4.661	6.727

An expanded table is presented in Appendix A of text.

II. Present Value of a Single Amount [pp. 241-242]

A. The present value of a future sum is the amount necessary such that if it were invested at a given interest rate today it would equal the future sum at the corresponding point in time.

B. Mathematically, present value can be determined by using the future value formula and solving for PV,

$$FV = PV(1 + 1)^n$$

$$PV = FV\left[\frac{1}{(1 + i)^n}\right]$$

Defining $\frac{1}{(1+i)^n}$ as the present value interest factor, PV_{IF}, the formula may be reduced to

$$PV = FV \times PV_{IF}.$$

TABLE 9-2
PRESENT VALUE OF $1

Periods	1%	2%	3%	4%	6%	8%	10%
1	.990	.980	.971	.962	.943	.926	.909
2	.980	.961	.943	.925	.890	.957	.826
3	.971	.942	.915	.889	.840	.794	.751
4	.961	.924	.889	.855	.792	.735	.683
5	.951	.906	.863	.822	.747	.681	.621
10	.905	.820	.744	.676	.558	.463	.386
20	.820	.673	.554	.456	.312	.215	.149

An expanded table is presented in Appendix B of text.

The present value of $2,382 to be received three years hence is $2,000 if the amount could be employed to earn a 6% return annually.

$PV = FV \times PV_{IF}$
$PV = (2,382)(.84)$
$PV = \$2,000.88$ (Note differences between tables are due to rounding)

Study Note: An alternative approach to solving for present value is available by simply expressing the equation as

$$PV = \frac{FV}{(1 + i)^n} \, .$$

Writing this equation in this form allows determination of present value using only the future value table where $(1 + i)^n$ equals the future value interest factor from Table 9-1.

$$PV = \frac{2,382}{1.191} = 2,000$$

The equivalency of the computation can be seen by studying the following relationship:

$$PV = FV\left[\frac{1}{(1 + i)^n}\right] \quad or \quad \frac{FV}{(1 + i)^n}$$

$$PV = 2,382\left[\frac{1}{1.191}\right] \quad or \quad \frac{2,382}{1,191}$$

$$PV = 2,382(.840) \quad or \quad \frac{2,382}{1,191}$$

$$PV = 2,000 \text{ (slight differences due to rounding)}$$

III.   Future Value--Annuity [pp. 242-244]

  A.   Business actions frequently generate a stream of inflows or outflows rather than a single payment or receipt.

  B.   A series of consecutive end-of-period payments or receipts of equal amount is called an **annuity**.

  C.   The future value of an annuity is the amount one would have at the end of the annuity period if each payment (receipt) were invested at a given interest rate and held to the end of the annuity period.

FIGURE 9-1
COMPOUNDING PROCESS FOR ANNUITY

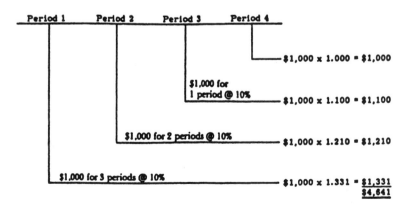

D. Mathematically, the future value of an annuity is determined as follows:

$$FV_A = A(1 + i)^{n-1} + A(1 + i)^{n-2} + \ldots + A(1 + i)^1 + A(1 + i)^0$$

where FV_A = future value of an annuity
A = annual annuity payment (receipt)
i = interest rate
n = number of periods

Study Note: By definition of an annuity, the A_s are equal; therefore, the future value of an annuity equation may be written as follows:

$$FV_A = A[(1 + i)^{n-1} + (1 + i)^{n-2} + \ldots + (1 + i)^1 + (1 + i)^0]$$

Notice that the first payment earns interest for one less period than the total annuity periods and the last payment does not earn any interest. This is a result of receiving payments at the end of the period. The future value of an annuity equation may be shortened by defining the sum of the values inside the bracket as the interest factor. The equation then is $FV_A = A \times FV_{IFA}$. The interest factor can be readily found in a future value of an annuity table.

TABLE 9-3
FUTURE VALUE OF AN ANNUITY OF $1

Periods	1%	2%	3%	4%	6%	8%	10%
1	1.000	1.000	1.000	1.000	1.000	1.000	1.000
2	2.010	2.020	2.030	2.040	2.060	2.080	2.100
3	3.030	3.060	3.091	3.122	3.184	3.246	3.310
4	4.060	4.122	4.184	4.246	4.375	4.506	4.641
5	5.101	5.204	5.309	5.416	5.637	5.867	6.105
10	10.462	10.950	11.464	12.006	13.181	14.487	15.937
20	22.019	24.297	26.870	29.778	36.786	45.762	57.275

An expanded table is presented in Appendix C of text.

E. The future value of a 10-year annuity of $3,000 per year with each payment invested at 8% would be:

$$FV_A = \$3,000(14.487) = \$43,461$$

IV. Present Value of an Annuity [p. 245]

A. Assuming a specific rate of interest, the present value of an annuity is the amount required today to permit payments (receipts) of equal amounts (A) at the end of each of n periods.

B. The equation for the present value of an annuity is:

$$PV_A = A\left[\frac{1}{(1 + i)}\right] + A\left[\frac{1}{(1 + i)}\right]^2 + \ldots + A\left[\frac{1}{(1 + i)}\right]^n$$

where PV_A = present value of an annuity
A = annual end-of-year payment
I = interest rate
n = number of periods

105

The equation can be expressed as follows since the A values are equal.

$$PV_A = A\left[\frac{1}{(1 + i)} + \frac{1}{(1 + i)^2} + \ldots + \frac{1}{(1 + i)^n}\right]$$

$$PV_A = A \times PV_{IFA}$$

TABLE 9-4
PRESENT VALUE OF AN ANNUITY OF $1

Periods	1%	2%	3%	4%	6%	8%	10%
1	0.990	0.980	0.971	0.962	0.943	0.926	0.909
2	1.970	1.942	1.913	1.886	1.833	1.783	1.736
3	2.941	2.884	2.829	2.775	2.673	2.577	2.487
4	3.902	3.808	3.717	3.630	3.465	3.312	3.170
5	4.853	4.713	4.580	4.452	4.212	3.993	3.791
8	7.652	7.325	7.020	6.733	6.210	5.747	5.335
10	9.471	8.983	8.530	8.111	7.360	6.710	6.145
20	18.046	16.351	14.877	13.590	11.470	9.818	8.514

An expanded table is presented in Appendix D of text.

C. The present value of an annuity can be determined handily by using the appropriate table (Table 9-4). The present value of an annuity of $6,000 for four years assuming an interest rate of 6% is:

$PV_A = \$6,000(3.465) = \$20,790$

V. Determining an Annuity Value [p. 249]

A. Sometimes the future value or present value of an annuity is known, and the annuity payment (A) must be determined.
B. To determine the annuity payment necessary to accumulate a specific sum at a given interest rate, we solve the future value of an annuity equation for A.

$$FV_A = A \times FV_{IFA}$$

$$A = \frac{FV_A}{FV_{IFA}}$$

Suppose we wish to accumulate $10,000 by depositing end-of-year payments in a savings account for four years. If 8% interest is paid on deposits, what is the required annual deposit?

$\$10,000 = A \times FV_{IFA}$
$\$10,000 = A(4.506)$

$A = \dfrac{\$10,000}{4.506} = \$2.219.26$

The $FV_{IFA} = 4.506$ is found in row four of the 8% column of Table 9-3.

C. Mechanically, computation of the annuity payment is the same when given the present value of an annuity as when given the future value of an annuity. The only difference is the table from which the IF is derived.

$$PV_A = A \times PV_{IFA}$$

$$A = \frac{PV_A}{PV_{IFA}}$$

where PV_{IFA} is derived from a present value of an annuity table (Table 9-4).

VI. Determining the Yield on an Investment [p. 254]

A. In each of the equations used so far to illustrate time value of money, there have been four variables. Whenever three of the four variables are given, the other can be found.

B. If a lender agreed to lend $1,000 now with a lump-sum payment of principal and interest of $1,404.49 at the end of three years, what rate of interest is being charged?

$$PV = FV \times PV_{IF}$$

$$\$1,000 = \$1,404.49(PV_{IF})$$

$$PV_{IF} = \frac{PV}{FV} = \frac{\$1,000}{\$1,404.49} = .712$$

To find the interest rate, read across row three (3 years) of the present value of $1 table (see appendix of text) until .712 is found. The value is found in the 12% column. The lender is charging a 12% rate of interest.

C. By solving for the IF and then locating the value in the appropriate table, the yield on an annuity may also be determined.

VII. Special Considerations in Time Value Analysis [p. 256]

A. More frequent than annual compounding.
1. Multiply the number of years by the number of compounding periods during the year
2. Divide the stated interest rate by the number of compounding periods during the year. The future value of $10,000 after three years at 8% annual interest, compounded quarterly would be:

$$FV = 10,000\left(1 + \frac{.08}{4}\right)^{(3)(4)}$$

$$FV = 10,000(1 + .02)^{12}$$

$$FV = 10,000(1.268) = 12,680$$

B. Present value of series of unequal payments.
1. Many business transactions generate differing cash flows each year. In such cases, the present value of each payment must be computed individually and summed.

Assume a 10% discount rate:
1   8,000 x .909 = 7,272
2   6,000 x .826 = 4,956
3   3,000 x .751 = 2,253
                      14,481

107

2. Some series of payments may combine an annuity with unequal payments. The present value of the annuity may be determined and added to the present value of the other payments.

Assume a 12% discount rate:

1	8,000
2	6,000
3	6,000
4	6,000
5	3,000

Present value = 8,000(.893) + 6,000(3.037 - .893) + 3,000(.567)
Present value = \$7,144 + \$12,864 + \$1,701 = \$21,709

VIII. Key Formulas

A. Future value of a single amount [p. 240]

$$FV = PV \times FV_{IF}$$

B. Present value of a single amount [p. 241]

$$PV = FV \times PV_{IF}$$

C. Future value of an annuity [p. 243]

$$FV_A = A \times FV_{IFA}$$

D. Present value of an annuity [p. 245]

$$PV_A = A \times PV_{IFA}$$

E. Annuity equaling a future value [p. 252]

$$A = \frac{FV_A}{FV_{IFA}}$$

F. Annuity equaling a present value [p. 253]

$$A = \frac{PV_A}{PV_{IFA}}$$

G. Determining the yield on an investment [pp. 254-255]

$$PV_{IF} = \frac{PV}{FV} \qquad PV_{IFA} = \frac{PV_A}{A}$$

H. Less than annual compounding periods [p. 256]

Multiply n by compounding frequency per year. Divide i by compounding frequency per year. After the above adjustments, use the normal formula.

I.   Patterns of payment-deferred annuity [pp. 256-258]

$$PV_A = A \times PV_{IFA}$$

$$PV = FV \times PV_{IF}$$

Study Note: Refer to the special review of the formulas in the text for guidance as to when to use each formula. [pp. 256-258]

Study Hints for Time Value of Money

1.   The key to using future-value and present-value tables efficiently is to be thoroughly familiar with their characteristics. Study them closely.

   a.   Each table has three dimensions: interest rate, number of periods, and an internal value called the interest factor.
   b.   Whenever two of the three dimensions of a table are known, the third is also determined. The process is similar to determining the mileage between two cities on a roadmap mileage chart.

2.   Knowing the relationship between the present-value tables is particularly important in solving present value problems that combine annuity streams with uneven payments. An interest factor in the present value of an annuity table is the summation of the interest factors in the corresponding column of the present value of $1 table.

| | *Present Value of $1* | | | *Present Value of Annuity of $1* | |
	10%			*10%*	
1	.909		1	.909	
2	.826	→1.736	2	1.736	
3	.751	→ 2.487	3	2.487	

3.   Notice that the present-value interest factor for any particular year may be determined from the present value of an annuity table.

IF(n = 3, i = 10%) = 2.487 - 1.736 = .751

4.   Today, most students use calculators extensively to make time value of money related calculations. In fact, many professors require the use of calculators and sometimes preclude the use of future-value and present-value tables. Other professors require students to do the calculations the "hard" way--with paper and pencil.

   While efficiency argues for the use of calculators, it is very important for the student to understand the mathematics involved--in other words, avoid the "black box" syndrome. Study the equations so that you may have insight as to the range of a reasonable answer. Such study will help you recognize hastily made, embarrassing errors.

   A real world experience will further indicate the need to understand the mathematics of your calculator generated answer. The author once received a phone call from the senior loan officer of a billion dollar lending institution asking for help in the calculation of an interest rate on a loan. A customer had demanded to see the interest rate calculated by hand--paper and pencil, not by the calculator. The loan officer had used the calculator and/or computer for so long, he could not calculate the interest rate by hand. Needless to say, he was embarrassed.

If you are required or choose to use a calculator for your calculations, you should become thoroughly familiar with the instrument prior to an exam. Purchasing a calculator the day before the exam is risky business. Block and Hirt provide basic instructions for using two commonly-used calculators in Appendix E of the text.

Chapter 9 - Multiple Choice Questions

1. The formula for computing the present value of a single amount is: [p. 241]
    a. $PV = FV \times PV_{IF}$.
    b. $FV = PV \times FV_{IF}$.
    c. $FV_A = A \times FV_{IFA}$.
    d. $PV_A = A \times PV_{IFA}$.
    e. None of the above are correct.

2. To determine the future value of an amount that will earn 8% interest paid quarterly for five years, the number of periods and discount rate will be: [p. 256]
    a. 8%, 5.
    b. 2%, 5.
    c. 32%, 20.
    d. 8%, 20.
    e. 2%, 20.

3. The owner of a building that costs $100,000 who wishes to determine the annual rent necessary to earn a 10% return on the investment in 10 years should use the: [pp. 252-253]
    a. Present value formula (solve for FV).
    b. Present value of annuity formula (solve for A).
    c. Future value of annuity formula (solve for A).
    d. Future value formula (solve for PV).
    e. Any of the above are correct.

4. The time value of money must be considered in capital outlay decisions because: [Chpt. 9]
    a. Accounting rules require it.
    b. Cash flows are not known with certainty.
    c. Cash inflows and cash outflows occur at different points in time.
    d. Inflation greatly reduces the outflows.
    e. A dollar received in the future is more valuable than a dollar received today.

5. One seeking to find the amount that must be deposited each year at 12% interest in order to accumulate $500,000 by retirement in 30 years should use which of the following formulas? [p. 252]
    a. $PV_A = A \times PV_{IFA}$.
    b. $FV = PV \times FV_{IF}$.
    c. $FV_A = A \times FV_{IFA}$.
    d. $PV = FV \times PV_{IF}$.
    e. Either *b* or *d* may be used.

6. The interest rate used to determine the present value of future cash flows is known as the: [p. 241]
    a. Annuity.
    b. Interest factor.
    c. Internal value.
    d. Discount rate.
    e. Interpolation.

7. A series of consecutive end-of-period payments or receipts of equal amount is called a(n): [p. 242]
    a. Annuity.
    b. Future value.
    c. Present value.
    d. Uneven series.
    e. Annuity due.

8. The values found in the present value and compound value tables are called: [p. 240]
    a. Interest rates.
    b. Interest factors.
    c. Discount rates.
    d. Annuities.
    e. Present values.

9. As long as an individual or business can employ dollars to earn a positive return, money will have: [p. 239]
    a. Time value.
    b. Present value greater than future value.
    c. Future value less than beginning value.
    d. Present value greater than beginning value.
    e. All of the above are correct.

10. The present value of a 10-year annuity is $100,000. The future value of the annuity is $500,000. If the appropriate interest rate is 8%, which formula would be appropriate to compute annual annuity payment (or receipt)? [pp. 251-254]
    a. Present value of an annuity.
    b. Present value.
    c. Future value.
    d. Future value of an annuity.
    e. Either present value of an annuity or future value of an annuity may be used.

Multiple Choice Answer Key - Chapter 9

1. a	2. e	3. b	4. c	5. c
6. d	7. a	8. b	9. a	10. e

Chapter 9 - Problems

9-1. Mark Anderson deposits $5,000 in a savings account earning 8% interest annually.

   (a) How much will be in the account at the end of the twelfth year?

   (b) How many years would be required to accumulate $20,000 under the same assumptions?

9-2. Shorty Stop, a professional baseball rookie, has just signed a five-year contract for $200,000 per year.

(a)   Assuming an opportunity rate of 12%, what is the present value of Mr. Stop's contract?

(b)   Suppose that Mr. Stop's contract requires a salary of $200,000 in each of the first three years and $400,000 in the latter two years, what is the present value of the contract?

9-3.   Mr. Paul Bearer may elect to take a lump-sum payment of $25,000 from his insurance policy or an annuity of $3,200 annually as long as he lives. How long must Mr. Bearer anticipate living for the annuity to be preferable to the lump sum if his opportunity rate is 8%?

9-4.   Ms. Erica Barham wishes to retire upon accumulation of $1,000,000.

(a)   How many years must she work if she is able to save and invest $6,080 at 10% interest compounded annually?

(b)   Suppose Ms. Barham wishes to retire in 40 years; how much must she save annually if the amount can be employed to earn 12%?

9-5.   The B&H Company recently issued $5,000,000 of 20-year bonds. The bond contract requires that a sinking fund be established that will enable the firm to pay off the bonds upon maturity.

(a)   If the firm can earn 6% on the sinking fund payments, what annual payment will be required?

(b)   Suppose the firm is not required to make the first sinking fund payment until the end of the sixth year. What annual payment would be required?

9-6.   Ms. Kristy Doler purchased 100 acres of land in 1990 for $100,000. If she sells the land for $5,000 per acre in 2010, what rate of return will she have earned on her investment? (Disregard property and income taxes.)

9-7.   Roy and Dale saved $5,000 per year for the first five years of their marriage. After the arrival of twin boys, Dale took a sabbatical from her job until the boys were six years old. Because of the decline in family income, saving was not possible, and withdrawals of $3,000 per year for six years were necessary. After Dale returned to a "paying" job, Roy and Dale were able to save $8,000 each year for the next 19 years before retiring.

(a)   Using 10% as the appropriate interest rate, how much will Roy and Dale have accumulated at retirement?

(b)   Assuming investment of their accumulated savings at 12%, how much can be withdrawn each year for 20 years? (Assume all contributions and withdrawals at the end of the year and disregard taxes.)

9-8.   Alicia Price just won the U.S. Publishers' Sweepstakes. She must decide whether to take a lump sum payment of $5,000,000 now or $1,000,000 at the end of each year for 25 years.

(a)   If Alicia uses a discount rate of 14%, which payment plan should she choose? (Ignore tax effects--in the real world, however, taxes may be a major factor in the decision.)

(b)   If Alicia assumes a discount rate of 20%, does your advice remain the same?

(c)   If taxes at a rate of 30% must be paid on the lump sum or stream of receipts, will your choice in (a) above change?

9-9.   ˌ Jared Beville recently sold his baseball card collection for $10,000.

(a)   If he reinvests the money in a mutual fund and earns 12% per year until he retires 40 years later, what is the value of his account? (Ignore taxes.)

(b)   At retirement Jared will roll his investment into a fixed return account paying 8% per year. How much will he be able to withdraw each year over his projected 30-year retirement?

9-10.   Brandon Blow recently graduated with a B.S. in Finance. He is suffering from a malady common to new graduates--Car Fever. Brandon is trying to decide between two automobiles -a $20,000 ZZZ or a $15,000 XXX. Brandon must finance his purchase over a three-year period regardless of his choice of cars.

(a)   Assuming an interest rate of 12%, what will Brandon's annual payment be on each car? (You may wish to calculate monthly payments to be more realistic.)

(b)   Brandon plans to buy a new car every three years. If the difference in the price of cars is maintained through Brandon's 40-year career, how much could he accumulate if he always bought the cheaper car and earned 8% on the difference in annual payments. (Ignore resale values.)

9-11.   Smokey Stack smokes a pack of cigarettes a day. Each pack of cigarettes costs $2.50. Smokey is wondering how much money she could accumulate if she quit smoking and invested the money.

(a)   Assuming the saved amount is invested at the end of the year at a 6% rate of return, how much could she accumulate during the next 40 years. (Assume 365-day year; ignore taxes.)

(b)   How much could Smokey accumulate if she was able to earn 10%?

(c)   If Smokey earns 6% on the accumulated amount from (b) above, how much can she withdraw each year for the next 20 years before depleting her accumulation? (Ignore taxes.)

9-12.   Gretchan Cooper is considering opening a savings account as a precaution against unexpected expenses. Busy Bank promises to pay 8% compounded quarterly on amounts deposited for one year. Gretchan can earn 8% paid annually on deposits in her credit union without the one-year restriction on withdrawals.

(a)   In which of the institutions will Gretchan earn the most interest on a $2,000 deposit?

(b)   In which institution should Gretchan deposit her money?

9-13. Dana Gulley is considering purchasing a house. Dana does not want to pay more than 25% of her income in annual house payments (principal and interest). Dana has determined that she can obtain a 30-year mortgage at a 10% interest rate.

    (a)   If Dana's annual income for the foreseeable future is $50,000, can she purchase a $140,000 home and remain within her limit?

    (b)   What is the maximum price that Dana can pay for a house without exceeding her limit?

9-14. Stacey Katz wishes to retire in 40 years. She is trying to determine what amount must be accumulated to provide $60,000 annually in **today's** dollars. (Ignore taxes.)

    (a)   If Stacey assumes a 5% inflation rate, what annual income will be required to provide an amount equivalent in purchasing power to $60,000 today?

    (b)   Stacey wishes to withdraw the amount calculated in (a) each year over her expected 30-year life span after retirement. If she expects to earn 8% interest on her portfolio during retirement, how much must she have accumulated at retirement.

    (c)   The amount that Stacey calculated in (b) above is certainly eye-opening (scary even!). Can she possibly accumulate such a large sum? If she can earn 12% on her savings (investments), how much would she have to save each year to achieve her goal?

Chapter 9 - Solutions

9-1.   (a)   *Future value*

$$FV = PV(1 + i)^n$$
$$FV = \$5,000(1 + .08)^{12}$$
$$FV = \$5,000(2.518)$$
$$FV = \textbf{\$12,590}$$

    (b) $\$20,000 = \$5,000(1 + .08)^n$

$$\frac{\$20,000}{5,000} = (1 + .08)^n$$

$$4 = (1.08)^n$$

Read down the 8% column of the future value table until the value 4 is found. The value 4 is not found exactly, but it can be determined that N is approximately **18 years**.

9-2.   (a)   *PV of an annuity*

$$PV_A = A \times PV_{IFA} \ (n = 5, i = 12\%)$$
$$PV_A = \$200,000 \times 3.605$$
$$PV_A = \textbf{\$721,000}$$

(b)   Present value of salary contract

Year	Salary	PV Factor 12%	Present Value
1	$200,000	.893	$178,600
2	200,000	.797	159,400
3	200,000	.712	142,400
4	400,000	.636	254,400
5	400,000	.567	226,800
			$961,600

An alternative way of computing the present value of the salary contract (b) is

PV of contract $= \$200,000 \times 2.402 + 400,000(3.605 - 2.402)$
$= \$480,400 + \$481,200$
$= \mathbf{\$961,600}$

9-3. $PV_A = A \times PV_{IFA}(n = ?, i = 8\%)$

$\$25,000 = \$3,200(PV_{IFA})$

$PV_{IFA} = \dfrac{\$25,000}{\$3,200}$

$PV_{IFA} = 7.813$

N = **approximately 13 years**

Mr. Bearer must expect to live more than 13 years for the annuity to be preferable.

9-4.   (a)   *Future value of an annuity*

$FV_A = A \times FV_{IFA}$

$\$1,000,000 = \$6,080 \times FV_{IFA}(n = ?, i = 10\%)$

$\dfrac{\$1,000,000}{\$6,080} = FV_{IFA}$

$164.474 = FV_{IFA}$

N = **approximately 30 years**

(b) $\$1,000,000 = A \times FV_{IFA}(n = 40, i = 12\%)$

$\$1,000,000 = A \times 767.09$

$A = \dfrac{\$1,000,000}{767.09} = \mathbf{\$1,303.63}$

9-5.   (a)   *Future value annuity*

$FV_A = A \times FV_{IFA}$

$\$500,000 = A \times 36.786$

$$A = \frac{\$5,000,000}{36.786} = \mathbf{\$135,921.27}$$

(b) $FV_A = A \times FV_{IFA}(n = 15, i = 6\%)$

$\$5,000,000 = A \times 23.276$

$$A = \frac{\$5,000,000}{23.276} = \mathbf{\$214,813.54}$$

The first payment would not be made until the end of the sixth year.

9-6. *Selling price of land* = $\$5,000 \times 100 = \$500,000$

Future value

$FV = PV\,(1 + i)^{20}$

$$\frac{\$500,000}{\$100,000} = (1 + i)^{20}$$

$5 = (1 + i)^{20}$

Read across the twentieth row of the future value tables. The factor lies approximately halfway between the interest factors for 8% and 9%. Approximate rate of return = **8.5%**.

The rate of return can be determined more accurately by interpolation.

8%	4.661		
		.339	
	5.000		.943
9%	5.604		

$$\text{Rate of return} = 8\% + \frac{.339}{.943}(1\%)$$

$$= 8\% + .359(1\%) = \mathbf{8.36\%}$$

9-7. (a) *Accumulation at retirement*

Future value of an annuity

$FV_A = A \times FV_{IFA}(n = 5, i = 10\%)$
$FV_A = \$5,000 \times 6.105$
$FV_A = \$30,525$

There are several ways to "handle" the next step of this problem. You may prefer a different procedure than the one shown.

Present value of an annuity

$PV_A = A \times PV_{IFA}(n = 6, i = 10\%)$
$PV_A = \$3,000 \times 4.355$

$PV_A = \$13,065$

$\$30,525 - \$13,065 = \$17,460$

Future value

$FV = PV \times FV_{IF} \ (n = 25, i = 10\%)$
$FV = \$17,460 \times 10.835 = \mathbf{\$189,179.10}$

An alternative approach to these steps follows.

Year	Beginning Amount	Interest Factor	Compound Amount	Withdrawal	Ending Amount
1*	$30,525.00	1.1	$33,577.50	$3,000	$30,577.50
2	$30,577.50	1.1	$33,635.25	$3,000	$30,635.25
3	$30,635.25	1.1	$33,698.78	$3,000	$30,698.78
4	$30,698.78	1.1	$33,768.66	$3,000	$30,768.66
5	$30,768.66	1.1	$33,845.53	$3,000	$30,845.53
6	$30,845.53	1.1	$33,930.08	$3,000	$30,930.08

*Year 1 (Year 6--first year after twins are born.

$FV = PV \times FV_{IF}(n = 19, i = 10\%)$
$FV = \$30,930.08 \times 6.116 = \mathbf{\$189,168.37}$

The $10.73 difference from the original calculation is due to rounding differences in the tables. Although both approaches yield the "same" result, the ease of the first approach should be obvious to the student.

To conclude the problem, the future value of the savings after Dale returns to the work force must be computed.

Future value of an annuity

$FV_A = A \times FV_{IFA}(n = 19, i = 10\%)$
$FV_A = \$8,000 \times 51.159 = \mathbf{\$409,272}$

Accumulation at retirement = $189,179.10 + $409,272 = **$598,451.10**

(b) Withdrawal each year for 20 years after retirement

Present value of an annuity

$PV_A = A \times PV_{IFA} \ (n = 20, i = 12\%)$
$\$598,451.10 = A \times 7.469$

$A = \dfrac{\$598,451.10}{7.469} = \mathbf{\$80,124.66}$

Author's Note: This problem is not intended to be sexually discriminatory. If you are concerned with Dale's staying home to take care of the twins, simply change the names and let Roy remain at home or recompute the answer assuming that Dale returns to the work force immediately and savings contributions continue (less child-care expenses, of course).

9-8. **(a)** **Choose the annuity stream**

PV_A = $1,000,000 x 6.873 = **$6,873,000**

Although the 25 $1,000,000 payments may seem much greater than the lump-sum, once they are time-adjusted, the difference is much less.

(b) PV_A = $1,000,000 x 4.948 = **$4,948,000**

At the higher discount rate of 20%, the lump sum has a higher present value. **Choose the lump sum**.

(c) *Taxes on lump sum* = $5,000,000 x .30 = $1,500,000
Net receipt = **$3,500,000**

Taxes on annual receipt = $1,000,000 x .30 = $300,000
Net annual receipt = $700,000

PV_A = $700,000 x 6.873 = **$4,811,100**

The difference in the present values = $4,811,000 - $3,500,000 = $1,311,000. This difference equals (1 - tax rate) x the difference when taxes were ignored: ($6,873,000 $5,000,000) x (1 - .3) = $1,311,000.

9-9. **(a)** $FV = PV \times FV_{IF}$

FV = $10,000 x 93.051 = **$930,510**

(b) $PV_A = A \times PV_{IFA}$, solve for A

$930,510 = A \times 11.258$

A = **$82,653.22**

9-10. **(a)** $PV_A = A \times PV_{IFA}$

$20,000 = A \times 2.402$

A = **$8,326.39** = annual payment on ZZZ

$15,000 = A \times 2.402$

A = **$6,244.80** annual payment on XXX

(b) *Difference in annual payments* = $8,326.39 - $6,244.80 = $2,081.59

$FV_A = A \times FV_{IFA}$

FV_A = $2,081.59 x 259.06 = **$539,256.71**

That's a lot of money. Brandon had better really enjoy driving the more expensive car. Note that the price of the cars is not relevant to the calculation. As long as a $5,000 difference exists, the difference in financing costs will be the same.

9-11. (a) *Annual cost of cigarettes* = $2.50 x 365 = $912.50

$$FV_A = A \times FV_{IFA}$$

$$FV_A = \$912.50 \times 154.76 = \mathbf{\$141{,}218.50}$$

(b) $FV_A = \$912.50 \times 442.59 = \mathbf{\$403{,}863.38}$

(c) $PV_A = A \times PV_{IFA}$

$\$403{,}863.38 = A \times 11.47$

$$A = \frac{\$403{,}863.38}{11.47} = \mathbf{\$35{,}210.41}$$

Of course, Smokey may need to plan for a longer life span if she stops smoking.

9-12. (a) Credit Union:

Interest = .08 x $2,000 = **$160**

Busy Bank:

$$FV = 2{,}000\left(1 + \frac{.08}{4}\right)^4 =$$

$FV = 2{,}000(1.082) = 2{,}164$

Interest = **$164**

(b) Although Gretchan will earn $4 more (actually more if calculated without using tables) because of quarterly compounding, she must consider the need to access the money quickly. In this situation, the lower interest may be the better choice.

9-13. (a) *Annual limit* = .25 x 50,000 = $12,500

Annual house payments

$PV_A = A \times PV_{IFA}$

$\$140{,}000 = A \times 9.427$

$$A = \frac{\$140{,}000}{9.427} = \mathbf{\$14{,}850.96}$$

No, he could not purchase a $140,000 home under the specified terms without exceeding his self-imposed limit.

(b) $PV_A = A \times PV_{IFA}$

$PV_A = \$12{,}500 \times 9.427$

$PV_A = \mathbf{\$117{,}837.50}$

9-14. (a) $FV = PV \times FV_{IF}$

       $FV = \$60,000 \times 7.040 = \mathbf{\$422,400}$

       At an annual inflation rate of 5%, it will take $422,400 forty years from now to maintain $60,000 purchasing power in today's dollars.

     (b) $PV_A = A \times PV_{IFA}$

       $PV_A = \$422,400 \times 11.258$

       $PV_A = \mathbf{\$4,755,379.20}$

       Note: This calculation ignores any inflation during the retirement period. In the presence of inflation (which is probable), a larger amount would be necessary to maintain purchasing power.

     (c) $FV_A = A \times FV_{IFA}$

       $\$4,755,379.20 = A \times 767.09$

$$A = \frac{\$4,755,379.20}{767.09} = \mathbf{\$6,199.25}$$

       The amount, though significant, is not nearly as large as one might initially think. Of course, Stacey might not be able to save much in the early years of her career, but may be able to save much more in the latter years. The problem also ignores several important components of retirement income, such as employer retirement plans and social security.

       Study Note: To avoid additional complexity, most of these problems explicitly or implicitly ignore taxes. In the "real world," this should never be done.

Chapter 10

Summary: Valuation is the key concept of finance. This chapter focuses on how financial assets are valued and how investors establish the rate of return they demand.

I.　　Valuation Concepts [p. 267]

　　A.　The value of an asset is the present value of the expected cash flows (inflows and outflows) associated with the asset. In order to compute the present value of an asset, an investor must know or estimate the amount of expected cash flows, the timing of expected cash flows and the risk characteristics of the expected flows.

　　B.　Actually, the price (present value) of an asset will be based on the collective assessment of the asset's cash flow characteristics by the many capital market participants.

II.　　Valuation of Bonds [p. 268]

　　A.　The value of a bond is derived from cash flows composed of periodic interest payments and a principal payment at maturity.

　　B.　The present value (price) of a bond can be expressed as follows:

$$P_b = \sum_{t=1}^{n} \frac{I_t}{(1+Y)^t} + \frac{P_n}{(1+Y)^n}$$

　　　　where　P_b　= the market price of the bond
　　　　　　　　I_t　= the periodic interest payments
　　　　　　　　P_n　= the principal payment at maturity
　　　　　　　　t　= the period from 1 to n
　　　　　　　　n　= the total number of periods
　　　　　　　　Y　= the yield to maturity (required rate of return)

　　C.　The present value tables may be used to compute the price of a bond. The stream of periodic interest payments constitutes an annuity. The present value of the stream of interest payments may be computed by multiplying the periodic interest payment by the present value of an annuity interest factor.

　　　$PV_A = A \times PV_{IFA}(n,i)$

　　　　where　PV_A　= present value of a stream of n interest payments
　　　　　　　　A　= periodic interest payment (same as I_t above)
　　　　　　　　i　= the market required rate of return (yield to maturity)

The present value of the principal payment may be computed by applying the present value of a $1 formula.

　　　$PV = FV \times PV_{IF}(n,i)$

　　　　where　PV　= present value of principal payment
　　　　　　　　FV　= the principal payment at the end of the nth period
　　　　　　　　i　= the market required rate of return (yield to maturity)

The present value (price) of the bond will be the sum of the present value of the interest payments plus the present value of the principal.

Example: Compute the present value (price) of a bond that is paying $100 annually (assume a $1,000 par value bond and a 10% coupon rate) in interest if the bond will mature in eight years and the market determined required rate of return (yield to maturity) is 12%.

$P_b = \$100 \times PV_{IFA}(n = 8, i = 12\%) + \$1,000 \times PV_{IF}(n = 8th, i = 12\%)$

$P_b = \$100(4.968) + \$1,000(.404)$

$P_b = \$496.80 + \$404 = \$900.80$

D.   An understanding of the relationships between the **required rate of return (yield to maturity)** and the **coupon rate** (the annual interest payment divided by the par value) will allow one to "anticipate" the value of a bond prior to calculation.

If the market rate is > the coupon rate, the bond will sell at a discount (below par value).
If the market rate = the coupon rate, the bond will sell at par value.
If the market rate is < the coupon rate, the bond will sell at a premium (above par value).

In the example above, the market rate, 12%, was greater than the coupon rate, 10%; therefore, the bond sold at a discount ($900.80 which is less than the par value of $1,000).

E.   Yield to maturity. [pp. 269-272]
 1.   Three factors influence an investor's required rate of return on a bond.
    a.   The required *real* rate of return--the rate of return demanded for giving up current use of funds on a noninflation-adjusted basis.
    b.   An **inflation premium**--a premium to compensate the investor for the effect of inflation on the value of the dollar.
    c.   **Risk premium**--all financial decisions are made within a risk-return framework. An astute investor will require compensation for risk exposure. There are two types of risk of primary concern in determining the required rate of return (yield to maturity) on a bond:
        (1)   Business risk--the possibility of a firm not being able to sustain its competitive position and growth in earnings.
        (2)   Financial risk--the possibility that a firm will be unable to meet its debt obligations as they come due.
 2.   Bond prices are inversely related to required rates of return. A change in the required rate of return will cause a change in the bond price in the opposite direction. The impact of the change in required rate of return on the bond price is dependent upon the remaining time to maturity. The impact will be greater the longer the time to maturity.

F.   Determining yield to maturity. [pp. 274-277]
 1.   If the bond price, coupon rate, and number of years to maturity are known, the yield to maturity (market-determined required rate of return) can be computed.
    a.   Trial and error process. This process requires one to "guess" various yields until the yield to maturity that will cause the present value of the stream of interest payments plus the present value of principal payment to equal the bond price is determined. The initial "guess" is not completely blind, however, since the relationship between the coupon rate, yield to maturity (market rate), and the bond price is known. For example, if a $1,000 par value bond maturing in 20 years with a coupon rate of 10% was priced in the

market at $800, we would know that the yield to maturity was greater than 10%. As an initial guess, try 14%.

$$\$800 \overset{?}{=} \$100(PV_{IFA}, n = 20, i = 14\%) + \$1,000(PV_{IF}, n = 20, i = 14\%)$$

$$\$800 = \$100(6.623) + \$1,000(.073)$$

$$\$800 \neq \$662.30 + \$73 = \$735.30$$

The initial estimate of 14% is too high. A lower rate must be "tried." Try 12%.

$$\$800 \overset{?}{=} \$100(7.469) + \$1,000(.104) = \$850.90$$

Now we know that the yield to maturity is less than 14% but more than 12%. Try 13.%

$$\$800 \overset{?}{=} \$100(7.025) + \$1,000(.087) = \$702.50 + \$87 = \$789.50$$

Again, 13% does not exactly equal the yield to maturity. The actual yield to maturity is slightly less than 13%. Interpolation, as illustrated in problem *9-6*, will allow a more exact calculation.

    b.   Often, a less exact calculation of the yield to maturity is sufficient. Using the approximate yield to maturity approach (AYTM): [p. 276]

$$AYTM = \frac{annual\ interest\ payment + \dfrac{principal\ payment - price\ of\ bond}{number\ of\ years\ till\ maturity}}{.6(price\ of\ bond) + .4(principal\ payment)}$$

Using the previous bond example, to illustrate:

$$AYTM = \frac{\$100 + \dfrac{\$1,000 - \$800}{20}}{.6(\$800) + .4(\$1,000)}$$

$$AYTM = \frac{\$100 + \$10}{\$480 + \$400} = \frac{\$110}{\$880} = 12.5\%$$

    c.   An exact calculation of the yield to maturity can be made using a good calculator or computer.

G.   Often interest payments are made more frequently than once a year. Semiannual interest payments are common. To compute the price of such a bond, we divide the annual amount of interest by the frequency of payment to arrive at the amount of payment. A $1,000 bond with a 10% coupon rate would pay $100 per year. The bondholder would receive, however, $50 at the end of the first six months and the remaining $50 at the end of the year. Stated differently, the bondholder would receive a 5% payment each six months. In II.C., a $1,000 bond with a 10% coupon rate and eight years to maturity was found to have a present value of $900.80 when the market required rate of return was 12%. Assuming that the bond has the same characteristics but pays $50 semiannually and the market rate of return is 12% compounded semiannually, the price of the bond would be:

$$BP = \$50(PV_{IFA}, n = 16, i = 6\%) + \$1,000(PV_{IF}, n = 16, i = 6\%)$$

$$BP = \$50(10.106) + \$1,000(.394)$$

$$BP = \$505.30 + \$394 = \$899.30$$

III. Valuation of Preferred Stock [pp. 278-279]

A. Preferred stock is usually valued as a perpetual stream of fixed dividend payments.

$$P_p = \frac{D_p}{(1 + K_p)^1} + \frac{D_p}{(1 + K_p)^2} + \frac{D_p}{(1 + K_p)^3} + \ldots + \frac{D_p}{(1 + K_p)^\infty}$$

where P_p = the price of preferred stock
D_p = the annual dividend for preferred stock
K_p = the required rate of return (discount rate) applied to preferred stock dividends

B. Since the dividend stream is a perpetuity, the preferred stock valuation formula can be reduced to a more usable form:

$$P_p = \frac{D_p}{K_p}$$

An investor who required an 8% rate of return would value a share of preferred stock paying $5 in dividends per year as follows:

$$P_p = \frac{\$5}{.08} = \$62.5$$

If the investor's required rate of return increased to 12%, he would be willing to pay only $41.67 for a share of the stock.

C. If the market price of preferred stock and the annual dividend are known, the market determined required rate of return may be computed by using the valuation equation and solving for K_p.

$$P_p = \frac{D_p}{K_p}$$

$$K_p = \frac{D_p}{P_p} = \frac{\$5}{41.67} = 12\%$$

IV. Valuation of Common Stock [pp. 279-285]

A. The value of a share of common stock is the present value of an expected stream of dividends.

$$P_o = \frac{D_1}{(1 + K_e)} + \frac{D_2}{(1 + K_e)^2} + \frac{D_3}{(1 + K_e)^3} + \ldots + \frac{D_\infty}{(1 + K_e)^\infty}$$

where P_o = price of the stock at time zero (today)
   D = dividend for each year
   K_e = the required rate of return for common stock

B. Unlike dividends on most preferred stock, common stock dividends may vary. The value formula may be applied, with modification, to three different circumstances: **no growth in dividends, constant growth in dividends**, and **variable growth in dividends**
 1. No growth in dividends. Common stock with constant (no growth) dividends is valued in the same manner as preferred stock.

$$P_o = \frac{D_o}{K_e}$$

  where P_o = price of common stock
     D_o = current annual dividend on common stock = D_1(expected to remain the same in the future)
     K_e = required rate of return for common stock

 2. Constant growth in dividends. The price of common stock with constant growth in dividends is the present value of an infinite stream of growing dividends. Fortunately, in this circumstance the basic valuation equation can be reduced to the more usable form below if the discount rate (K_e) is assumed to be greater than the growth rate.

$$P_o = \frac{D_1}{K_e - g}$$

  where D_1 = dividend expected at the end of the first year = $D_o(1 + g)$
     g = constant growth rate in dividends
   P_o, K_e = same as previously defined

Rearrangement of the constant growth equation allows the calculation of the required rate of return, K_e, when P_o, D_1, and g are given.

$$K_e = \frac{D_1}{P_o} + g$$

The first term represents the dividend yield that the stockholder expects to receive; and the second term represents the anticipated growth in dividends, earnings, and stock price.

 3. Variable growth in dividends. The present value of any pattern of dividends can be computed. Some variable patterns, however, are assumed to occur more often than others. Supernormal growth and the "no dividend" approach are the patterns most often assumed.

  a. **Supernormal growth**--an exceptional rate of dividend growth is initially expected followed by a constant rate thereafter. Suppose a firm's current dividend of $2 is expected to increase by 14% each year for the next five years before settling down to a 5% rate of growth thereafter.

$$P_0 = \frac{\$2(1.14)}{(1 + K_e)} + \frac{\$2(1.14)^2}{(1 + K_e)^2} + \frac{\$2(1.14)^3}{(1 + K_e)^3} + \frac{\$2(1.14)^4}{(1 + K_e)^4}$$

$$+ \frac{\$2(1.14)^5}{(1 + K_e)^5} + \frac{\$2(1.14)^5(1.05)}{(1 + K_e)^6} + \ldots + \frac{\$2(1.14)^5(1.05)^\infty}{(1 + K_e)^\infty}$$

Assuming a required rate of return of 12%, the price of a share of the firm's stock can be computed as follows:

$$P_0 = \$2.28(.893) + \$2.60(.797) + \$2.96(.712) + \$3.37(.636) + \$3.84(.567)$$

$$+ \frac{D_6}{(1 + K_e)^6} + \ldots + \frac{D^\infty}{(1 + K_e)^\infty}$$

Beginning with the sixth year, the dividend is assumed to grow at a constant rate.

$D_6 = D_5(1.05)$
$D_6 = \$3.84(1.05) = \$4.03$

Using the constant growth formula previously discussed, the price of the firm's stock at the end of the fifth year can be computed. The price at the end of the fifth year, of course, is the present value (at the end of year 5) of dividends D_6 through D_∞.

$$P_5 = \frac{D_6}{(1 + K_e)} + \ldots + \frac{D_\infty}{(1 + K_e)^\infty}$$

$$P_5 = \frac{D_6}{(K_e - g)} = \frac{\$4.03}{(.12 - .05)} = \$57.57$$

P_5, \$57.57, must be discounted (present valued), however, to determine the value at time zero.

$P_0 = \$2.28(.893) + \$2.60(.797) + \$2.96(.712) + \$3.37(.636)$
$\quad + \$3.84(.567) + \$57.57(.567)$

$P_0 = \$2.03 + \$2.07 + \$2.11 + \$2.14 + \$2.18 + \$32.64$

$P_0 = \$43.17$

b. "No dividend" pattern.

    (1) Suppose a firm will not pay a dividend during the next ten years but beginning in year eleven the firm will pay a \$10 dividend each year. This is a "no-dividend-no-growth" situation.

$$P_0 = \frac{P_{10}}{(1 + K_e)^{10}}$$

$$P_{10} = \frac{\$10}{K_e}$$

If an investor's required rate of return is 15%, P_{10} would be P_{10} = $10/.15 = $66.67. The present value of this delayed dividend stream would be found as follows:

$$P_o = \frac{P_{10}}{(1 + K_e)^{10}} = \frac{\$66.67}{(1 + .15)^{10}} = \$66.67(.247)$$

$$P_o = \$16.47$$

(2) Instead of a fixed dividend following a no-dividend period, a firm's dividend may grow at a constant rate. Replacing the assumption of a constant dividend in (1) above with an expectation of a 5% constant dividend growth rate, the present value (price of stock) of the expected dividends is:

$$P_o = \frac{P_{10}}{(1 + K_e)^{10}}$$

P_{10}, however, in this situation is:

$$P_{10} = \frac{D_{11}}{(K_e - g)} = \frac{\$10}{(.15 - .05)} = \frac{\$10}{.10} = \$100$$

and $P_o = \$100(.247) = \$24.70$

V.   Key Formulas

A.   Price of corporate bond [p. 268]

$$P_b = \sum_{t=1}^{N} \frac{I_t}{(1 + Y)^t} + \frac{P_N}{(1 + Y)^N}$$

An equivalent expression using the tables is:

$P_b = PV_A + PV$

where PV_A is present value of the interest payment annuity and PV is the present value of the principal payment.

B.   Approximate yield to maturity [p. 276]

$$AYTM = \frac{annual\ interest\ payment + \dfrac{principal\ payment - price\ of\ bond}{number\ of\ years\ till\ maturity}}{.6(price\ of\ bond) + .4(principal\ payment)}$$

C.   Price of preferred stock [p. 278]

$$P_p = \frac{D_p}{K_p}$$

127

D. Required rate of return on preferred stock [p. 279]

$$K_p = \frac{D_p}{P_p}$$

E. Price of common stock [pp. 280, 281, 297]

(a) No growth

$$P_o = \frac{D_o}{K_e}$$

(b) Constant growth

$$P_o = \frac{D_1}{(K_e - g)}$$

(c) Supernormal growth

$$P_o = \sum_{t=1}^{n} \frac{D_t}{(1 + K_e)^t} + P_n \left(\frac{1}{(1 + K_e)} \right)^n$$

F. Required rate of return on common stock [p. 283]

$$K_e = \frac{D_1}{P_o} + g$$

Chapter 10 - Multiple Choice Questions

1. Which of the following is considered to be a hybrid security? [p. 278]
   a. Corporate bond
   b. Common stock
   c. Preferred stock
   d. Treasury bond
   e. None of the above are correct.

2. Which of the following describes the relationship between bond prices and interest rates? [pp. 271-273]
   a. Bond prices move in the same direction as interest rates.
   b. Bond prices may go up or down when interest rates rise (all other factors held constant).
   c. Bond prices move inversely with interest rates.
   d. Bond prices are independent of interest rates.
   e. All of the above are correct.

3. A $1,000 30-year corporate bond that pays $80 annually in interest is current selling for $892. Which of the following relationships is correct? [pp. 271-273]
   a. Market rate > coupon rate.
   b. Market rate = coupon rate.
   c. Market rate < coupon rate.
   d. Market rate may be more or less than the coupon rate.
   e. Market rate plus inflation premium = coupon rate.

4.   The required rate of return on a corporate bond is often called the: [p. 268]
        a.   Risk premium.
        b.   Yield to maturity.
        c.   Real rate of return.
        d.   Approximate yield to maturity.
        e.   Present value.

5.   Which of the following is the valuation equation for common stock expected to have
        constantly growing dividends? [p. 281]
        a. $P_o = D_o/K_e$
        b. $P_o = D_1/g$
        c. $P_o = D_1/K_e$
        d. $P_o = D_1/(K_e - g)$
        e. $P_o = D_o/(K_e - g)$

6.   The primary determinant of the value of a share of stock is the: [p. 279]
        a.   P/E ratio.
        b.   EPS.
        c.   Discount rate.
        d.   Present value of an expected stream of future dividends.
        e.   Risk premium.

7.   The key concept of finance is: [p. 266]
        a.   Profit.
        b.   Rate of return.
        c.   Revenues.
        d.   Risk.
        e.   Valuation.

8.   Because of its normally fixed dividend and lack of maturity, preferred stock is often called
        a(n): [p. 278]
        a.   Perpetuity.
        b.   Bond.
        c.   No-growth common stock.
        d.   Money market security.
        e.   Interpolation.

9.   The possibility that a firm will be unable to meet its debt obligations is: [p. 270]
        a.   Business risk.
        b.   Financial risk.
        c.   Purchasing power risk.
        d.   Interest rate risk.
        e.   Inflation risk.

10.   The DCA Corporation issued bonds (20-year bonds, five years ago) with a coupon rate of
        12%. The market-required rate of return on the bonds is currently 9%. The bonds will be
        priced: [pp. 268-272]
        a.   At par.
        b.   Below par.
        c.   Above par.
        d.   Above and below par.
        e.   As a perpetuity.

Chapter 10 - Problems

10-1. The BJS Company is issuing preferred stock that will pay an annual dividend of $5.

    (a)   If you require a 12% return on the stock, what is the most you would be willing to pay for the stock?

    (b)   If rates of return available in the market decline and you now require only a 10% rate of return, what would you be willing to pay for the stock?

    (c)   Suppose that BJS experiences a severe financial decline, and you require a 20% return on the stock. What is the most you would pay for the stock?

10-2. Doldrum Plastics has been paying a $3 dividend each year and company reports indicate that management intends to continue this dividend payment for the foreseeable future.

    (a)   If the market-determined required rate of return on Doldrum's common stock is 15%, what will be the price of a share of stock?

    (b)   Suppose that an aggressive new Chief Executive Officer is hired by Doldrum. Because of the productive policies and processes instituted, capital market partici-pants anticipate that Doldrum's earnings and dividends will increase continuously at an 8% rate. What would be the price of a share of Doldrum common stock if the required rate of return remains at 15%?

    (c)   Instead of the 8% continuous growth rate in part (b), assume that earnings and dividends are expected to grow at a 12% rate for 6 years before declining to a constant rate of 5% growth each year thereafter. What will be the price of the stock?

10-3. The common stock of Knicely, Inc. is selling for $53 per share. If the recent dividend of $3 is expected to grow at a constant rate of 6% in the future, determine the required rate of return on the stock.

10-4. A corporate bond bearing a 10% coupon rate will mature in 10 years.

    (a)   If the current market rate is 8%, what is the current value of the bond (assume annual interest payments)?

    (b)   If interest payments are made semiannually, what is the value of the bond?

    (c)   Under the conditions in (b), what would the price of the bond be if market interest rates rose to 12%?

10-5. Brad Couvillon recently bought 100 shares of IMH preferred stock. The preferred stock pays $6 in dividends annually and is currently selling for $75.

      (a)   What is Brad's expected rate of return on the stock?

      (b)   If his required return of the stock was 6%, how much would he be willing to pay per share?

      (c)   If under current business conditions Brad's required real rate of return is 3%, he expects inflation to be 4% annually and he assigns a risk premium of 2% to IMH, how much would he pay for a share?

10-6. Ashleigh Williams is interested in buying some bonds of Bienville, Inc. The bonds have a 12% coupon and mature in 20 years. If the bonds have a par value of $1,000 and are currently selling for $1,160, what is the approximate yield to maturity on the bonds?

Chapter 10 - Solutions

10-1.   (a)

$$P_o = \frac{D_p}{K_p} = \frac{\$5}{.12} = \mathbf{\$41.67}$$

      (b)

$$P_o = \frac{\$5}{.10} = \mathbf{\$50}$$

      (c)

$$P_o = \frac{\$5}{.20} = \mathbf{\$25}$$

10-2.   (a)

$$P_o = \frac{D_1}{(K_e - g)} \quad \text{With this situation } D_o = D_1 = \$3, \, g = 0.$$

$$P_o = \frac{\$3}{(.15 - 0)} = \frac{\$3}{.15} = \mathbf{\$20}$$

      (b)

$$P_o = \frac{D_1}{(K_e - g)}$$

$$D_1 = D_o(1 + g) = \$3(1.08) = \$3.24$$

$$P_o = \frac{\$3.24}{(.15 - .08)} = \frac{\$3.24}{.07} = \mathbf{\$46.29}$$

(c)

$$P_o = \frac{D_1}{(1 + K_e)} + \frac{D_2}{(1 + K_e)^2} + \ldots + \frac{D_6}{(1 + K_e)^6} + \frac{P_6}{(1 + K_e)^6}$$

$$P_6 = \frac{D_7}{(K_e - g)}$$

$$D_1 = \$3.00(1.12) = \$3.36$$

$$D_2 = \$3.36(1.12) = \$3.76$$

$$D_3 = \$3.76(1.12) = \$4.21$$

$$D_4 = \$4.21(1.12) = \$4.71$$

$$D_5 = \$4.71(1.12) = \$5.28$$

$$D_6 = \$5.28(1.12) = \$5.91$$

$$D_7 = \$5.91(1.05) = \$6.21$$

$$P_6 = \frac{D_7}{(K_e - g)} = \frac{\$6.21}{(.15 - .05)} = \frac{\$6.21}{.10} = \$62.10$$

$$P_o = \frac{\$3.36}{(1.15)} + \frac{\$3.76}{(1.15)^2} + \frac{\$4.21}{(1.15)^3} + \frac{\$4.71}{(1.15)^4} + \frac{\$5.28}{(1.15)^5} + \frac{\$5.91}{(1.15)^6} + \frac{\$62.10}{(1.15)^6}$$

$$P_o = \$3.36(.870) + \$3.76(.756) + \$4.21(.658) + \$4.71(.572) + \$5.28(.497)$$
$$+ \$5.91(.432) + \$62.10(.432)$$

$$P_o = \$2.92 + \$2.84 + \$2.77 + \$2.69 + \$2.62 + \$2.55 + \$26.83$$

$$P_o = \mathbf{\$43.22}$$

10-3. $D_1 = D_o(1 + g) = \$3.00(1.06) = \$3.18$

$$P_o = \frac{D_1}{(K_e - g)}$$

$$\$53 = \frac{\$3.18}{(K_e - .06)}$$

$$K_e = \frac{D_1}{P_o} + g$$

$$K_e = \frac{\$3.18}{\$53} + .06$$

$$K_e = .06 + .06 = \mathbf{.12}$$

10-4. (a)   Bond price = $100(IF_{PVA}$, $n = 10$, $i = 8\%) + (IF_{PV}$, $n = 10$, $i = 8\%)$
             Bond price = $100(6.710) + \$1,000(.463)$
             Bond price = $671 + \$463 = \mathbf{\$1,134}$

      (b)   Bond price = $50(IF_{PVA}$, $n = 20$, $i = 4\%) + \$1,000(IF_{PV}$, $n = 20$, $i = 4\%)$
             Bond price = $50(13.59) + \$1,000(.456)$
             Bond price = $679.50 + \$456 = \mathbf{\$1,135.50}$

      (c)   Bond price = $50(IF_{PVA}$, $n = 20$, $i = 6\%) + \$1,000(IF_{PV}$, $n = 20$, $i = 6\%)$
             Bond price = $50(11.47) + \$1,000(.312)$
             Bond price = $573.50 + \$312 = \mathbf{\$885.50}$

10-5. (a)

$$P_p = \frac{D_p}{K_p}$$

$$\$75 = \frac{\$6}{K_p}$$

$$K_p = \frac{\$6}{\$75} = .08 = \mathbf{8\%}$$

      (b)

$$P_p = \frac{\$6}{.06} = \mathbf{\$100}$$

      (c)

        Required rate of return $= 3\% + 4\% + 2\% = 9\%$

$$P_p = \frac{\$6}{.09} = \mathbf{\$66.67}$$

10-6.

$$AYTM = \frac{annual\ interest\ payment + \dfrac{principal\ payment - price\ of\ bond}{number\ years\ till\ maturity}}{.6(price\ of\ bond) + .4(principal\ payment)}$$

$$AYTM = \frac{\$120 + \dfrac{\$1,000 - \$1,160}{20}}{.6(\$1,160) + .4(\$1,000)}$$

$$= \frac{\$120 + (-\$8)}{\$696 + \$400} = \frac{\$112}{\$1,096} = \mathbf{10.22\%}$$

Summary: The purpose of this chapter is to examine the processes for determining the appropriate discount rate that a firm should apply in evaluating investment opportunities.

I.   Introduction

    A.   A business firm must strive to earn at least as much as the cost of the funds that it uses.

    B.   Usually a firm has several sources of funds, and each source may have a different cost.

    C.   The overall cost of the funds employed is a proportionate average of the various sources.

    Assume that you borrow money from three friends in the following amounts and costs:

Source	Amount	Interest Rate
Larry	$5,000	10%
Curly	2,000	6%
Moe	3,000	8%

If the $10,000 is invested, what rate of return must be earned to enable you to pay your friends their required rate of interest?

Weighted cost of borrowing:

(1) Source	(2) Cost	(3) Amount Borrowed	(4) Proportion	(5) Weighted Average Cost (2 x 4)
Larry	.10	$ 5,000	$\frac{\$5,000}{\$10,000} = .5$	.050
Curly	.06	$ 2,000	$\frac{\$2,000}{\$10,000} = .2$	.012
Moe	.08	$\frac{\$ 3,000}{\$10,000}$	$\frac{\$3,000}{\$10,000} = \frac{.3}{1.0}$	$\frac{.024}{.086}$

The average cost is 8.6%. The cost can also be found by expressing the aggregate interest cost as a ratio of the amount borrowed.

Source	Interest Rate	Amount Borrowed	Interest
Larry	.10	$ 5,000	$500
Curly	.06	2,000	120
Moe	.08	$\frac{3,000}{\$10,000}$	$\frac{240}{\$860}$

$$Weighted\ cost = \frac{\$860}{10,000} = 8.6\%$$

In order to pay your friends their required interest, you must invest the borrowed funds to earn at least 8.6%. Suppose you also invest $10,000 of your own money and seek to earn 20% on your investment, what is the required rate of return?

| (1) | (2) | (3) | (4) | (5) Weighted Average |
Source	Cost	Amount	Proportion	Cost (2 x 4)
Larry	.10	$ 5,000	$\frac{\$5,000}{\$20,000}$ = .25	.025
Curly	.06	$ 2,000	$\frac{\$2,000}{\$20,000}$ = .10	.006
Moe	.08	$ 3,000	$\frac{\$3,000}{\$20,000}$ = .15	.012
You	.20	$\frac{\$10,000}{\$20,000}$	$\frac{\$10,000}{\$20,000}$ = $\frac{.50}{1.00}$	$\frac{.100}{.143}$

Notice that due to financial leverage (fixed payments to lenders) the required rate of return on the total investment is less than your required return. The above computation may be validated as follows:

Dollar return required = .143 x $20,000 = $2,860
Interest payments to lenders   860
Return to you $2,000

Your rate of return = $\frac{\$2,000}{\$10,000}$ = 20%.

D. The firm's **required rate of return** that will satisfy all suppliers of capital is called its **cost of capital**.

E. There are several steps in measuring a firm's cost of capital. [p. 302]
1. Compute the cost of each source of capital.
2. Assign weights to each source.
3. Compute the weighted average of the component costs.

II. Interdependence of Valuation and Cost of Capital

A. To achieve the goal of the firm, maximization of stockholder's wealth, the firm's assets must be employed to earn at least the required rate of return (cost of capital).

B. A firm's required rate of return (cost of capital) is determined in the market by the suppliers of capital.

C. The market-determined required rate of return for each source of capital depends upon the market's perceived level of risk associated with the individual securities.

D. The market allocates capital at varying rates of return based on perceptions of an individual firm's riskiness, efficiency, and expected returns.

III. The Cost of Debt [pp. 302-304]

A. The basic cost of debt to the firm is the effective yield to maturity. The yield to maturity is a market-determined rate and can be found by examining the relationships of security price, periodic interest payments, maturity value, and length of time to maturity. The yield to maturity for a corporate bond may be found by solving for Y in the following equation:

$$P_b = \sum_{t=1}^{n} \frac{I_t}{(1 + y)^t} + \frac{P_n}{(1 + y)^n}$$

where P_b = the market price of the bond
I_t = the periodic interest payments
P_n = the principal at maturity
t = the period from 1 to n
n = the total number of periods
y = the yield to maturity

B. Since interest is tax deductible, the actual cost of debt to the firm is less than the yield to maturity.

C. The aftertax cost of debt is:

K_d *(cost of debt) = yield* x *(1 - tax rate)*.

The aftertax cost to a firm of bonds issued at par paying $100 annually in interest would be 6.6% if the firm's marginal tax rate were 34%.

$K_d = .10(1 - .34) = .066$

IV. The Cost of Preferred Stock [p. 305]

A. Preferred stock is similar to debt in that the preferred dividend is fixed but dissimilar in that dividends are not tax deductible.

B. The cost of preferred stock to a firm may be determined by examining the relationship of its annual (usually fixed) dividend and its market-determined price. Preferred stock, unlike debt, has no maturity and, therefore, the dividends are expected to be perpetual.

C. The cost of preferred stock is computed by dividing the annual dividend payment by the net proceeds received by the firm in the sale of preferred stock.

$$K_p \text{ (cost of preferred stock)} = \frac{D_p}{P_p - F}$$

where D_p = preferred stock dividend
F = flotation costs per share
P_p = market price of preferred stock

V. The Cost of Common Equity [pp. 305-310]

A. The basis of computation of the price of common stock is the Dividend Valuation Model.

$$P_o = \frac{D_1}{(1 + K_e)^1} + \frac{D_2}{(1 + K_e)^2} + \ldots + \frac{D_\infty}{(1 + K_e)^\infty}$$

The current price of the stock, P_o, is the present value of the expected future stream of dividends, $D_1 \ldots D_\infty$. The discount rate is K_e, the cost of common stockholders' equity.

B. Assuming constant growth, the **Dividend Valuation Model** can be reduced to:

$$P_o = \frac{D_1}{K_e - g}$$

and then solved for K_e

$$K_e = \frac{D_1}{P_o} + g$$

D_1 = expected dividend in first year
P_o = price per share of stock
g = growth rate in dividend

C. The equation for common stock cost is composed of two parts, the dividend yield, D_1/P_o, plus the anticipated growth rate, g, of dividends.

D. One must be careful not to misinterpret the K_e equation. It appears at first glance, that the lower g is, the lower the cost of common stock.

$$K_e = \frac{D_1}{P_o} + g$$

To avoid this mistake, examine the equation from which the one above is derived.

$$P_o = \frac{D_1}{K_e - g}$$

E. Common stock financing is available through the retention of earnings belonging to present stockholders or by issuing new common stock.
   1. The cost of new common stock is higher than the cost of retained earnings because the firm's proceeds from sale of the stock is less than the price paid by the stockholder due to **flotation costs**. The cost of new common stock, K_n, is:

$$K_n = \frac{D_1}{P_o - F} + g$$

   2. Earnings of a firm belong to the owners. The owners of a corporation are the stockholders. If a corporate decision is made to retain earnings, the stockholders expect a return on this indirect investment.
   3. Since retained earnings are not reduced by floatation costs, the cost to the corporation is less than new common stock financing.

F. An alternative calculation of the required return on common equity is presented in VIII.

VI. Methods of Weighting Costs [pp. 310-312]

A. A firm should seek to minimize its cost of capital by employing the optimal mix of capital financing.

B. Although debt is the cheapest source of capital, there are limits to the amount of debt capital that lenders will provide (recall the D/E relationship discussed in Chapter 3). The cost of both debt and equity financing rise as debt becomes a larger portion of the capital structure.

C. Traditional financial theory maintains that the **weighted average cost of capital** declines as lower costing debt is added to the capital structure. The optimum mix of debt and equity corresponds to the minimum point on the average cost of capital curve (see Figure 11-1 below).

FIGURE 11-1
COST OF CAPITAL CURVE

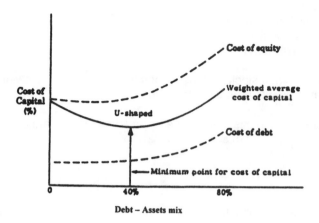

D. The optimal debt utilization varies among industries. The more cyclical the business, the lower the debt ratio is required to be.

E. The weights applied in computing the weighted average cost should be market value weights.

VII. Capital Acquisition and Decision Making [pp. 314-319]

A. The discount rate used in evaluating capital projects should be the weighted average cost of capital.

B. If the cost of capital is earned on all projects, the residual claimants of the earnings stream, the owners, will receive their required rate of return. If the overall return of the firm is less than the cost of capital, the owners will receive less than their desired rate of return because providers of debt capital must be paid.

FIGURE 11-2
COST OF CAPITAL OVER TIME

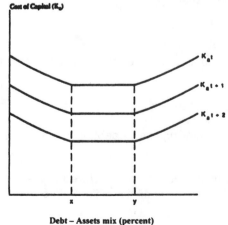

C. For most firms, the cost of capital is fairly constant within a reasonable range of debt/equity mixes (flat portion of curve in Figure 11-2). Changes in money and capital market conditions (supply and demand for money), however, cause the cost of capital for all firms to vary upward and downward over time (t, t + 1, t + 2).

D. Cost of capital in the capital budgeting decision.
1. It is the *current* cost of each source of funds that is important.
2. The cost of each source of capital will vary with the amount of capital derived from that source. The **marginal cost of debt** (the cost of the last amount of debt financing) will rise as more debt financing is used. The **marginal cost of equity** also rises when the shift from retained earnings to external (common stock) equity financing is necessary. The maximum capital structure that can be supported by using the lower costing internal equity (retention of earnings) can be projected by using the following formula:

$$X = \frac{retained\ earnings}{\%\ of\ retained\ earnings\ of\ the\ capital\ structure}$$

Beyond the capital structure calculated by the following formula, the firm's marginal cost of debt will rise.

$$Z = \frac{amount\ of\ lower-cost\ debt}{\%\ of\ debt\ of\ the\ capital\ structure}$$

E. It is very important to recognize that a firm's weighted average cost of capital is a weighted average of marginal costs.

VIII. Appendix 11A: Cost of Capital and the Capital Asset Pricing Model [pp. 330-337]

A. The **Capital Asset Pricing Model (CAPM)** relates the risk-return tradeoffs of individual assets to market returns.

B. The CAPM encompasses all types of assets but is most often applied to common stock.

C. The basic form of the CAPM is a linear relationship between returns on individual stocks and the market over time. Using least squares regression analysis, the return on an individual stock K_j is:

$$K_j = \alpha + \beta K_m + e$$

where K_j = return on the individual common stock of the company
α = alpha, the intercept on the Y axis
β = beta, the coefficient--a measurement of the return performance of a given stock relative to the return performance in the market
K_m = return on the market (usually an index of stock prices is used)
e = error term of the regression equation

D. Using historical data, the beta coefficient is computed. The beta coefficient is a measurement of the return performance of a given stock relative to the return performance of the market.

E. The CAPM is an expectational model. There is no guarantee that historical data will be repeated.

F. The CAPM evolved into a risk premium model.

1. Investors expect (require) higher returns if higher risks are taken.
2. The minimum return expected by investors will never be less than can be obtained from a riskless asset (usually considered to be U.S. Treasury bills). The relationship is expressed as follows:

$$K_j = R_f + \beta(K_m - R_f)$$

where
R_f = the risk-free rate of return
β = the beta coefficient
K_m = the return on the market index
$(K_m - R_f)$ = the premium or excess return of the market versus the risk-free rate
$\beta(K_m - R_f)$ = the expected return above the risk-free rate for the stock of company j, given the level of risk

3. Beta measures the sensitivity of an individual security's return relative to the market.
    a. By definition, the market beta = 1.
    b. A security with a beta = 1, is expected to have returns equal to and as volatile as the market. One with a beta of 2 is twice as volatile (up or down).
4. Beta measures the impact of an asset on an individual's portfolio of assets.

G. A risk-return graph can be derived from the risk premium model. The graphed relationship between risk (measured by beta) and required rates of return is called the Security Market Line (SML). [p. 334]

FIGURE 11-A-1
THE SECURITY MARKET LINE (SML)

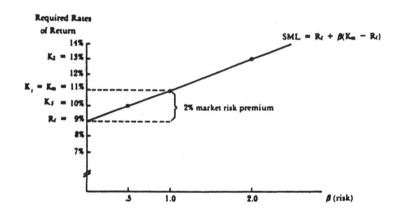

H. Cost of capital considerations
    1. If required returns rise, prices of securities fall to adjust to the new equilibrium return level; and as required returns fall, prices rise.
    2. A change in required rates of return is represented by a shift and/or a change in slope of the SML.
        a. The new SML will be parallel to the previous one if investors attempt to maintain the same risk premium over the risk-free rate and maintain purchasing power.

b. An investor's required rate of return and thus a firm's cost of capital will also change if investors risk preferences change. The slope of the SML would change even if the risk-free rate remained the same.

IX. Key Formulas

A. Aftertax cost of debt [p. 304]

$$K_d = Y(1 - T)$$

B. Cost of preferred stock [p. 305]

$$K_p = \frac{D_p}{P_p - F}$$

C. Cost of common equity--retained earnings [p. 308]

$$K_e = \frac{D_1}{P_o} + g$$

D. Cost of common equity--new common stock [p. 309]

$$K_e = \frac{D_1}{P_o - F} + g$$

E. CAPM--required return on common stock [pp. 307, 332]

$$K_j = R_f + \beta(K_m - R_f)$$

F. Size of capital structure that retained earnings will support [p. 316]

$$X = \frac{retained\ earnings}{\%\ retained\ earnings\ of\ the\ capital\ structure}$$

G. Size of capital structure that lower-cost debt will support (page 317)

$$Z = \frac{amount\ of\ debt}{\%\ of\ debt\ of\ the\ capital\ structure}$$

Chapter 11 - Multiple Choice Questions

1. The primary determinant of the value of a share of stock is the: [p. 306]
   a. Revenues of the firm.
   b. EPS of the firm.
   c. Present value of an expected stream of future dividends.
   d. Present value of expected net income.
   e. P/E ratio.

2. Which of the following is correct? [Chpt. 11]
   a. The cost of retained earnings is normally higher than the cost of new common stock.
   b. The cost of preferred stock is normally lower than the aftertax cost of debt.
   c. Floatation costs raise the cost of capital.
   d. The current yield on a share of stock is the stock price divided by earnings per share.
   e. The use of debt always raises a firm's cost of capital.

3. The graphical representation of the capital asset pricing model is called the: [p. 334]
   a. CAPM.
   b. SML.
   C. IS-LM.
   d. Beta.
   e. NOI.

4. Which of the following equations is the CAPM? [p. 332]

   a. $K_e = \dfrac{D_1}{P_o} + g$

   b. $P_o = \dfrac{D_1}{K_e - g}$

   c. $K_d = Y(1 - T)$

   d. $K_j = R_f + \beta(K_m - R_f)$

   e. $F = \sqrt{GPA}$

5. Which of the following should be used to evaluate capital projects? [p. 313]
   a. The cost of the specific source of capital used to finance the project
   b. The cost of common equity
   c. The SML
   d. The risk-free rate + inflation premium
   e. The weighted-average cost of capital

6. When investors expect a rise in the inflation rate and also become more risk sensitive, the SML will: [pp. 334-336]
   a. Shift upward and become more steeply sloped.
   b. Shift upward only.
   c. Become more steeply sloped but the vertical intercept will remain the same.
   d. Shift downward only.
   e. Shift downward and become less steeply sloped.

7. The firm's cost of capital is also called its: [p. 313]
   a. Required rate of return.
   b. Beta.
   c. K_e.
   d. NOI.
   e. M&M.

8. A firm's cost of capital is: [Chpt. 11]
   a. Set by its board of directors.
   b. Market determined.
   c. Set by the management of the firm.
   d. The same for each firm in an industry.
   e. Set by the Securities Exchange Commission.

9. The appropriate cost of each source of capital for a firm is the: [Chpt. 11]
   a. Average cost.
   b. Marginal cost.
   c. Historical cost.
   d. Weighted average cost.
   e. Floatation cost.

10. Which of the following statements is incorrect? [Chpt. 11]
    a. A firm's cost of capital is fairly constant within a reasonable range of debt-equity mixes.
    b. The cost of each source of capital may vary with the amount derived from that source.
    c. Owners are residual claimants on the earnings stream.
    d. When a firm earns less than its cost of capital, it has negative net income.
    e. Changes in capital market conditions cause the cost of capital of a firm to vary upward and downward over time.

Multiple Choice Answer Key - Chapter 11

1. c	2. c	3. b	4. d	5. e
6. a	7. a	8. b	9. b	10. d

Chapter 11- Problems

11-1. The aftertax cost of Par Value Corporation's outstanding bond is 6.6%. If the firm is in the 34% tax bracket, what is the *before*tax cost (yield) of that debt?

11-2. The Dowel Jones Company is planning to issue 10,000 shares of $100 preferred stock.

   (a) If flotation costs amount to 3%, what will be the net proceeds of the issue to the firm?

   (b) If the dividend is $7 annually, what will be the effective cost of preferred stock to the firm?

11-3. Stable Corporation has been paying an annual dividend of $3 per share for 10 years and is expected to continue such payment in the future.

   (a) If the firm's shares are selling for $20 per share, what is the cost of common stock?

   (b) If instead of the no-growth situation, the firm were growing at an annual rate of 5% and increasing its dividends at the same rate, what would be the price of the firm's stock (assume stockholders' desire a 15% rate of return)?

11-4. Bond Industries issued $10,000,000 of 30-year, $1,000 bonds 20 years ago. The bonds carry a 6% coupon rate and are currently selling for $670 per bond. Bond is in a 30% tax bracket.

   (a) If Bond issued new bonds today, what would be the approximate aftertax cost of debt? (Assume new bonds are viewed as equally risky as the old bonds in the market.)

   (b) What coupon rate would they need to place on new bonds for the bonds to sell at par value?

11-5. Alsup Manufacturing stock is selling for $28 per share. The firm's last dividend was $4 and is expected to grow at a 5% rate constantly.

(a) What is the firm's cost of equity?

(b) Assuming a 10% floatation cost, what is the firm's cost of new common stock?

11-6. The characteristics of the capital sources of the Eoff Corporation are listed below.

Source	Cost	Proportion
Debt	.08	30%
Preferred stock	.09	10%
Common equity	.15	60%

Assuming Eoff's tax rate is 30%, calculate the firm's weighted-average cost of capital.

11-7. The common stock of Soar Corporation is $100 per share. The expected dividend on its stock in the current period is $5, and the firm's cost of common stock is 12%. Determine the firm's dividend growth rate (assume that the growth rate is constant).

11-8. Solar Utility is a rapidly expanding supplier of energy in the southwestern United States. The firm has 5,000,000 shares of common stock outstanding on which it recently paid a $2 dividend. The common stock currently is priced at $30 per share. The firm wishes to maintain a payout ratio of 50%. The current earnings per share of $4 are expected to increase at an annual rate of 6% for the foreseeable future.

The firm also has two long-term bond issues outstanding. An issue of $100,000,000 bearing a 12% interest rate has been outstanding for two years, and the bonds are selling at face value. A prior bond issue of $60,000,000 will mature in the forthcoming period and must be refunded with a new issue of bonds. The new 10-year bonds will have a coupon rate of 10% and are expected to sell for $900.

Solar Utility utilizes preferred stock as a financing source and has 300,000 shares of $100 par value preferred shares outstanding. The firm pays an annual dividend of $6 on the preferred stock which is currently selling at $75.

The firm expects to continue to provide capital financing in the following proportions in the future: long-term debt, 40%; preferred stock, 10%; common stock, 20%; and retention of earnings, 30%.

If the issue costs of common and preferred stock average 8% and 4% of the amount issued, respectively, and the firm is in a 34% tax bracket, compute the minimum return that the firm should strive to earn.

11-9. (This problem relates to the appendix.) Using the capital asset pricing model, compute the required rate of return on investment j given the following information.

(a) R_f = 8%
K_m = 14%
β = 1.0

(b) Recalculate the required rate of return in (a) assuming β is .5 and 1.8.

(c)   If R_f = 6% and K_m = 12%, what value of beta, β, would yield a required return of 15%?

11-10. The market-determined required rate of return on the common stock of M. Hartsfield, Inc., is 18%. The expected return of the market is 12%, and the risk-free rate is currently 6%.

(a)   What is the beta of M. Hartsfield?

(b)   If the beta of Hartsfield were .8, what would be its required return on common stock?

Chapter 11 - Solutions

11-1.

$$K_d = yield(1 - T)$$

$$.066 = yield(1 - .34)$$

$$yield = \frac{.066}{(1 - .34)} = \frac{.066}{.66} = .10 = \textbf{10\%}$$

11-2. (a)

$$(10,000)(\$100) = \$1,000,000$$

$$(\$1,000,000)(1 - .03) = \textbf{\$970,000}$$

(b)

$$\frac{\$970,000}{10,000} = \$97 \text{ proceeds per share}$$

$$K_p = \frac{\$7}{\$97} = .072 = \textbf{7.2\%}$$

11-3. (a)

$$K_e = \frac{D_1}{P} + g$$

$$K_e = \frac{\$3}{\$20} + 0 = .15 = \textbf{15\%}$$

(b)

$$P_o = \frac{D_1}{K_e - g}$$

$$P_o = \frac{\$3(1.05)}{.15 - .05} = \frac{\$3.15}{.10} = \textbf{\$31.50}$$

11-4. (a)

$$AYTM = \frac{\$60 + \dfrac{\$1,000 - \$670}{10}}{.6(\$670) + .4(\$1,000)}$$

$$AYTM = \frac{\$60 + \$33}{\$402 + \$400} = \frac{\$93}{802} = 11.6\%$$

$$K_d = .116(1 - .3) = .0812 = \textbf{8.12\%}$$

(b) **11.6%**

11-5. (a)

$$K_e = \frac{D_1}{P_o} + g$$

$$K_e = \frac{\$4(1.05)}{\$28} + .05$$

$$K_e = \frac{\$4.20}{\$28} + .05 = .20 = \textbf{20\%}$$

(b)

$$K_N = \frac{\$4.20}{\$28(1 - .1)} + .05$$

$$K_N = \frac{\$4.20}{\$25.20} + .05 = .2167 = \textbf{21.67\%}$$

11-6. Eoff Corporation

Source	Cost	Aftertax Cost	Proportion	WACC
Debt	.08	.056	.3	.0168
Preferred stock	.09	.090	.1	.0090
Common equity	.15	.150	.6	.0900
				.1158

11-7.

$$K_e = \frac{D_1}{P_o} + g$$

$$.12 = \frac{\$5}{\$100} + g$$

$$.12 = .05 + g$$

$$\textbf{.07} = g$$

11-8.

$$\text{Cost of new common stock} = \frac{D_1}{P_o - F} + g$$

$$K_N = \frac{\$2(1 + .06)}{\$30(1 - .08)} + .06 = \frac{2.12}{\$27.60} + .06$$

$$K_N = .077 + .06 = .137 = 13.7\%$$

Note: If the firm's earnings increase at a constant rate and the payout ratio is maintained, the dividends will increase at the same rate.

Example: If the earnings per share increase by 6% in the coming year, new earnings per share will be:

$EPS_1 = \$4(1.06) = 4.24.$

Maintaining the 50% payout ratio:

$DPS_1 = (.5)(4.24) = \$2.12$

which equals the previous dividend increased by 6%:

$DPS_1 = \$2(1.06) = \$2.12.$

Cost of retained earnings = K_e

$$K_e = \frac{D_1}{P_o} + g$$

$$K_e = \frac{\$2.12}{\$30} + .06$$

$$K_e = .071 + .06 = .131 = 13.1\%$$

Cost of preferred stock

$$K_p = \frac{D}{P - F}$$

$$K_p = \frac{\$6}{75(1 - .04)} = \frac{\$6}{\$72} = .0833 = 8.33\%$$

Cost of long-term debt

$$AYTM = \frac{\text{amount of interest payment} + \dfrac{\text{principal payment} - \text{price of bond}}{\text{number of years till maturity}}}{.6(\text{price of the bond}) + .4(\text{principal payment})}$$

$$AYTM = \frac{\$100 + \dfrac{\$1,000 - \$900}{10}}{.6(\$900) + .4(\$1,000)} = \frac{\$110}{\$940} = .117$$

$K_d = yield(1 - T)$

$K_d = (.117)(1 - .34) = .0772 = 7.72\%$

Capital Structure Components	Aftertax Costs	Weights	Weighted Cost of Capital
Long-term debt	.0772	.4	.0309
Preferred stock	.0833	.1	.0083
New common stock	.1370	.2	.0274
Retained earnings	.1310	.3	.0393
			.1059

Weighted cost of capital = **10.59%**

11-9. (a) $K_j = R_f + \beta(K_m - R_f)$

$K_j = 8\% + 1.0(14\% - 8\%) = \textbf{14\%}$

(b) $K_j = 8\% + .5(14\% - 8\%) = \textbf{11\%}$

$K_j = 8\% + 1.8(14\% - 8\%) = \textbf{18.8\%}$

(c) $15\% = 6\% + \beta(12\% - 6\%)$

$15\% - 6\% = \beta(6\%)$

$\dfrac{9\%}{6\%} = \beta$

$\beta = \textbf{1.5}$

11-10. (a)

$$K_j = R_f + \beta(K_m - R_f)$$

$$.18 = .06 + \beta(.12 - .06)$$

$$.18 - .06 = .06\beta$$

$$.12 = .06\beta$$

$$\frac{.12}{.06} = \beta$$

$$\beta = \mathbf{2}$$

(b)

$$K_j = .06 + .8(.12 - .06)$$

$$K_j = .06 + .048 = .108 = \mathbf{10.8\%}$$

Chapter 12

Summary: Capital budgeting involves planning capital expenditures that will generate future benefits. In this chapter the various techniques employed to evaluate the acceptability of capital projects are discussed and compared.

I.   Characteristics of Capital Budgeting Decisions [p. 338]

      A.   **Capital expenditures** are outlays for projects with lives extending beyond one year and perhaps for many years.

      B.   Extensive planning is required.

      C.   Capital expenditures usually require initial cash flows, often large, with the expectation of future cash inflows. The differing time periods of inflows and outflows require present-value analysis.

      D.   The lengthier the time horizon associated with a capital expenditure, the greater the uncertainty. Areas of uncertainty are:
         1.   Annual costs and inflows.
         2.   Product life.
         3.   Interest rates.
         4.   Economic conditions.
         5.   Technological change.

II.   Administrative Considerations [pp. 339-340]

      A.   Search and discovery of investment opportunities.

      B.   Collection of data.

      C.   Evaluation and decision making.

      D.   Reevaluation and adjustment.

III.   Accounting Flows Versus Cash Flows [pp. 340-342]

      A.   The capital budgeting process focuses on **cash flows** rather than income. Income figures do not reflect the cash available to a firm due to the deduction of noncash expenditures such as depreciation.

      B.   Accounting flows are not totally disregarded in the capital budgeting process.
         1.   Investors' emphasis on earnings per share may, under certain conditions, require use of income rather than cash as the decision criterion.
         2.   Top management may elect to glean the short-term personal benefits of an income effect rather than the more beneficial (from the owner's viewpoint) long-run cash-flow effects.

      C.   Only incremental cash flows are relevant in a capital budgeting decision. A cash flow is incremental and relevant if it will only occur because of the capital expenditure decision. Any cash flows that will occur regardless of the capital expenditure are nonincremental and irrelevant to the decision.

FIGURE 12-1
CAPITAL BUDGETING PROCEDURES

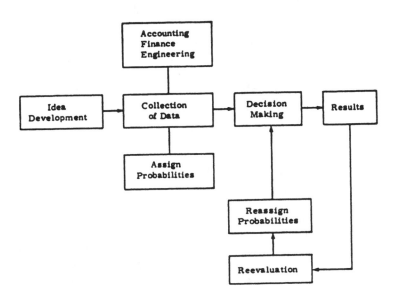

IV.   Methods for Ranking Investment Proposals [pp. 342-346]

   A.   **Payback method** [pp. 342-343]
         1.   The payback period is the length of time necessary for the sum of the expected
               annual cash inflows to equal the cash investment. A cutoff period is established
               for comparison. Capital proposals with a payback in excess of the cutoff are
               rejected.
         2.   Deficiencies of the method.
               a.   Inflows after the cutoff period are ignored.
               b.   The pattern of cash flows is ignored; therefore, time value of money is not
                     considered.
         3.   Though not conceptually sound, the payback method is frequently used.
               a.   Easy to use.
               b.   Emphasizes liquidity.
               c.   Quick return is important to firms in industries characterized by rapid
                     technological development.

   B.   **Internal rate of return (IRR)** [pp. 343-345]
         1.   The IRR method requires calculation of the rate that equates the cash investment
               with the expected cash inflows.
         2.   The calculation procedure is the same as the yield computation given in Chapter 9.
               a.   If the inflows constitute an annuity, the IRR may be computed directly.

$$\frac{Investment}{Annuity} = PV_{IFA}$$

                     The PV_{IFA} may then be found in the present value of an annuity table and its
                     correspondent interest rate (IRR).
               b.   If the cash inflows do not constitute an annuity, determination of IRR (without
                     a calculator) is a trial-and-error process.

151

(1) Choose an interest rate and apply the appropriate interest factors (from present-value table) to the corresponding annual cash flows.

(2) The initial choice (guess) of an interest rate may be obtained by averaging the cash flows and acting as if the investment yielded an annuity equal to the computed average. Assume an investment of $14,000 and the following cash inflows:

$$\begin{array}{r} \$\ 7,000 \\ 7,000 \\ \underline{4,000} \\ \$18,000/3 = \$6,000 \end{array}$$

Dividing the investment by the "assumed" annuity, a PV_{IFA} is found.

$$\frac{Investment}{Annuity} = \frac{\$14,000}{\$6,000} = 2.33 = PV_{IFA}$$

Referring to Appendix D of *Foundations of Financial Management*, 2.33 is found between the PV_{IFA} values for 13% and 14%. The process yields a first approximation only. The actual IRR will be higher since our approximation is understated by the lower third year inflow of $4,000. Now the trial-and-error process continues. Since the actual rate of return will be higher than the initial estimate, we will try a higher rate, 16%.

Year	16%		Year	15%
1	$7,000 x .862 = $ 6,034		1	$7,000 x .870 = $6,090
2	7,000 x .743 = 5,201		2	7,000 x .756 = 5,292
3	4,000 x .641 = 2,564		3	4,000 x .658 = 2,632
	$13,799			$14,014

At 16%, the present value of the inflows is less than $14,000, use a lower discount rate.

At 15%, the present value of the inflows is more than $14,000--the discount rate is too low.

The actual internal rate of return lies between 15% and 16%.
The internal rate of return can be found more exactly if desired by interpolation.

Rate	Present Value	
15%	$14,014	
		14
?	$14,000	
		215
16%	$13,799	

15% + (14/215)(1%) = 15.07%

3. The IRR can be solved for directly with most financial calculators.
4. To apply the IRR method, a minimum acceptable rate of return must be established such as the firm's cost of capital. If the IRR exceeds the minimum rate, the proposal is acceptable.

C. **Net present value (NPV)** [pp. 345-346]
  1. In this method the cash inflows are discounted at the firm's cost of capital or some variation of that measure.
  2. If the present value of the cash inflows equals or exceeds the present value of the cash investment, the capital proposal is acceptable.

V. Selection Strategy [pp. 346-348]

  A. All nonmutually-exclusive projects having a NPV $\geq$ 0 (which also means IRR $\geq$ cost of capital) should be accepted under normal conditions.

  B. The NPV method and the IRR method always agree on the accept-reject decision on a capital proposal.

  C. A disagreement may arise between the NPV and IRR methods when a choice must be made from **mutually exclusive proposals** or all acceptable proposals are not taken due to capital rationing.
  1. The primary cause of disagreement is the differing **reinvestment assumptions** [p. 347]. The NPV method inherently assumes reinvestment of cash inflows at the cost of capital. The IRR method assumes reinvestment of cash inflows at the internal rate of return.
  2. The more conservative net present value technique is usually the recommended approach when a conflict in ranking arises.

VI. Capital Rationing [pp. 348-349]

  A. Management may implement **capital rationing** by artificially constraining the amount of investment expenditures.

  B. Under capital rationing, some acceptable projects may be declined due to management's fear of growth or hesitancy to use external financing.

  C. Under capital rationing, projects are ranked by NPV and accepted until the rationed amount of capital is exhausted.

VII. Net Present Value Profile [pp. 349-352]

  A. The characteristics of an investment may be summarized by the use of the net present value profile.

  B. The **NPV profile** provides a graphical representation of an investment at various discount rates.

  C. Three characteristics of an investment are needed to apply the net present value profile:
  1. The net present value at a zero discount rate.
  2. The net present value of the project at the normal discount rate (cost of capital).
  3. The internal rate of return for the investment.

  D. The NPV profile is particularly useful in comparing projects when they are mutually exclusive or under conditions of capital rationing.

VIII. Combining Cash Flow Analysis and Selection Strategy

  A. The cash flow effects of depreciation may be very significant in capital budgeting decisions. Depreciable assets are classified in nine categories. Each is referred to as a **modified accelerated cost recovery system (MACRS)** category and has its own rate of depreciation. [pp. 352-353]

B.   Since taxes are paid with cash, corporate tax rates are very important in capital budgeting decisions. Applicable tax rates vary greatly because of the nature and location of business firms.

C.   There are several cash flow computations (projections) that are required in a capital investment decision process. [pp. 354-359]
    1.   The cash outlay required to acquire new machinery or initiate a project must be projected. If a **replacement decision** is required, then projections of cash inflows from the sale of old assets is also necessary.
    2.   The annual incremental benefits (cash flows) must be projected throughout the life of the asset or project. This projection requires calculation of incremental cash flow effects of depreciation and taxes.
    3.   The projected cash inflows and outflows are employed in the capital budgeting methods discussed in the chapter to make an investment decision.

Chapter 12 - Multiple Choice Questions

1.   Which of the following statements is incorrect? [Chpt. 12]
    a.   The payback method is deficient because of its failure to incorporate the time value of money.
    b.   If the NPV > 0, the proposal is acceptable.
    c.   If the internal rate of return < cost of capital, the proposal should be rejected.
    d.   The NPV and IRR methods always agree when evaluating mutually exclusive projects.
    e.   The NPV and IRR methods always agree on the accept-reject decision.

2.   Constraining investment in acceptable investments is called: [p. 348]
    a.   Capital consumption.
    b.   Capital rationing.
    c.   Selection strategy.
    d.   Technological restriction.
    e.   A replacement problem.

3.   In the net present value method, cash flows are discounted at: [p. 345]
    a.   The cost of capital.
    b.   The internal rate of return.
    c.   The net profit margin.
    d.   The MACRS.
    e.   The ADR.

4.   Which of these statements comparing the NPV and IRR methods is correct? [pp. 346-348]
    a.   The NPV method assumes reinvestment of cash flows at the internal rate of return.
    b.   The IRR method assumes reinvestment of cash flows at the cost of capital.
    c.   The NPV method assumes reinvestment of cash flows at the cost of capital.
    d.   The IRR assumes reinvestment of cash flows at the internal rate of return.
    e.   Both *c* and *d* are correct statements.

5.   Which of the following should be emphasized when making a capital expenditure decision? [pp. 340-341]
    a.   Incremental income
    b.   Existing expenses
    c.   Incremental cash flows
    d.   The P/E ratio
    e.   The EPS

6. The NPV and IRR methods may provide different mutually exclusive project rankings because: [pp. 346-348]
   a. NPV incorporates time value of money, and IRR does not.
   b. IRR uses income, and NPV focuses on cash flow.
   c. NPV ignores cash flows beyond the crossover period.
   d. Differing reinvestment assumptions.
   e. IRR uses accelerated depreciation and NPV does not.

7. The payback method: [p. 342]
   a. Is deficient because it ignores cash flows beyond the payback period.
   b. Ignores time value of money.
   c. May be useful to firms in industries characterized by rapid technological development.
   d. Emphasizes liquidity.
   e. All of the above are correct statements.

8. The first step in the capital budgeting process is: [p. 339]
   a. Collection of data.
   b. Assignment of probabilities.
   c. Decision making.
   d. Idea development.
   e. Assessment of results.

9. When the NPV of a capital expenditure proposal is > zero, the IRR: [p. 347]
   a. Will be > the cost of capital.
   b. May be > or < the cost of capital.
   c. Cannot be determined from the NPV information.
   d. Will be = the cost of capital.
   e. Will be < the cost of capital.

10. When projects are mutually exclusive or capital rationing has been imposed, the preferred capital budgeting technique is the: [p. 348]
    a. Profitability index.
    b. IRR method.
    c. NPV method.
    d. Payback method.
    e. NOI method.

Multiple Choice Answer Key - Chapter 12

1. d	2. b	3. a	4. e	5. c
6. d	7. e	8. d	9. a	10. c

Chapter 12 - Problems

12-1. Recycle Paper Company utilizes the payback method to evaluate investment proposals. It is presently considering two investment opportunities:

	Investment A Net Investment = $100,000		Investment B Net Investment = $500,000
Year	Expected Cash Inflows	Year	Expected Cash Inflows
1	$25,000	1	$125,000
2	25,000	2	250,000
3	25,000	3	300,000
4	25,000	4	225,000
5	25,000	5	100,000
6	10,000	6	25,000
7	5,000	7	0

(a) Compute the payback period for each of the investments.

(b) If the firm utilized a payback cutoff standard of three years which, if either, of the investments would be acceptable?

12-2. As a recent employee of Recycle Paper Company (*12-1* above), you recognize the deficiencies of the payback method. After deriving the firm's required rate of return (cost of capital), you desire to illustrate alternative approaches to your boss.

(a) Assuming a cost of capital of 14%, calculate the NPV of investment proposals A and B.

(b) Should Recycle accept either of the investment proposals?

12-3. Capital budgeting decisions are very sensitive to the pattern of expected cash flows and to the discount rate (cost of capital) used in the analysis.

(a) Recompute the NPV of Investment A for Recycle using a discount rate of 10%. Would investment A be acceptable at the lower required rate of return?

(b) Recompute Investment B using the 14% required rate of return but interchange the Year 3 and Year 7 cash flows. In other words, the expected cash flow in Year 3 is 0 and in Year 7, $300,000. Is investment B acceptable?

12-4. Compute the internal rate of return of an investment of $30,000 that generates the following stream of cash inflows:

Year	Cash Inflows
1	$12,500
2	12,500
3	12,500

12-5. Rework Problem *12-4* using the following stream of cash inflows:

Year	Cash Inflows
1	$17,000
2	11,000
3	9,500

12-6. The Todd Corporation expects to generate the following cash flows from a $1,000,000 investment:

Year	Net Cash Inflows
1	$100,000
2	400,000
3	500,000
4	300,000
5	100,000

(a) Compute the net present value of the investment if the firm estimates its cost of capital to be 10%.

(b) Compute the internal rate of return of the investment.

(c) Compute the profitability index (see footnote #2 of Chapter 12 in the text).

12-7. The Noles Corporation is contemplating the purchase of a new milling machine. The machine will cost $600,000. The machine is expected to generate earnings before depreciation and taxes of $200,000 each year over its five-year economic life. Mr. Noles is aware that Congress is currently debating some tax law changes that may take effect prior to the acquisition of the new machine. Proposed changes would necessitate using five-year straight-line depreciation rather than the three-year MACRS schedule. Noles' tax rates would increase to 40% instead of the current 34%. Noles' cost of capital is 12%.

(a) Compute the NPV of the new machine under existing depreciation and tax laws.

(b) Compute the IRR of the new machine under existing depreciation and tax laws.

12-8. Compute the NPV of the milling machine for Noles Corporation (*12-7* above) assuming a five-year straight-line depreciation schedule is required (tax rates remain the same).

12-9. Assume that Congress passes tax legislation increasing the corporate tax rate of Noles (*12-7* above) to 40% and also requires five-year straight-line depreciation on equipment such as the milling machine.

(a) Compute the NPV of the milling machine.

(b) Compute the IRR of the milling machine.

12-10. The Tough Grip Tire Corporation is analyzing the proposed purchase of a new tire-forming machine for $60,000. The proposed machine has an estimated economic life of seven years but will be treated as five-year MACRS property for depreciation purposes. The machine will increase the firm's capacity, and it is expected to contribute $15,000 annually to earnings before depreciation and taxes. The firm is in a 34% tax bracket and estimates its cost of capital to be 12%.

(a) Compute the payback period for the investment.

(b) Compute the NPV of the investment.

(c) Compute the IRR of the investment.

(d) Should the machine be acquired?

12-11. Liquid Steel, a major steel fabricator, is evaluating a proposal to replace a major piece of equipment in its operation. The automated nature of the new equipment enables it to be operated with two less workers. Liquid Steel operates three shifts, and the purchase of the new machine will generate annual savings in salaries of $88,000. No additional maintenance costs are anticipated.

The new machine will cost $250,000 and is expected to be useful for five years (assume machine to be three-year MACRS property). The old machine which originally cost $100,000 one year ago also has a remaining useful life of five years. The old machine can be sold to a smaller manufacturer for $70,000. The old machine is being depreciated as five-year MACRS property. Liquid Steel is in the 34% tax bracket, and its estimated cost of capital is 10%.

Determine whether the replacement machine should be purchased by using the NPV method.

12-12. Knothole Furniture is analyzing a new $45,000 computer controlled lathe that will allow the firm to substantially reduce waste of wood materials in its furniture making process. Their existing lathe which is being depreciated as three-year MACRS property cost $27,000 one year ago and has a remaining life of four years. The new lathe is expected to reduce materials costs by $16,000 each year of its four-year useful life. The new lathe will be depreciated as three-year property. Although the old lathe can be used for four more years, it has no market value since furniture companies prefer to buy new, modern equipment. Knothole's financial manager estimates the company's cost of capital to be 13%. The firm is in a 34% tax bracket.

(a) Compute the net present value of the proposed lathe replacement. Should the lathe be replaced?

(b) Compute the internal rate of return of the proposal. Does it confirm your decision in (a)?

(c) Assume now that the old lathe could be sold for $20,000. Compute the net present value of the replacement.

Chapter 12 - Solutions

12-1.   (a)

$$PB_A = \frac{\$100,000}{\$25,000} = 4 \; years$$

$$PB_B = \begin{array}{l} \$125,000 \\ \$250,000 \\ \$300,000 \end{array} \begin{array}{l} \$375,000 \\ \$675,000 \end{array}$$

Payback occurs in **Year 3**

(b) **Investment B**

12-2.   (a) Investment A
$NPV = \$25,000(3.433) + \$10,000(.456) + \$5,000(.400) - \$100,000$
$NPV = \$92,385 - \$100,000 = \textbf{-\$7,615}$
Investment B
$NPV = \$125,000(.877) + \$250,000(.769) + \$300,000(.675) + \$225,000(.592)$
$\qquad + \$100,000(.519) + \$25,000(.456) - \$500,000$

$NPV = \$700,875 - \$500,000 = \textbf{\$200,875}$

(b) Recycle should accept **Investment B**.

12-3.   (a) Investment A

$NPV = \$25,000(3.791) + \$10,000(.564) + \$5,000(.513) - \$100,000$

$NPV = \$102,980 - \$100,000 = \textbf{\$2,980}$

Investment A is acceptable under these conditions.

(b) Investment B

$NPV = \$125,000(.877) + \$250,000(.769) + \$0(.675) + \$225,000(.592)$
$\qquad + \$100,000(.519) + \$25,000(.456) + \$300,000(.400) - \$500,000$

$NPV = \$618,375 - \$500,000 = \textbf{\$118,375}$

Investment B is still acceptable, but the NPV is considerably reduced.

An easier calculation to determine the change in NPV of Investment B follows:

$\Delta NPV = \$300,000(Year\;3\;PV_{IFA} - Year\;7\;PV_{IFA})$
$\qquad\quad = \$300,000(.400 - .675)$
$\qquad\quad = \$300,000(-.275)$
$\qquad\quad = \textbf{-\$82,500}$

This can be confirmed by subtracting the original NPV from the recomputed NPV
$\Delta NPV = \$118,375 - \$200,875 = \textbf{-\$82,500}$

12-4.   The stream of expected cash inflows constitutes an annuity.

$$\frac{Investment}{Annuity} = PV_{IFA}$$

$$\frac{\$30,000}{12,500} = 2.4$$

Refer to present value of an annuity table; 3 years, $PV_{IFA} = 2.4$.
IRR = approximately 12%

12-5.   Since the expected cash inflows do not constitute an annuity, the IRR must be determined by a trial and error process.

(1) Average the inflows:

$$\frac{17,000 + 11,000 + 9,500}{3} = 12,500$$

(2) Divide the investment by the average annnuity:

$$\frac{\$30,000}{\$12,500} = 2.4$$

(3) Refer to the present value of annuity table. The IRR indicated is approximately 12%, the same rate indicated in Problem *12-4*. Notice, however, that the returns take place sooner than in the previous situation. It should be expected that the actual rate of return will be greater than previously determined.

(4) Trial and error process.

Try 18%

Year		18%		
1	$ 17,000 x .847	=	$14,399
2	11,000 x .718	=	7,898
3	9,500 x .609	=	5,786
			$28,083

The amount $28,083 is less than the investment of $30,000; therefore, another "guess" must be made. The basic equation that is being used is:

$$\$30,000 = \frac{17,000}{(1 + r)} + \frac{11,000}{(1 + r)^2} + \frac{9,500}{(1 + r)^3}$$

We seek to find the value of r, the internal rate of return, that makes the equation hold. To increase the right side, we lower the denominator or, in other words, select a lower rate.

Try 14%

Year		14%		
1	$ 17,000 x .877	=	$14,909
2	11,000 x .783	=	8,459
3	9,500 x .675	=	6,413
			$29,781

Try 13%

Year		13%		
1	$ 17,000 x .885	=	$15,045
2	11,000 x .783	=	8,613
3	9,500 x .693	=	6,548
			$30,242

The rate lies **between 13% and 14%**.

12-6.   (a) *Net present value = present value of inflows - present value of outflows*

Present value of inflows

Year		10%		
1	$100,000 x .909	=	$ 90,900
2	$400,000 x .826	=	330,400
3	$500,000 x .751	=	375,500
4	$300,000 x .683	=	204,900
5	$100,000 x .621	=	62,100
			$1,063,800

Present value of inflows	$1,063,800
Present value of outflows	1,000,000
Net present value	$ 63,800

(b) Note: The NPV and IRR approaches may disagree on the ranking of projects, but they always agree on the accept-reject decision. Whenever you are asked to compute both NPV and IRR, it will be wise to compute the NPV first in order to have some direction in making your first trial-and-error guess. Since the NPV of this investment is positive, the IRR must be greater than the cost of capital.

Try 12%

Year		12%		
1	$100,000 x .893	=	$ 89,300
2	$400,000 x .797	=	318,800
3	$500,000 x .712	=	356,000
4	$300,000 x .636	=	190,800
5	$100,000 x .567	=	56,700
			$1,011,600

$1,011,600 exceeds investment of $1,000,000 so a higher rate should be selected.

Try 13%

Year	13%		
1	$100,000 x .885	=	$ 88,500
2	$400,000 x .783	=	313,200
3	$500,000 x .693	=	346,500
4	$300,000 x .613	=	183,900
5	$100,000 x .543	=	54,300
			$ 986,400

The IRR lies between 12% and 13%.

(c)

$$Profitability\ index\ =\ \frac{present\ value\ of\ the\ inflows}{present\ value\ of\ the\ outflows}$$

$$Profitability\ index\ =\ \frac{\$1,063,800}{\$1,000,000}\ =\ \mathbf{1.0638}$$

12-7.   (a)   Cash investment = purchase price

Cash investment = $600,000

Depreciation Schedule (3-year MACRS)

Year	Depreciation Base	Percentage	Depreciation
1	$ 600,000	.333	$ 199,800
2	600,000	.445	267,000
3	600,000	.148	88,800
4	600,000	.074	44,400
5	---	---	0
			$ 600,000

Expected Cash Flow Schedule

	Year 1	Year 2	Year 3	Year 4	Year 5
Earnings before depreciation & taxes	$200,000	$200,000	$200,000	$200,000	$200,000
Depreciation	199,800	267,000	88,800	44,400	0
Earnings before taxes	$ 200	($ 67,000)	$111,200	$155,600	$200,000
Taxes (34%)	68	(22,780)	37,808	52,904	68,000
Earnings after taxes	$ 132	($ 44,220)	$ 73,392	$102,696	$132,000
Add depreciation	199,800	267,000	88,800	44,400	0
Cash flow	$199,932	$222,780	$162,192	$147,096	$132,000

NPV = $199,932(.893) + $222,780(.797) + $162,192(.712) + $147,096(.636)
    + $132,000(.567) - $500,000

162

$NPV = \$178{,}539.28 + \$177{,}555.66 + \$115{,}480.70 + \$93{,}553.06$
$\quad + \$74{,}844 - \$500{,}000$

$NPV = \$639{,}972.70 - \$600{,}000 = \mathbf{\$39{,}972.70}$

(b) The internal rate of return must be > 12% since the NPV is positive.

Try 15%

$\$600{,}000 \overset{?}{=} \$199{,}932(.870) + \$222{,}780(.756) + \$162{,}192(.658)$
$\quad + \$147{,}096(.572) + \$132{,}000(.497)$

$\$600{,}000 \neq \$598{,}827.77$

Try 14%

$\$600{,}000 \overset{?}{=} \$199{,}932(.877) + \$222{,}780(.769) + \$162{,}192(.675)$
$\quad + \$147{,}096(.592) + \$132{,}000(.519)$

$\$600{,}000 \neq \$611{,}726.62$

The IRR is between 14% and 15%.

12-8. The depreciation base will be the same--$600,000.

$$Annual\ depreciation = \frac{\$600{,}000}{5} = \$120{,}000$$

Since the earnings before depreciation and taxes is the same each year and the depreciation expense is the same, the expected cash flow will be the same each year.

Expected Cash Flow Schedule

	Years 1-5
Earnings before depreciation & taxes	$ 200,000
Depreciation	120,000
Earnings before taxes	$ 80,000
Taxes (34%)	27,200
Earnings after taxes	$ 52,800
Add depreciation	120,000
Cash flow	$ 172,800

$NPV = \$172{,}800(3.605) - \$600{,}000$

$NPV = \$622{,}944 - \$600{,}000 = \mathbf{\$22{,}944}$

Although the NPV remains positive, the lower tax shields in the earlier years causes the NPV to decline.

12-9. (a) The depreciation base and anual depreciation is the same as in problem *12-8*.

Expected Cash Flow Schedule

	Years 1-5
Earnings before depreciation & taxes	$ 200,000
Depreciation	120,000
Earnings before taxes	$ 80,000
Taxes (40%)	32,000
Earnings after taxes	$ 48,000
Add depreciation	120,000
Cash flow	$ 168,000

$NPV = \$168,000(3.605) - \$600,000$

$NPV = \$605,640 - \$600,000 = \textbf{\$5,640}$

The NPV is still positive and the proposal is acceptable. Nevertheless, the changes in the tax law would make management more uncertain about capital expenditures.

(b) Since the expected cash flows constitute an annuity, the IRR can be solved directly.

$PV_A = A \times PV_{IFA}(N = 5, i = ?)$

$\$600,000 = \$168,000(PV_{IFA})$

$\dfrac{\$600,000}{\$168,000} = PV_{IFA}$

$3.571 = PV_{IFA}$

Go to row 5 of the present value of an annuity table. The value, 3.571, lies between 3.605 and 3.517--the interest factors for 12% and 13%. Since the NPV of the machine was positive but only slightly so, **the IRR between 12% and 13%** should have been anticipated since 12% is the firm's cost of capital.

12-10. (a) Cash investment = purchase price
Cash investment = $60,000
Depreciation base = purchase price = $60,000

Depreciation Schedule (see Depreciation Schedule in text)

Year	Depreciation Base	Percentage	Depreciation
1	$60,000	.200	$12,000
2	60,000	.320	19,200
3	60,000	.192	11,520
4	60,000	.115	6,900
5	60,000	.115	6,900
6	60,000	.058	3,480
7	---	---	---
			$60,000

Expected Cash Flow Schedule

	Year 1	Year 2	Year 3	Year 4-5	Year 6	Year 7
Earnings before depre.						
& taxes	$15,000	$15,000	$15,000	$15,000	$15,000	$15,000
Depreciation	12,000	19,200	11,520	6,900	3,480	0
Earnings before taxes	$ 3,000	($ 4,200)	$ 3,480	$ 8,100	$11,520	$15,000
Taxes (34%)	1,020	(1,428)	1,183*	2,754	3,917*	5,100
Earnings after taxes	$ 1,980	($ 2,772)	$ 2,297	$ 5,346	$ 7,603	$ 9,900
Add depreciation	12,000	19,200	11,520	6,900	3,480	0
Cash Flow	$13,980	$16,428	$13,817	$12,246	$11,083	$ 9,900

*Figures are rounded.

An alternative approach to calculating expected cash flows may also be used (only years 1, 2, and 7 are illustrated).

	Year 1		Year 2		Year 7	
	Income	Cash	Income	Cash	Income	Cash
Earnings before deprec.						
& taxes	$15,00	$15,000	$15,000	$15,000	$15,000	$15,000
Depreciation	0		19,200		0	
Earnings before taxes	12,000		($ 4,200)		$15,000	
Taxes (34%)	$ 3,000	1,020	(1,428)	(1,428)	5,100	5,100
Cash Flow	1,020	$13,980		$16,428		$ 9,900

Payback period:

Payback occurs in the 5th year.

(b) *Net Present Value*

Year	Expected Cash Inflows	Present Value Factor (12%)	Present Value
1	$13,980	.893	$12,484.14
2	16,428	.797	13,093.12
3	13,817	.712	9,837.70
4	12,246	.636	7,788.46
5	12,246	.567	6,943.48
6	11,083	.507	5,619.08
7	9,900	.452	4,474.80
			$60,240.78

Net present value = present value of inflows - present value of outflows

$NPV = \$60,240.78 - \$60,000 = \textbf{\$240.78}$

(c) Since NPV is positive but near zero, try a rate slightly above the cost of capital.

Try 13%

Year	Expected Cash Inflows	Present Value Factor (13%)	Present Value
1	$13,980	.885	$12,372.30
2	16,428	.783	12,863.12
3	13,817	.693	9,575.18
4	12,246	.613	7,506.80
5	12,246	.543	6,469.58
6	11,083	.480	5,319.84
7	9,900	.425	4,207.50
			$58,494.32

Since the present value of the expected cash inflows is more than $60,000 (NPV > 0) when discounted at 12% and less than $60,000 when discounted at 13, **the internal rate of return is between 12% and 13%**.

(d) NPV > 0: IRR > 12%: **YES**

12-11.   *Depreciation Schedule of Old Machine*

Year	Depreciation Base	Percentage	Depreciation
1	$100,000	.200	$ 20,000
2	100,000	.320	32,000
3	100,000	.192	19,200
4	100,000	.115	11,500
5	100,000	.115	11,500
6	100,000	.058	5,800
			$100,000

When originally acquired, the old machine had a 6-year useful life and a 5-year (6 years with half-year convention) depreciable life. Since the machine was acquired a year ago, one year of depreciation has been taken.

Book value of old machine = $100,000 - $20,000 = $80,000

Tax Effect on Sale of Old Machine

$ 70,000	selling price
80,000	book value
$ 10,000	loss on sale
.34	tax rate
$ 3,400	tax *savings* resulting from loss

Net Cash Outlay for the New Machine

$250,000   purchase price of new machine
- 70,000   selling price of old machine
$180,000
- 3,400   tax savings from loss
$176,600   net cash investment

Depreciation Schedule of New Machine

Year	Depreciation Base	Percentage	Depreciation
1	$250,000	.333	$ 83,250
2	250,000	.445	111,250
3	250,000	.148	37,000
4	250,000	.074	18,500
5	---	---	0
			$250,000

Incremental Depreciation from Replacement

Years New Machine	Years Remaining Old Machine	Depreciation on New Machine	Depreciation on Old Machine	Change in Depreciation
1	2	$ 83,250	$32,000	$51,250
2	3	111,250	19,200	92,050
3	4	37,000	11,500	25,500
4	5	18,500	11,500	7,000
5	6	0	5,800	(5,800)

Expected Cash Flow Schedule

	Year 1	Year 2	Year 3	Year 4	Year 5
Earnings before deprec. & taxes	$88,000	$88,000	$88,000	$88,000	$88,000
Incremental depreciation	51,250	92,050	25,500	7,000	(5,800)
Earnings before taxes	36,750	($ 4,050)	$62,500	$81,000	$93,800
Taxes (34%)	12,495	(1,377)	21,250	27,540	31,892
Earnings after taxes	$24,255	($ 2,673)	$41,250	$53,460	$61,908
Add incremental deprec.	51,250	92,050	25,500	7,000	(5,800)
Cash Flow	$75,505	$89,377	$66,750	$60,460	$56,108

Net Present Value

$NPV = \$75,505(.909) + \$89,377(.826) + \$66,750(.751) + \$60,460(.683) + \$56,108(.621) - \$176,600$

$NPV = \$68,643.05 + \$73,825.40 + \$50,129.25 + \$41,294.18 + \$34,843.07 - \$176,600$

$NPV = \$268,725.95 - \$176,600 = \mathbf{\$92,125.95}$

12-12. *Depreciation Schedule of Old Machine*

Year	Depreciation Base	Percentage	Depreciation
1	$27,000	.333	$ 8,991
2	27,000	.445	12,015
3	27,000	.148	3,996
4	27,000	.074	1,998
			$27,000

Book value of old machine = $27,000 - $8,991 = $18,009

Tax Effect on Disposal of Old Lathe

$ 0	market value
18,009	book value
$18,009	loss on disposal
.34	tax rate
$ 6,123	tax savings (rounded)

Net Cash Investment for the New Lathe

$45,000	purchase price
- 6,123	tax savings
$38,877	net cash investment

Depreciation Schedule of New Lathe

Year	Depreciation Base	Percentage	Depreciation
1	$45,000	.333	$14,985
2	45,000	.445	20,025
3	45,000	.148	6,660
4	45,000	.074	3,330
			$45,000

Incremental Depreciation

Years	Depreciation on New Machine	Depreciation on Old Machine	Incremental Depreciation
1	$14,985	$12,015	$ 2,970
2	20,025	3,996	16,029
3	6,660	1,998	4,662
4	3,330	0	3,330

Expected Cash Flow Schedule

	Year 1	Year 2	Year 3	Year 4
Earnings before depreciation & taxes	$16,000	$16,000	$16,000	$16,000
Incremental depreciation	2,970	16,029	4,662	3,330
Earnings before taxes	$13,030	($ 29)	$11,338	$12,670
Taxes (34%)	4,430*	(10)*	3,855*	4,308*
Earnings after taxes	$ 8,600	(19)	$ 7,483	$ 8,362
Add incremental depreciation	2,970	16,029	4,662	3,330
	$11,570	$16,010	$12,145	$11,692

*Figures are rounded.

Net Present Value = $11,570(.885) + $16,010(.783) + $12,145(.693)
                    + $11,692(.613) - $38,877

NPV = $38,358.96 - $38,877 = **($518.04)   The lathe should not be replaced.**

(b) Since the NPV was negative, the IRR must be less than the cost of capital.

Try 12%

$38,877 $\overset{?}{=}$ $11,570(.893) + $16,010(.797) + $12,145(.712) + $11,692(.636)
$38,877 ≠ $39,175.32

Since the NPV < 0 at 13% and a 12% rate provides a positive NPV ($39,175.32 - $38,877 = $298.32), **the internal rate of return is between 12% and 13%**. The decision in (*a*) is confirmed.

(c) The annual cash inflows will not be affected by the change in the disposal price of the old lathe. The cash investment will change.

Tax Effect on Sale of Old Lathe

$20,000	sales price
18,009	book value
$ 1,991	gain on sale
.34	tax rate
$ 677	tax on gain (rounded)

Net Cash Investment

$ 45,000	purchase price of new
- 20,000	lathe
$ 25,000	selling price of old lathe
+ 677	
$ 25,677	tax on gain
	net cash investment

Net Present Value

NPV = $38,358.96 - $25,677 = **$12,681.96**

Under these conditions the replacement should be made.

Summary: In this chapter the definitions of risk, its measurement and incorporation into the capital budgeting process, and the basic tenets of portfolio theory are examined.

I.   Risk in Capital Budgeting [p. 372]

    A.   Management's ability to achieve the goal of owner's wealth maximization will largely depend on success in dealing with risk.

    B.   Definition: Variability of possible outcomes. The wider the distribution of possible outcomes for a particular investment, the greater its **risk**.

FIGURE 13-1
VARIABILITY AND RISK

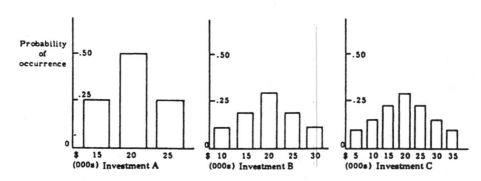

    C.   **Risk aversion** is a basic assumption of financial theory. Investors require a higher expected return the riskier an investment is perceived to be. [p. 372]

II.   Measurement of Risk [pp. 374-376]

    A.   A basic risk measurement is the **standard deviation**, which is a measure of dispersion around an expected value.
        1.   The **expected value** is a weighted average of the possible outcomes of an event times their probabilities.

$$\bar{D} \text{ (expected value)} = \Sigma DP$$

        2.   The steps for computing the standard deviation are:
            a.   Subtract the expected value, $\bar{D}$, from each possible outcome.
            b.   Square the deviations, $D - \bar{D}$.
            c.   Multiply the squared deviations, $(D - \bar{D})^2$, by the associated probability.
            d.   Sum the probability-weighted squared deviations.
            e.   Determine the square root

$$\sigma \text{(standard deviation)} = \sqrt{\Sigma(D - \bar{D})^2 P}$$

B. The Coefficient of Variation
1. The standard deviation is limited as a risk measure for comparison purposes. Two projects A and B may both be characterized by a standard deviation of $10,000 but A may have an expected value of $50,000 and B $100,000.
2. The size problem is eliminated by employing the **coefficient of variation**, V, which is the ratio of the standard deviation of an investment to its expected value. The higher the coefficient of variation, the higher the risk.

$$\text{Coefficient of Variation } (V) = \frac{\sigma}{\bar{D}}$$

$$
\begin{array}{cc}
A & B \\
V = \dfrac{\$10,000}{\$50,000} = .20 & V = \dfrac{\$10,000}{\$100,000} = .10
\end{array}
$$

C. Beta is another measure of risk that is widely used in portfolio management. Beta measures the volatility of returns on an individual stock relative to a stock market index of returns. (See Appendix 11A for a thorough discussion.)

III. Risk and the Capital Budgeting Process [pp. 377-383]

A. The expected inflows from capital projects usually are risky--they are not certain.

B. Cash flows of projects bearing a normal amount of risk undertaken by the firm should be discounted at the cost of capital.

C. The required rate of return of lenders and investors increases as the risk they are subjected to increases.

D. The cost of capital is composed of two components: the **risk-free rate** (time value of money only) and a **risk premium** (risk associated with usual projects of a business).

E. Adjustments must be made in the evaluation process for projects bearing risk levels (more or less) other than normal.
1. **Risk-adjusted discount rate approach**: The discount rate is adjusted upward for a more risky project and downward for projects bearing less than normal risk. A firm may establish a risk-adjusted discount rate for each of various categories of investment such as new equipment, new market, etc.
2. **Certainty equivalent approach**: Recognition of differing risk levels is made by multiplying the expected cash flow by a percentage figure indicating degree of certainty and discounting at the risk-free rate.
3. "Seat-of-the-pants" approach is based on experience and preference of decision maker.

F. The uncertainty associated with a capital budgeting decision may be reduced by projecting and preparing for the various possible outcomes resulting from the decision. **Simulation** models and **decision trees** enhance management's initial capital budget decision efforts and also expedite intermediate decisions (whether to continue, etc.) once the initial decision has been made.
1. Simulation models--various values for economic and financial variables affecting the capital budgeting decision are randomly selected and used as inputs in the simulation model. Although the process does not ensure that a manager's decision will be correct (in terms of actual events), decisions can be made with a greater understanding of possible outcomes.

2. Decision trees--the sequential pattern of decisions and resulting outcomes and associated probabilities (managerial estimates based on experience and statistical processes) are tracked along the branches of the decision tree. Tracing the sequence of possible events in this fashion is a valuable analytical tool in the decision-making process.

FIGURE 13-2
RELATIONSHIP OF RISK TO DISCOUNT RATE

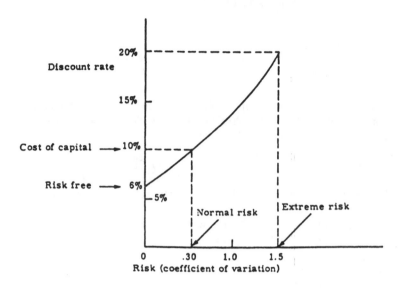

IV. The Portfolio Effect [pp. 383-386]

A. A risky project may actually reduce the total risk of the firm through the **portfolio effect**.

B. Projects that move in opposite directions in response to the same economic stimulus are said to be negatively correlated. Since the movement of negatively correlated projects are in opposite directions, the total deviation is less than the deviations of the projects individually.

C. The relationship between project movements is expressed by the **coefficient of correlation** which varies from the extremes of -1 (perfectly negative) to +1 (perfectly positive) correlation. Noncorrelated projects have a correlation coefficient of zero.

D. Although projects with correlation coefficients of -1 are seldom found, some risk reduction will occur, however minor, when projects are negatively correlated or have low positive correlation.

E. The firm should strive to achieve two objectives in combining projects according to their risk-return characteristics.
   1. Achieve the highest possible return at a given risk level.
   2. Allow the lowest possible risk at a given return level.

F. The various optimal combinations of projects are located along a risk-return line referred to as the **"efficient frontier."** [p. 386]

172

V.   The Share Price Effect [p. 396]

    A.   Higher earnings do not necessarily contribute to the firm's goal of owner's wealth maximization. The firm's earnings may be discounted at a higher rate because investors perceive that the firm is pursuing riskier projects to generate the earnings.

    B.   The risk aversion of investors is verified in the capital market. Firms that are very sensitive to cyclical fluctuations tend to sell at lower P/E multiples.

VI.   Key Formulas

    A.   Expected value [p. 374]

$$\bar{D} = \Sigma DP$$

    B.   Standard deviation [p. 374]

$$\sigma = \sqrt{\Sigma D - \bar{D})^2 P}$$

    C.   Coefficient of variation [p. 376]

$$V = \frac{\sigma}{\bar{D}}$$

Chapter 13 - Multiple Choice Questions

1.   When employing the certainty equivalent approach in capital budgeting: [p. 380]
    a.   Flows are discounted at the risk-adjusted discount rate.
    b.   Flows are discounted at the weighted-average cost of capital.
    c.   Flows are discounted at the marginal cost of capital.
    d.   Flows are discounted at the risk-free rate.
    e.   Flows are not discounted.

2.   If investors perceive that a firm has become more risky: [p. 377]
    a.   They will lower their discount rate when valuing the firm's stock.
    b.   They will raise their discount rate when valuing the firm's stock.
    c.   They may raise or lower their discount rate when valuing the firm's stock.
    d.   They will require a lower rate of return from the stock.
    e.   None of the answers above are correct.

3.   The coefficient of variation is computed by: [p. 376]
    a.   Dividing the expected value by the standard deviation.
    b.   Multiplying the firm's beta by its coefficient of correlation.
    c.   Dividing the standard deviation by the expected value.
    d.   Squaring the standard deviation.
    e.   Squaring the probability of graduating from college.

4.   A basic assumption of financial theory is that investors are: [p. 372]
    a.   Risk averse.
    b.   Risk neutral.
    c.   Risk seekers.
    d.   Risk ignorant.
    e.   Positively correlated with risk.

5. The returns of securities A and B have a zero correlation coefficient. The returns are: [pp. 383-386]
   a. Slightly positively correlated.
   b. Negatively correlated.
   c. Slightly negatively correlated.
   d. Positively correlated.
   e. Independent.

6. Optimal combinations of risk-return characteristics of investments are located along the: [p. 386]
   a. Risk-free curve.
   b. Efficient frontier.
   c. Certainty equivalent curve.
   d. Yield curve.
   e. Normal distribution.

7. Reduction in risk by combining risky securities with appropriate risk-return characteristics is called: [p. 383]
   a. Risk aversion.
   b. Correlation.
   c. The portfolio effect.
   d. The share price effect.
   e. The "seat of the pants" approach.

8. Which of the following is the correct relationship (choose the *best* answer). [p. 372]
   a. High risk, high return
   b. High risk, low return
   c. High risk, high required return
   d. Low risk, high return
   e. High risk, low required return

9. Firms (and investors) strive to combine projects (investments) such that they: [p. 386]
   a. Achieve the highest return at the highest risk.
   b. Achieve the highest return at a given level of risk.
   c. Allow the lowest possible risk at a given level of return.
   d. Answers *a* and *c* are correct.
   e. Answers *b* and *c* are correct.

10. Risk-adjusted discount rates are composed of: [Chpt. 13]
    a. The risk-free rate minus a risk premium.
    b. The risk-free rate plus beta.
    c. The required rate of return x beta plus the risk-free rate.
    d. The risk-free rate plus a risk premium.
    e. The risk premium minus the risk-free rate.

Multiple Choice Answer Key - Chapter 13

1. d	2. b	3. c	4. a	5. e
6. b	7. c	8. c	9. e	10. d

Chapter 13 - Problems

13-1. Zappa Manufacturing is evaluating an investment opportunity that would require an outlay of $100,000. The annual net cash inflows are estimated to vary according to economic conditions.

Economic Conditions	Probability	Cash Flow
very good	.10	40,000
good	.45	32,000
fair	.30	20,000
poor	.15	14,000

The firm's required rate of return is 14%. The project has an expected life of six years. Compute the expected NPV of the proposed investment.

13-2. Calculate the coefficient of variation of the cash flows of Zappa Manufacturing (*13-1* above).

13-3. Ringgold, Inc. is planning advertising campaigns in three different market areas. The estimates of probability of success and associated additional profits are provided below:

	Market 1		Market 2		Market 3	
	Profit	Probability	Profit	Probability	Profit	Probability
Fair	10,000	.40	5,000	.20	16,000	.50
Normal	18,000	.50	8,000	.60	20,000	.30
Excellent	25,000	.10	12,000	.20	25,000	.20

(a) Compute the expected value and standard deviation of profits resulting from advertising campaigns in each of the market areas.

(b) Rank the three markets according to riskiness using the coefficient of variation.

13-4. The Alphabet Soup Company is seeking to diversify its operations and is considering acquisition of three firms in unrelated fields. Alphabet's cost of capital is approximately 10% and the coefficient of variation associated with its usual investments averages .3. Using the information below, determine which, if any, of the three proposed acquisitions are acceptable investments.

(1)

Firm	Blue Boy Supermarkets	Acey-Ducey Electronics	Wild Cat Drilling
Required investment	$25,000,000	$40,000,000	$22,000,000
Expected life	12 years	8 years	6 years
Expected annual aftertax returns	3,000,000	8,000,000	5,000,000
Estimated standard deviation of returns	300,000	3,000,000	3,000,000

(2) Required rates of return on company investments:

Coefficient of variation	less than .2	.2 to .40	.4 to .55	above .55
Required rate of return	8%	10%	15%	20%

13-5. Moonshot, Inc., a venture capital firm, is considering investing in either a new space movie, *Star Raiders*, or sponsoring the development of an energy saving device that will be used in heavy manufacturing. Each project can be funded for $30 million. Using the information below, compute the net present value of each of these projects.

		(1)	(2)	(3)
		Expected Sales	*Probability*	*Present Value of Cash Flow from Sales*
MOVIE		Blockbuster	.30	$80 million
		Average box office	.50	$40 million
		Popcorn only	.20	$15 million
ENERGY DEVICE		Peak demand	.50	$60 million
		Check the meter	.20	$35 million
		Power failure	.30	$20 million

13-6. Plummer Chemicals employs the internal rate of return method to evaluate capital expenditure proposals. Plummer adjusts its acceptable rate of return to accommodate varying degrees of risk. The cash flow characteristics of a capital proposal and required rate of return are presented below.

Coefficient of Variation of Cash Flow	Required Rate of Return
.10 to .15	.12
.16 to .35	.14
.36 to .50	.18
> .50	.24

Expected Cash Flows Each Year from Proposal for 10 Years	Probability
$400,000	.20
$600,000	.40
$800,000	.30
$900,000	.10

The capital expenditures proposal will require a cash investment of $3,000,000. Utilizing the internal rate of return method and information above, should Plummer accept the proposal?

Chapter 13 - Solutions

13-1.

Expected Annual Net Cash Inflow

Conditions	Probability	Cash Inflows	Expected Annual Flow
Very good	.10	$40,000	$ 4,000
Good	.45	32,000	14,400
Fair	.30	20,000	6,000
Poor	.15	14,000	2,100
			$26,500

$NPV = \$26,500 \times PV_{IFA}(n = 6, r = 14\%) - \$100,000$

$NPV = \$26,500 \times 3.889 - \$100,000$

$NPV = \$103,058.50 - \$100,000 = \mathbf{\$3,058.50}$

13-2.   Zappa Manufacturing

D	$\bar{D}$	$D - \bar{D}$	$(D - \bar{D})^2$	P	$(D - \bar{D})^2 P$
$40,000	$26,500	$13,500	$182,250,000	.10	$18,225,000
32,000	26,500	5,500	30,250,000	.45	13,612,500
20,000	26,500	(6,500)	42,250,000	.30	12,675,000
14,000	26,500	(12,500)	156,250,000	.15	23,437,500
					$67,950,000

$$\sigma = \sqrt{\$67,950,000} = \$8,243 \ (rounded)$$

$$V = \frac{\sigma}{\bar{D}} = \frac{\$8,243}{\$26,500} = \mathbf{.31}$$

13-3.   (a)   *Exp. Val. Mkt. 1* = 10,000(.40) + 18,000(.50) + 25,000(.10)
          Exp. Val. Mkt. 1 = 4,000 + 9,000 + 2,500 = **15,500**

   Standard deviation of profits in Market 1:

$$\sigma = \sqrt{(10,000 - 15,500)^2(.4) + (18,000 - 15,500)^2(.5) + (25,000 - 15,500)^2(.10)}$$

$$\sigma = \sqrt{12,100,000 + 3,125,000 + 9,025,000}$$

$$\sigma = \sqrt{24,250,000} = \mathbf{4,924}$$

   Exp. Val. Mkt. 2 = (5,000)(.2) + (8,000)(.6) + (12,000)(.2)
   Exp. Val. Mkt. 2 = 1,000 + 4,800 + 2,400 = **$8,200**

   Standard deviation of profits in Market 2:

$$\sigma = \sqrt{(5,000 - 8,200)^2(.2) + (8,000 - 8,200)^2(.6) + (12,000 - 8,200)^2(.2)}$$

$$\sigma = \sqrt{2,048,000 + 24,000 + 2,888,000}$$

$$\sigma = \sqrt{4,960,000} = \mathbf{2,227}$$

   Exp. Val. Mkt. 3 = 16,000(.5) + 20,000(.3) + 25,000(.2)
   Exp. Val. Mkt. 3 = 8,000 + 6,000 + 5,000 = **19,000**

   Standard deviation of profits in Market 3:

$$\sigma = \sqrt{(16,000 - 19,000)^2(.5) + (20,000 - 19,000)^2(.3) + (25,000 - 19,000)^2(.2)}$$

$$\sigma = \sqrt{4,500,000 + 300,000 + 7,200,000}$$

$$\sigma = \sqrt{12,000,000} = \mathbf{3,464}$$

(b)

$$Coefficient\ of\ variation\ of\ 1 = \frac{\$4,924}{\$15,500} = \mathbf{.32}$$

$$Coefficient\ of\ variation\ of\ 2 = \frac{\$2,227}{\$8,200} = \mathbf{.27}$$

$$Coefficient\ of\ variation\ of\ 3 = \frac{\$3,464}{\$19,000} = \mathbf{.18}$$

13-4. (a)

$$Coefficient\ of\ variation = \frac{\$300,000}{\$3,000,000} = .10$$

Required rate of return = 8%

$NPV = \$3,000,000(7.536) - \$25,000,000$

$NPV = \$22,608,000 - \$25,000,000 = \mathbf{(\$2,392,000)}$

Supermarket investment is unacceptable even though the required rate of return, 8% is less than normally required of investments.

(b)

$$Coefficient\ of\ variation = \frac{\$3,000,000}{\$8,000,000} = .375$$

Required rate of return = 10%.

$NPV = \$8,000,000(5.335) - \$40,000,000$

$NPV = \$42,680,000 - \$40,000,000 = \mathbf{\$2,680,000}$

Acey-Ducey Electronics is an acceptable investment.

(c)

$$Coefficient\ of\ variation = \frac{\$3,000,000}{\$5,000,000} = .6$$

Required rate of return = 20%.

$$NPV = \$5,000,000(3.326) - \$22,000,000$$

$$NPV = \$16,630,000 - \$22,000,000 = (\$5,370,000)$$

13-5.   Moonshot, Inc.

	(1)	(2)	(3) Present Value of	(4) Initial	(5) NPV	(6) Expected
	Expected Sales	Prob	Cash Flow fr Sales	Invest.	(3-4)	NPV (2x5)
MOVIE	Blockbuster	.30	$80 mil.	$30 mil.	$50 mil.	$15 mil.
	Avg box office	.50	$40 mil.	$30 mil.	$10 mil.	$ 5 mil.
	Popcorn only	.20	$15 mil.	$30 mil.	$(15) mil.	$(3) mil. $17 mil.
ENERGY DEVICE	Peak demand	.50	$60 mil.	$30 mil.	$30 mil.	$15 mil.
	Check meter	.20	$35 mil.	$30 mil.	$ 5 mil.	$ 1 mil.
	Power failure	.30	$20 mil.	$30 mil.	$(10) mil.	$(3) mil. $13 mil.

13-6.   Plummer Chemicals

Expected Cash Flow Each Year

$400,000	x	.20	=	$ 80,000
600,000	x	.40	=	240,000
800,000	x	.30	=	240,000
900,000	x	.10	=	90,000
				$650,000

Internal Rate of Return

$$PV_A = A \times PV_{IFA}(n = 10, i = ?)$$

$$\$3,000,000 = \$650,000\ PVA_{IFA}$$

$$PV_{IFA} = \frac{\$3,000,000}{\$650,000} = 4.615$$

IRR is **between 17% and 18%.**

Standard Deviation of Cash Flows

D	D̄	(D - D̄)	(D - D̄)²	P	P(D - D̄)²
$400,000	$650,000	($250,000)	$62,500,000,000	.20	$12,500,000,000
600,000	650,000	(50,000)	2,500,000,000	.40	1,000,000,000
800,000	650,000	150,000	22,500,000,000	.30	6,750,000,000
900,000	650,000	250,000	62,500,000,000	.10	6,250,000,000
					$26,500,000,000

$$\sigma = \sqrt{\$26,500,000,000} = \$162,788 \ (rounded)$$

Coefficient of Variation

$$V = \frac{\sigma}{\bar{D}} = \frac{\$162,788}{\$650,000} = .25$$

The required rate of return of the project is 14% according to Plummer's schedule. The IRR of this proposal which is between 17% and 18% exceeds the requirement. **The proposal is acceptable**.

Chapter 14   Capital Markets

Summary: The role of the various participants in the markets and their structure are discussed in this chapter.

I.   Money and Capital Markets [p. 404]

     A.   **Money market:** Short-term market comprised of securities maturing in a year or less.

     B.   **Capital market:** Long-term market consisting of securities having maturities greater than one year.

II.   International Capital Markets [pp. 404-405]

     A.   An increasing international demand for capital has resulted in the rapid growth and development of capital markets worldwide. Several important events have significantly impacted international capital markets.
         1.   Iron curtain "collapse."
         2.   Reunification of East and West Germany.
         3.   A more competitive and tariff-free Europe.
         4.   The North American Free Trade Agreement (NAFTA).
         5.   Economic growth of Asian countries led by China.

     B.   The initiation of the European Monetary Union (EMU) in January 1999 created a new economic order for Europe. If the EMU rises above nationalistic feelings, its economic impact will be felt worldwide. The new European Central Bank will be responsible for monetary policy throughout the Euro zone. Securities markets in Europe may eventually rival Wall Street.

     C.   Companies search international markets for borrowing opportunities at the lowest cost and list their common stock on international exchanges.

     D.   By the end of 1999, foreign investors had made net investments in the United States totaling $7.8 trillion. At the same time, U.S. investors had made investments in foreign countries totaling $7.2 trillion. The excess inflow of more than $600 billion has significantly impacted U.S. businesses and has provided a large portion of federal government financing.

III.   Competition for Funds in the Capital Market [pp. 405-408]

     A.   Government securities.
         1.   The U.S. Treasury manages the federal government's debt. The Treasury sells short-term or long-term securities to finance deficits. In recent years, the U.S. has experienced annual fiscal surpluses and the Treasury has reduced the federal debt by repurchasing securities in the capital market.
         2.   Federally sponsored credit agencies, charged with funding the large numbers of federal programs, are heavy issuers of securities in the capital markets. Agencies such as the Federal National Mortgage Association (Fannie Mae), the Federal Home Loan Banks (FHLB), Farm Credit Banks, and the Student Loan Marketing Association issue securities separately from the U.S. Treasury. Although not directly backed by the Treasury, no issue has ever failed.
         3.   Municipal securities which are exempt from federal income taxes are issued by state and local governments. Such federal tax-exempt securities tend to be purchased by investors in high marginal tax brackets.

B. Corporate securities.
   1. Contrary to popular belief, the majority of external financing by U.S. corporations is through bonds not common stock.
   2. Preferred stock is the least used of long-term corporate securities.
   3. Corporations seeking new equity capital may sell common stock in the capital market. The first common stock issue of a firm is referred to as an initial public offering (IPO). Subsequent stock issues are called secondary offerings.

C. Other very important sources of long-term funds for corporations are internally generated funds. Funds are provided internally through retention of earnings and through the depreciation process. During the decade of the nineties, 40% of corporate long-term financing was internally generated. Typically, retention of earnings is less than 50% of internally generated funds; but in the highly profitable years of 1994 and 1995, retained earnings accounted for more than 60% of such funds. (See Figure 14-1 in text.)

   Study Note: Students should be very careful in interpreting internally generated funds from depreciation. A corporation's internally generated funds come from its operations. Depreciation in and of itself does not provide any funds to a firm. The net income measure from which retained earnings is derived, however, does not capture all internally generated funds. Depreciation expense reduces reported net income, but it is a noncash expense and does not reduce funds available to the firm. To appropriately measure internally generated funds, depreciation and other noncash expenses must be added to retention of earnings.

IV. The Supply of Capital Funds [pp. 408-409]

   A. *Business* and *government* have been net demanders of funds and the *household* sector the major supplier of funds in our **three-sector economy**.

   B. Household-sector savings are usually channeled to demanders of funds through financial institutions such as commercial banks, savings & loans, mutual savings banks, and credit unions.

   C. Other intermediaries in the flow-of-funds process include mutual funds, pension plans, and insurance firms.

   D. International savers/investors are very important suppliers of capital to the U.S. economy and currently supply 10.84% of funds in the U.S. capital markets. (See Figure 14-3 in text.)

V. The Role of the Security Markets [p. 410]

   A. Security markets facilitate the allocation of capital between the sectors of the economy with the aid of **financial intermediaries**.

   B. Security markets enable the demanders of capital to issue securities by providing the necessary liquidity for investors in two ways:
   1. Corporations are able to sell new issues of securities rapidly at fair competitive prices.
   2. The markets allow the purchaser of securities to convert the securities to cash with relative ease through **secondary trading** activities..

VI. The Organization of the Security Markets [p. 410]

   A. Several national and regional exchanges provide a centrally located auction market for buyers and sellers of securities who use the services of brokers having representatives on the floor of the exchanges.

1. The primary U.S. exchanges are the New York Stock Exchange (NYSE) and the American Stock Exchange (AMEX).
2. Exchanges of lesser importance include the Chicago, Pacific, Boston, and Cincinnati exchanges.

B. In 1998 the American Stock Exchange and the National Association of Securities Dealers (NASD) merged their markets as the Nasdaq-AMEX Market Group. While AMEX continues as a stock exchange with a physical location in New York City, Nasdaq is the largest screen-based market in the United States. Screen-based markets have no physical location and trading is based on computers and other communication mediums.

C. Regional exchanges trade stock in the same companies that trade on the New York Stock Exchange. This **dual trading** accounts for over 90% of stocks traded on the Chicago and Pacific Exchanges. Because all listed stock trades on all regional exchanges, the NYSE, and Nasdaq are reported on a consolidated tape, stock prices are very competitively and efficiently determined. In addition to the consolidated tape, there is the Intermarket Trading System (ITS) which links nine markets–NYSE, AMEX, Boston, Chicago, Cincinnati, Pacific, and Philadelphia stock exchanges, the Chicago Board Options Exchange, and the Nasdaq.

D. New York Stock Exchange (NYSE).
1. The NYSE is the largest and most important of all the global stock exchanges.
2. To be listed on the NYSE, firms must meet certain minimum requirements pertaining to earning power, level of assets, market value, publicly-held common stock, and monthly trading volume.
3. Traditionally, the NYSE has quoted stock prices in ⅛ fractions. The Securities and Exchange Commission (SEC) mandated a switch to quotations in decimals. The phasing in of **decimalization** of price quotes began in August 2000. The effects of decimalization are debated between two groups. One group, the market makers, feel that lower profits resulting from decimalization will force them out of the market and liquidity will decline. Others think that the more easily understood decimals will attract more investors and enhance capital markets.

E. The global nature of capital markets is evidenced by the increasing volume and security listings on stock markets around the world. The Tokyo stock exchange is extremely large and companies such as Intel, IBM, and McDonald's trade there and on the Frankfurt stock exchange. Likewise, many foreign companies trade on the NYSE. As more companies trade on exchanges around the world in multiple time zones, it will be easier for trading to be continuous for 24 hours per day.

F. Corporations that do not meet listing requirements or choose not to be listed on the exchanges are traded in the **over-the-counter market (OTC)**.
1. The OTC market is a national network of dealers linked by computers and telephones.
2. OTC dealers own the securities they trade and seek to earn a profit from their buying and selling, whereas brokers receive a commission as an agent of the buyer or seller of securities.
3. The **National Association of Securities Dealers (NASD)**, which supervises the OTC market, has divided the OTC market into groups based on size and trading requirements:
   a. The Nasdaq National Market comprised of the biggest companies.
   b. The Nasdaq Small-Cap Market composed of smaller companies.
4. Due to the great amount of debt securities traded OTC, the OTC market is the largest market for all security transactions in total dollars although the NYSE is the largest for stocks.

G. Electronic Communication Networks (ECNs), also known as alternative trading systems

(ATS), are electronic trading systems that automatically match buy and sell orders at specified prices. If a subscriber seeks to buy through an ECN and there are no matching sell orders, the order cannot be executed. The ECN may wait for a match or when possible, the order will be routed to another market. There are nine ECNs, the largest is Instinet <www.instinet.com> which is owned by Reuters. Seeking to protect itself from an expected loss of volume as more trading moves to ECNs, the NYSE has developed its own electronic trading system which will be used to extend its trading hours into the evening.

VII. **Market Efficiency** [p. 416]

    A.   Criteria of efficiency:
        1.   Rapid adjustment of prices to new information.
        2.   Continuous market; successive prices are close.
        3.   Market is capable of absorbing large dollar amounts of securities without destabilizing the price.

    B.   The more certain the income stream, the less volatile price movements will be and the more efficient the market will be.

    C.   Trading in the U.S. has become cheaper and more efficient as a result of decimalization, ECNs, and online brokerage.

    D.   The efficiency of the stock market is stated in three forms.
        1.   Weak form: Past price information is unrelated to future prices, trends cannot be predicted and taken advantage of by investors.
        2.   Semi-strong form: Prices reflect all *public* information.
        3.   Strong form: Prices reflect all public and private information.

    E.   The efficiency of the market is debatable, but most would agree that the movement is toward greater efficiency.

VIII. Regulation of the Security Markets [pp. 416-419]

    A.   Organized securities markets are regulated by the **Securities and Exchange Commission (SEC)** and through self-regulation. The OTC market is regulated by the National Association of Securities Dealers (NASD).

    B.   Three major laws govern the sale and trading of securities.
        1.   The **Securities Act of 1933:** This act was a response to abuses present in the securities market during the Wall Street "Crash" era. Its purpose was to provide full disclosure of all pertinent investment information on new corporate security issues.
        2.   The **Securities Exchange Act of 1934** created the Securities and Exchange Commission (SEC) and empowered it to regulate the securities markets.
        3.   The **Securities Acts Amendments of 1975** directed the SEC to supervise the development of a national securities market, prohibited fixed commissions on public transactions, and prohibited financial institutions and insurance companies from buying stock exchange memberships to save commission costs.

Chapter 14 - Multiple Choice Questions

1. The majority of external financing by U.S. corporations is through the issuance of: [p. 407]
    a. Common stock.
    b. Bonds.
    c. Preferred stock.
    d. ECNs.
    e. Options.

2. Which of the following levels of market efficiency is based on past price information being unrelated to future prices? [p. 416]
    a. Weak form
    b. Strong form
    c. Illegal form
    d. Insider trading
    e. Semi-strong form

3. The over-the-counter market is primarily regulated by the: [p. 416]
    a. OTC.
    b. NYSE.
    c. SEC.
    d. FTC.
    e. NASD.

4. Which of the following terms best describes Nasdaq stock trading? [Chpt. 14]
    a. Screen-based
    b. Dual
    c. Regional
    d. Strong form
    e. Broker-based

5. The primary benefit provided investors by security markets is: [p. 410]
    a. Guaranteed returns.
    b. Liquidity.
    c. Riskless trading.
    d. Costless trading.
    e. Access to all relevant security information.

6. Which of the following markets is the largest market for all security transactions in total dollars? [p. 415]
    a. Tokyo
    b. NYSE
    c. OTC
    d. AMEX
    e. London

7. The Securities Exchange Commission was created by the: [p. 418]
    a. NAFTA.
    b. Securities Act of 1933.
    c. Securities Exchange Act of 1934.
    d. Securities Acts Amendments of 1975.
    e. Financial Intermediary Act of 1929.

185

8. The market for securities having maturities of more than one year is called the: [p. 404]
   a. Intermediate market.
   b. Money market.
   c. International market.
   d. Capital market.
   e. Domestic market.

9. Which of the following merged their markets in 1998? [p. 411]
   a. AMEX and Nasdaq
   b. France and Australia
   c. NYSE and CBOE
   d. Chicago Exchange and Pacific Exchange
   e. SEC and OTC

10. Which of the following owns securities and seeks to earn a profit from buying and selling? [p 414]
    a. Brokers
    b. SEC
    c. OTC
    d. Dealers
    e. National Association of Securities Dealers

Multiple Choice Answer Key - Chapter 14

1. b	2. a	3. e	4. a	5. b
6. c	7. c	8. d	9. a	10. d

Chapter 15

Summary: This chapter discusses the role of the investment banker, the advantages and disadvantages of selling securities to the public, and the private placement of securities with various institutions.

I.   The Role of Investment Banking [p. 424]

    A.   The **investment banker** serves as a middleman in channeling funds from the investor to the corporation.

    B.   Changes in investment banking: [pp.424-427]
        1.   Concentration of capital allows larger firms to take additional risks and satisfy the needs of capital markets. Top ten underwriters (see Table 15-1 in text) control 83 percent of the U.S. market for stocks and bonds and almost 74 percent of the global market.
        2.   Gramm-Leach-Bliley Act repeals depression-era laws, including the Glass-Stegal Act. The repeals reduce the competitive disadvantage of U.S. commercial and investment banks against large European and Japanese banks.

    C.   Functions of the investment banker: [pp.427-428]
        1.   **Underwriter**: The risk-taking function. The underwriter bears the risk of fluctuations in the selling price of the security issue. The investment banker may handle the issues of unknown corporations on a nonrisk-bearing **"best efforts"** basis only.
        2.   **Market maker**: The investment banker may engage in buying and selling of a security to ensure an available market.
        3.   **Advising**: Corporations may seek an investment banker's advice on the size, timing, and marketability of security issues. Advice is also rendered pertaining to merger and acquisition decisions, leveraged buyouts, and corporate restructuring.
        4.   **Agency functions**: As an agent, the investment banker assists in the private placement of security issues and in the negotiating process of merger and acquisition transactions.

    D.   The Distribution Process [p. 428]
        1.   The **managing investment banker** forms an **underwriting syndicate** of investment bankers to increase marketability of the issue and spread the risk.
        2.   Syndicate members, acting as wholesalers, sell the securities to brokers and dealers who eventually sell the securities to the public.

    E.   The **underwriting spread** is the difference in the price of a security to the public and the amount paid to the issuing firm and represents the compensation of those participating in the distribution.
        1.   The spread is divided among the distribution participants. The lower a party falls in the distribution hierarchy, the lower the portion of the spread received.
        2.   Usually, the larger the dollar value of an issue, the smaller the spread.
        3.   The spread on equity issues is greater than on debt issues because of the greater price uncertainty.

    F.   Several factors must be considered by the managing investment banker when negotiating the issue price of a security of a first-time issue.
        1.   An industry analysis.

2. Financial characteristics.
3. Expected earnings and dividends.
4. P/E multiples of firms in the same industry.
5. Anticipated public demand.

G. The issue price of securities of firms with existing securities outstanding are usually determined by "underpricing."
   1. Price is set slightly below current market value.
   2. Underpricing is partially a result of the dilutive effect of spreading earnings over a greater number of shares of stock.

H. The managing investment banker seeks to **stabilize the market** (keep the sales price up) by repurchasing securities while at the same time selling them. The investment banker's reputation rests, to a large extent, on how well a security is priced after the distribution period in the **aftermarket**.

I. **Shelf registration**. [p. 433]
   1. Large companies are permitted to file one comprehensive registration statement and then wait (hold securities on shelf) until market conditions are favorable before issuing securities without further SEC approval. Previously, a registration statement had to be filed for each security issue. Shelf registration has been used primarily for debt issues.
   2. A greater concentration of business among the stronger firms in the investment banking industry has resulted from the shelf registration process.

II. Public Versus private Financing [pp. 433-439]

A. Advantages of being public.
   1. Greater availability of funds.
   2. Prestige.
   3. Higher liquidity for stockholders.
   4. Established price of public issues aids a stockholder's estate planning.
   5. Enables a firm to engage in merger activities more readily.

B. Disadvantages of being public.
   1. Company information must be made public through SEC and state filings.
   2. Accumulating and disclosing information is expensive in terms of dollars and time.
   3. Short-term pressure from security analysts and investors.
   4. Embarrassment from public failure.
   5. High cost of going public.

C. **Private placement** refers to selling securities directly to insurance companies, pension funds, and others rather than going through security markets.
   1. Used more for debt than equity issues.
   2. Advantages:
      a. Eliminates the lengthy, expensive registration process with the SEC.
      b. Greater flexibility in negotiating terms of issue.
      c. Costs of issue are less.
   3. The usually higher interest cost on a privately placed debt instrument is a disadvantage.

D. Firms that elect to go private are usually small companies that are seeking to avoid large auditing and reporting expenses. In the 1980s, however, large firms began going private. There are two basic ways to go private. The public firm can be purchased by a private firm or the company can repurchase all publicly traded shares from the stockholders.

E.   Many firms have gone private through **leveraged buyouts**. Management or some external group borrows the needed cash to repurchase all shares of the company. Frequently, the management of the private firm must sell off assets in order to reduce the heavy debt load.

F.   Several firms that went private during the 1980s have restructured and returned to the public market at an increased market value. In some cases the firm was divided and the divisions were sold separately. The "breakup value" of some firms such as Beatrice Foods was substantially higher than the market value of the unified entity.

III.   Privatization: The collapse of the USSR and other communist countries has created a need to privatize companies previously owned by the government. The process of selling government ownership interests to the public occurred in countries such as Great Britain, France, and Japan many years before.

Chapter 15 - Multiple Choice Questions

1.   Setting a price of a new security below current market value is called: [p. 432]
   a.   Syndicating.
   b.   Underwriting.
   c.   Stabilizing.
   d.   Spreading.
   e.   Underpricing.

2.   Many firms have gone private through: [p. 439]
   a.   Shelf registration.
   b.   Leverage buyouts.
   c.   Consolidation.
   d.   Syndicating.
   e.   Merger.

3.   Selling securities directly to firms such as insurance companies is called: [p. 436]
   a.   Private placement.
   b.   Public placement.
   c.   Syndication.
   d.   Intermediation.
   e.   Best efforts.

4.   Which of the following is an investment banker's risk-bearing function? [p. 427]
   a.   Buying and selling to insure a market.
   b.   Price support.
   c.   Underwriting.
   d.   Providing size and timing advice.
   e.   Accepting deposits.

5.   A managing investment banker may seek to spread the risk by: [p. 428]
   a.   Underpricing.
   b.   Utilizing a leveraged buyout.
   c.   Spreading.
   d.   Forming a syndicate.
   e.   Going public.

6. Which of the following is not an advantage of being a publicly traded firm? [p. 434]
    a. Prestige
    b. Higher liquidity for stockholders
    c. Frequent SEC filings
    d. Greater availability of funds
    e. Increased ability to engage in merger activity

7. If the investment banker does not bear the risk of fluctuations in the selling price of the security issue, the issue is handled: [p. 427]
    a. On a best-efforts basis.
    b. By syndication.
    c. By shelf registration.
    d. By underwriting.
    e. By consolidation.

8. Permission to large firms by the SEC to file a comprehensive registration statement and then wait until the market is "right" to issue a security is called: [p. 433]
    a. Private placement.
    b. Stabilizing the market.
    c. Market making.
    d. Shelf registration.
    e. Preselling.

9. Which of the following types of securities is most often involved in a private placement? [p. 436]
    a. Corporate bonds
    b. Common stock
    c. Preferred stock
    d. Treasury bills
    e. Municipal bonds

10. A firm that elects to buy-in all shares of stock in the public's hands is said to be: [pp. 438-439]
    a. Consolidating.
    b. Leveraging.
    c. Going private.
    d. Spreading.
    e. Shrinking.

Multiple Choice Answer Key - Chapter 15

1. e   2. b   3. a   4. c   5. d
6. c   7. a   8. d   9. a   10. c

Chapter 15 - Problems

15-1. The Tims Corporation expects earnings of $8,000,000 in the current year on 6,000,000 shares of common stock. The company is considering the effects on reported earnings of issuing an additional 2,000,000 shares of common stock.

   (a) What will be the initial dilution in earnings per share?

(b)   If the firm sells the stock for a net price of $23 per share and is able to earn 6% *aftertax* on the proceeds before year end, what will be the earnings per share?

15-2. Eighteen Wheeler Corporation has recently received approval from regulatory authorities to expand its territory. The firm needs $30,000,000 to acquire trucks and other equipment for their expanded route.

Company officials are confident that a 12-year term loan can be negotiated with a national insurance firm at an annual rate of 10%. Alternatively, an investment banking firm has indicated that it will underwrite a common stock issue for a gross spread of 5%. The firm currently has 2,000,000 shares of stock outstanding.

(a)   If Eighteen's stock can be sold for $30, how many shares of stock must be sold to *net* *$30,000,000* assuming out-of-pocket costs are $600,000?

(b)   If the firm's earnings before interest and taxes increase to $10,000,000 and the applicable tax rate is 34%, what would the earnings per share be under each financing alternative? (Assume annual interest before financing of $1,000,000.)

(c)   Compute the approximate market price of the common stock if the P/E ratio remains at 10 if stock is issued but falls to 9.5 if debt is privately placed.

15-3. K. O'Neal Metalworks is planning a multiple security issue to raise $50,000,000. Following the advice of an investment banker, the company will seek to issue $20,000,000 in 20-year corporate bonds with a 9% coupon rate and $10,000,000 (par value at $100 per share) of preferred stock with a $5 per share fixed dividend. The remainder of the $50,000,000 will come from the sale of common stock. The firm's common stock is currently selling at $32 per share.

(a)   If the current yield to maturity on similar bonds is 11% and the management estimates floatation costs to be 2%, what amount will K. O'Neal Metalworks receive from the sale of bonds?

(b)   The yield demanded in the market on comparable preferred stock is 8%. What is the expected selling price of the preferred stock? If the floatation cost of preferred stock averages 10%, what will be the net proceeds to the firm?

(c)   If the investment banker agrees to handle the common stock issue for a commission of $1.50 per share and advises K. O'Neal that underpricing of $2 per share will be necessary to sell the new stock, how many shares of common stock must be sold?

15-4. Prior to the issuance of the securities indicated (*15-3* above), K. O'Neal projected its operating earnings to be $18,000,000 for the coming year. It had annual interest payments of $2,200,000 and 4,000,000 shares of common stock outstanding. The firm had not issued preferred stock previously. The firm is in the 34% tax bracket.

(a)   What was the projected EPS prior to the issuance of the securities indicated in *Problem 15-3?*

(b) At what beforetax rate must the $50,000,000 be invested to maintain EPS available to common stock?

(c) If the P/E ratio falls from 15 to 12 due to the market's risk perception, what will be the percentage decline in the price per share?

Chapter 15- Solutions

15-1. (a) Initial dilution

Projected EPS prior to issue of new stock

$$EPS = \frac{\$8,000,000}{6,000,000} = \$1.33$$

Projected EPS after issue of new stock

$$EPS = \frac{\$8,000,000}{8,000,000} = \$1$$

The dilution effect = $1.33 - $1.00 = **$.33 per share**

As a percent the dilution effect $= \dfrac{\$.33}{\$1.33} =$ **25%**

(b) *Net proceeds* = $23 x 2,000,000 = $46,000,000

Additional aftertax earnings = $46,000,000 x .06 = $2,760,000

New EPS $= \dfrac{\$8,000,000 + \$2,760,000}{8,000,000} =$ **$1.345**

15-2. (a) $30.00
   <u> .95</u>
$28.50 proceeds/share of stock issued

Number of shares that must be issued $= \dfrac{\$30,000,000 + \$600,000}{\$28.50} =$ **1,073,684 shares**

(b)

	Stock		*Debt*
EBIT $10,000,000		EBIT $10,000,000	
Interest 1,000,000		Interest 4,000,000	
Taxable income . . . . . . $ 9,000,000		Taxable income . . . . . . $ 6,000,000	
Taxes 3,060,000		Taxes 2,040,000	
Net income . . . . $ 5,940,000		Net income . . . . $ 3,960,000	

$$EPS = \frac{\$5,940,000}{3,073,684} = \mathbf{\$1.93}$$

$$EPS = \frac{\$3,960,000}{2,000,000} = \mathbf{\$1.98}$$

(c) Stock
$$Stock\ price = 10 \times \$1.93 = \mathbf{\$19.30}$$

Debt
$$Stock\ price = 9.5 \times \$1.98 = \mathbf{\$18.81}$$

Note the possible conflict between maximizing EPS and maximizing the market value of owner's equity (market price).

15-3. (a)

$$P_b = \$90(7.963) + \$1,000(.124)$$

$$P_b = \$716.67 + \$124 = \$840.67$$

$$Number\ of\ bonds\ sold = \frac{\$20,000,000}{\$1,000} = 20,000$$

$$Net\ proceeds\ per\ bond = \$840.67 \times (1 - .02) = \$823.86$$

$$Total\ proceeds\ from\ sale\ of\ bonds = 20,000 \times \$823.86 = \mathbf{\$16,477,200}$$

(b)

$$P_p = \frac{\$5}{.08} = \mathbf{\$62.50}$$

$$Net\ proceeds\ per\ preferred\ stock\ share = \$62.50 \times (1 - .1) = \$56.25$$

$$Number\ of\ shares\ of\ preferred\ stock\ sold = \frac{\$10,000,000}{\$100} = 100,000$$

$$Net\ proceeds\ from\ sale\ of\ preferred\ stock = 100,000 \times \$56.25 = \mathbf{\$5,625,000}$$

(c) Amount that must be raised from the sale of common stock:

$50,000,000	amount needed
- 16,477,200	net proceeds from sale of bonds
- 5,625,000	net proceeds from sale of preferred stock
$27,897,800	amount to be raised from selling common stock

Net proceeds per share of common stock = $32.00 - $2.00 - $1.50 = $28.50

Number of common stock shares needed to be sold = $27,897,800/$28.50 = **978,871** (rounded)

15-4. (a) EPS prior to raising $50,000,000

$18,000,000	projected operating earnings (EBIT)
2,200,000	annual interest payments
$15,800,000	taxable income
5,372,000	taxes (34%)
$10,428,000	net income

$$\text{Projected EPS} = \frac{\$10,428,000}{4,000,000} = \mathbf{\$2.607}$$

(b) *Number of common shares after financing* = 4,000,000 + 978,871 = 4,978,871

Required net income to maintain EPS = 4,978,871 x $2.607 = $12,979,916.70

Since the $50,000,000 is to be acquired from multiple sources, the payments to each source must be considered.

Annual interest on the <u>new</u> bonds = .09 x $20,000,000 = $1,800,000

Annual dividend payments on preferred stock = 100,000 x $5 = $500,000

The preferred stock dividends, however, are not tax deductible as are the interest payments. To determine the amount of beforetax earnings necessary, the dividend payments must be divided by (1 - tax rate).

Beforetax earnings to pay preferred dividends = $500,000/(1 - .34) = $757,575.76

Required increase in net income = $12,979,916.70 - $10,428,000 = $2,551,916.70

The required increase in aftertax income is $2,551,916.70. The required increase in beforetax income will be $2,551,916.70/(1 - .34) = $3,866,540.46.

Beforetax required return on the $50,000,000 to maintain EPS =

$$\frac{\$1,800,000 + \$757,575.76 + \$3,866,540.46}{\$50,000,000} = \frac{\$6,424,116.22}{\$50,000,000} = .1285 = \mathbf{12.85\%} \ (rounded)$$

This calculation can be confirmed as follows:

$24,424,116.22	EBIT = ($18,000,000 + $6,424,116.22)
4,000,000.00	interest = ($2,200,000 + $1,800,000)
$20,424,116.22	taxable income
6,944,199.52	taxes (34%)
$13,479,916.70	net income
500,000.00	preferred dividends
$12,979,916.70	net income available to common stockholders

$$EPS \text{ available for common stockholders} = \frac{\$12,979,916.70}{4,978,871} = \$2.607$$

(c)   Price of stock before raising $50,000,000:

$P = 15 \times \$2.607 = \$39.11$ *(rounded)*

Price of stock after issue of new securities:

$P = 12 \times \$2.607 = \$31.28$

$$Percentage \text{ decline of stock price} = \frac{\$39.11 - \$31.28}{\$39.11} = \mathbf{20\%}$$

Summary: This chapter considers the importance of debt in the U.S. economy, the nature of long-term debt instruments, the mechanics of bond yield and pricing, the bond refunding decision, and the use of leasing as a special case of long-term debt financing.

I.   The Expanding Role of Debt [p. 453]

    A.   Corporate debt has expanded dramatically in the last 3 decades.

    B.   The rapid expansion of corporate debt is the result of:
        1.   Rapid business expansion.
        2.   Inflation.
        3.   At times, inadequate funds generated from the internal operations of business firms.

II.   Debt Contract Terminology and Provisions [pp. 453-456]

    A.   **Par value**--the face value of a bond.

    B.   **Coupon rate**--annual interest divided by face value.

    C.   **Maturity date**--the final date on which repayment of the debt principal is due.

    D.   **Indenture**--lengthy, legal agreement detailing the issuer's obligations pertaining to a bond issue. The indenture is administered by an independent trustee.

    E.   Security provisions:
        1.   Secured debt--specific assets are pledged to bondholders in the event of default.
        2.   **Mortgage agreement**--real property is pledged as security for loan.
        3.   *Senior* claims require satisfaction in liquidation proceedings prior to *junior* claims.
        4.   New property may become subject to a security provision by an "*after acquired property clause*."

    F.   Unsecured debt.
        1.   **Debenture**--an unsecured, long-term corporate bond.
        2.   **Subordinated debenture**--an unsecured bond in which payment will be made to the bondholder only after the holders of designated senior debt issues have been satisfied.

    G.   Methods of repayment of principal:
        1.   **Lump-sum** payment at maturity.
        2.   **Serial payments**--bonds are paid off in installments over the life of the issue; each bond has a predetermined maturity date.
        3.   **Sinking fund**--the issuer is required to make regular contributions to a fund under the trustee's control. The trustee purchases (retires) bonds in the market with the contributions.
        4.   **Conversion**--retirement by converting bonds into common stock; this is the option of the holder, but it may be forced. (See Chapter 19.)
        5.   **Call feature**--an option of the issuing corporation allowing it to retire the debt issue prior to maturity. Requires payment of a call premium over par value of 5% to 10% to the bondholder. The call is usually exercised by the firm when interest rates have fallen.

III. Bond Prices, Yields, and Ratings [pp. 456-461]

    A. Bond prices are largely determined by the relationship of their coupon rate to the going market rate and the number of years until maturity.
        1. If the market rate for the bond exceeds the coupon rate, the bond will sell below par value. If the market rate is less than the coupon rate, the bond will sell above par value.
        2. The more distant the maturity date of a bond, the farther below or above par value the price will be given the coupon rate and market rate relationship.

    B. Bond yields are quoted on three different bases. Assume a $1,000 par value bond pays $100 per year interest for 10 years. The bond is currently selling at $1,200 in the market.
        1. **Coupon rate** (nominal yield)--

$$\textit{Stated interest payment divided by par value} \quad \frac{\$100}{\$1,000} = 10\%$$

        2. **Current yield**--

$$\textit{Stated interest payment divided by the current price of the bond} \quad \frac{\$100}{\$1,200} = 8.33\%$$

        3. **Yield to maturity**--the interest rate that will equate future interest payments and payment at maturity to current market price (the internal rate of return). The yield to maturity may be computed *approximately* by the following formula.

$$\textit{Approximate YTM} = \frac{\textit{annual interest payment} + \dfrac{\textit{principal payment} - \textit{market value}}{\textit{number of years till maturity}}}{.6(\textit{market value}) + .4(\textit{principal payment})}$$

$$AYTM = \frac{\$100 + \dfrac{\$1,000 - \$1,200}{10}}{.6(\$1,200) + .4(\$1,000)}$$

$$AYTM = \frac{\$100 + \dfrac{-\$200}{10}}{\$1,120} = \frac{\$100 - \$20}{\$1,120} = \frac{\$80}{\$1,120} = 7.14\%$$

    C. Bond ratings.
        1. There are two major bond rating agencies--Moody's Investor Service and Standard and Poor's Corporation.
        2. The higher the rating, the lower the interest rate that must be paid.
        3. The ratings are based on:
            a. The firm's ability to make interest payments.
            b. Its consistency of performance.
            c. Its size.
            d. Its debt/equity ratio.
            e. Its working capital position.
            f. And other factors.

IV. The Refunding Decision [pp. 461-465]

    A. The process of calling outstanding bonds and replacing them with new ones is termed **refunding**. This action is most likely to be pursued by businesses during periods of declining interest rates.

B.   Interest savings from refunding can be substantial over the life of a bond, but the costs of refunding can also be very large.

C.   A refunding decision is a capital budgeting problem. The refunding costs constitute the investment, and the net reduction in annual cash expenditures are the inflows.

D.   A major difference in evaluating a capital expenditure for refunding is that the discount rate applied is the aftertax cost of debt rather than the cost of capital because the annual savings are known with greater certainty.

V.   Other Forms of Bond Financing [pp. 465-466]

A.   **Zero-coupon rate bonds**.
   1.   Do not pay interest; sold at deep discounts from face value.
   2.   These bonds provide immediate cash inflow to the corporation (sell bonds) without any outflow (interest payments) until the bonds mature.
   3.   Since the difference between the selling price and the maturity value is amortized for tax purposes over the life of the bond, a tax reduction benefit occurs without a current cash outflow.
   4.   Allows investor to "lock-in" a multiplier of the initial investment.
   5.   Most investors in these bonds have tax-exempt or tax-deferred status because the annual interest in bond value is taxed as ordinary income even though no payment is received.

B.   **Floating rate bonds**.
   1.   The interest rate varies with market conditions.
   2.   Unless market rates move beyond floating rate limits, the price of the floating rate bond should not change; therefore, the investor is assured (within limits) of the market value of his investment.

VI.   Advantages and Disadvantages of Debt [pp. 466-467]

A.   Advantages:
   1.   Tax deductibility of interest.
   2.   The financial obligation is specific and fixed (with the exception of floating rate bonds).
   3.   In an inflationary economy, debt may be repaid with "cheaper dollars."
   4.   Prudent use of debt may lower the cost of capital.

B.   Disadvantages:
   1.   Interest and principal payments must be met when due regardless of the firm's financial position.
   2.   Burdensome bond indenture restrictions.
   3.   Imprudent use of debt may depress stock prices.

VII.   Leasing as a Form of Debt [pp. 469-472]

A.   A long-term, noncancellable lease has all the characteristics of a debt obligation.

B.   The position of the accounting profession that companies should fully divulge all information about leasing obligations was made official for financial reporting purposes in November 1976. The Financial Accounting Standards Board (FASB) issued *Statement of Financial Accounting Standards (SFAS) No. 13*.
   1.   Prior to *Statement No. 13*, lease obligations could be divulged in footnotes to financial statements.

2. *SFAS No. 13* requires that certain types of leases be shown as long-term obligations on a firm's financial statements.

C. Leases that substantially transfer all the benefits and risks of ownership from the owner to the lessee must be capitalized. A **capital lease** is required whenever any one of the following conditions exists.
  1. Ownership of the property is transferred to the lessee by the end of the lease term.
  2. The lease contains a bargain purchase price (sure to be purchased) at the end of the lease.
  3. The lease term is equal to 75% or more of the estimated life of the leased property.
  4. The present value of the minimum lease payments equals or exceeds 90% of the fair value of the leased property at the beginning of the lease.

D. A lease that does not meet any of the four criteria is an **operating lease**.
  1. Usually short-term.
  2. Often cancelable at the option of the lessee.
  3. The lessor frequently provides maintenance.
  4. Capitalization and presentation on the balance sheet is not required.

E. Impact of capital lease on the income statement.
  1. The intangible leased property under capital lease (asset) amount is amortized and written off over the life of the lease.
  2. The obligation under capital lease (liability) is written off through amortization with an "implied" interest expense on the remaining balance.

F. Advantages of leasing.
  1. Lessee may not have sufficient funds to purchase or borrowing capability.
  2. Provisions of lease may be less restrictive.
  3. May be no down payment.
  4. Expert advice of leasing (lessor) company.
  5. Creditor claims on certain types of leases are restricted in bankruptcy and reorganization procedures.
  6. Tax considerations.
    a. Obtain maximum benefit of tax advantages.
    b. Tax deductibility of lease payments for land.
  7. Infusion of capital through a sale-leaseback.

VIII. Appendix 16A: Financial Alternatives for Distressed Firms [pp. 479-484]

A. Financial distress.
  1. **Technical insolvency**--firm has positive net worth but is unable to pay its bills as they come due.
  2. **Bankruptcy**--a firm's liabilities exceed the value of its assets--negative worth.

B. Out-of-court settlements.
  1. **Extension**--creditors allow the firm more time to meet its financial obligations.
  2. **Composition**--creditors agree to accept a fractional settlement on their original claim.
  3. **Creditor committee**--a creditor committee is established to run the business in place of the existing management.
  4. **Assignment**--a **liquidation** of the firm's assets without going through formal court action.

C. In-court settlements--formal bankruptcy.
  1. Bankruptcy proceedings may be initiated voluntarily by the firm or forced by the creditors--involuntary bankruptcy.

2. The decisions of a court-appointed referee who arbitrates the bankruptcy proceedings are final, subject to court review.
3. Reorganization--a fair and feasible plan to reorganize the bankrupt firm.
    a. **Internal reorganization**--necessitates an evaluation of existing management and policies. An assessment and possible redesign of the firm's capital structure is also required.
    b. **External reorganization**--a financially strong and managerially competent merger partner is found for the bankrupt firm.
4. Liquidation--if reorganization of the firm is determined to be infeasible, the assets of the firm will be sold to satisfy creditors. The priority of claims is:
    a. Bankruptcy administrative costs (legal fees).
    b. Wages of workers earned within 3 months of bankruptcy declaration.
    c. Federal, state, and local taxes.
    d. Secured creditors--designated assets.
    e. General creditors--there is a priority within this category also.
    f. Preferred stockholders.
    g. Common stockholders.

IX. Appendix 16B: Lease versus Purchase Decision [pp. 485-487]

A. Leasing as a means of financing is often compared to borrow-purchase arrangements when assets are to be acquired. This procedure is appropriate for comparing an operating lease to purchasing.

B. The present value of all aftertax cash outflows associated with each form of financing is computed. The procedure requires consideration of all tax shields for each method. Since all outflows are fixed by contract, the discount rate employed in computing the present value of the outflows is the aftertax cost of debt.

C. Although qualitative factors must be considered, the usual decision criterion is to accept the financing method, leasing or borrow-purchase, that has the lowest present value of cash outflows. The cash inflows should be the same whether the asset is leased or purchased.

Chapter 16 - Multiple Choice Questions

1. Which of the following is a long-term unsecured bond? [p. 454]
    a. First mortgage bond
    b. Commercial paper
    c. Indenture
    d. Serial bond
    e. Debenture

2. Which of the following is usually a characteristic of an operating lease? [p. 470]
    a. The lessee provides maintenance.
    b. The lease term is equal to 75% or more of the estimated life of the property.
    c. It is cancelable by lessee.
    d. Capitalization is required.
    e. Ownership is transferred to lessee at end of lease.

3. The bond yield found by dividing the annual interest payment by the current price of a bond is called the: [p. 460]
    a. Current yield.
    b. Yield to maturity.
    c. Approximate yield to maturity.
    d. Coupon rate.
    e. Historical yield.

4. New property may become subject to a security provision by a(n): [p. 454]
    a. Acceleration clause.
    b. Debenture.
    c. Subordinated debenture.
    d. After-acquired property clause.
    e. Sinking fund.

5. Which of the following debt instruments is most likely to maintain a constant price? [p. 466]
    a. Zero-coupon bond
    b. Floating rate bond
    c. Convertible bond
    d. Corporate bond with a fixed annual interest payment
    e. Eurobond

6. An issuer may be required to fund the retirement of a bond issue by (a): [p. 455]
    a. Conversion.
    b. Call feature.
    c. Mortgage agreement.
    d. Sinking fund.
    e. Refunding.

7. Which of the following indicates the status of a firm which has positive net worth but is unable to pay its bills? [p. 479]
    a. Extension
    b. Composition
    c. Technical insolvency
    d. Bankruptcy
    e. Assignment

8. The legal agreement that details a security issuer's obligation is called a(n): [p. 454]
    a. Indenture.
    b. Trustee.
    c. Covenant.
    d. Pledge.
    e. Assignment.

9. In the liquidation of a firm's assets, which of the following will have the highest priority of claim? [p. 481]
    a. Legal fees
    b. Federal, state, and local taxes
    c. Common stockholders
    d. Wages of workers earned within three months
    e. Secured creditors

10. The call premium that a firm pays when refunding a bond issue is: [p. 462]
    a. Spread over the life of the new issue for tax purposes.
    b. A noncash cost.
    c. A tax deductible expense at the time of refunding.
    d. Required by law.
    e. A non-tax-deductible expense.

Chapter 16 - Problems

16-1. The Reynolds Corporation issued $1,000-thirty-year bonds which pay $120 annually in interest The bonds are currently selling at par.

    (a)   What is the coupon rate?

    (b)   What is the current price of the bonds?

    (c)   What is the current yield?

    (d)   What is the yield to maturity?

16-2. Referring to Table 16-1 in the text, answer the following questions.

    (a)   When does May Department Stores 10.75% debenture mature?

    (b)   What was the high price (in dollars) of McDonalds' 7.375% debenture in 2000?

    (c)   Are Maytag's 9.75% notes that mature in 2002 selling at a premium or at a discount?

    (d)   What is Moody's rating of MBIA's 7.15% debentures?

16-3. CBA Corporation issued a 20-year bond 10 years ago. The bond, which pays $80 interest annually, was issued at par.

    (a)   What was the yield to maturity on the bond at time of issue?

    (b)   If the bond is currently selling for $820, is its yield to maturity greater or less than the coupon rate?

    (c)   What is the approximate yield to maturity on the bond at the present time?

    (d)   If the firm were to issue a similar bond today, approximately what yield to maturity would be required for the bond to sell at par?

    (e)   What is the current yield on the bond if the bond price is $820?

16-4. What would be the market price of a 20-year bond that pays $80 interest annually if the market rate of interest on bonds of similar risk were (a) 6%, (b) 8%, and (c) 10%?

16-5. In 1998, National Utility issued $60,000,000 of 12% 25-year bonds at par. The current market rate on bonds with the same rating is 10%. The bond contract will allow refunding of these bonds in 2003. Company officers have estimated the floatation costs of a 20-year refunding bond issue to be $1,500,000. The underwriting costs on the old issue were $1,000,000. The terms of the current bond contract require the payment of a 6% call premium.

(a) Assuming that the utility firm's tax rate is 30%, would a decision to refund the outstanding bonds be acceptable?

(b) Would your answer be the same under the following conditions?

	Old Issue	New Issue
Size	$60,000,000	$60,000,000
Interest rate	7%	6%
Total life	25 years	10 years
Remaining life	10 years	10 years
Call premium	10%	---
Underwriting costs	$1,000,000	$2,000,000

(Round discount rate to nearest whole rate.)

16-6. The Cap-Short Corporation is debating whether to acquire an asset through an operating lease arrangement or to borrow funds and purchase the asset. The purchase price of the asset, $100,000, can be financed with a four-year, 15% bank loan. If purchased, the asset will be depreciated as three-year property with no expected salvage at the end of its four-year life. Alternatively, the firm can obtain the use of the asset through two operating leases of two years each. The lease payments would be $30,000 per year on the first lease and $35,000 per year on the second lease. The firm's tax rate is approximately 34%. Which alternative should be selected based on minimizing the present value of aftertax costs?

(Round discount rate to nearest whole rate.)

Chapter 16 - Solutions

16-1. (a)

$$Coupon\ rate = \frac{\$120}{\$1,000} = \textbf{12\%}$$

(b)

Bonds are selling at par = **$1,000**

(c)

$$Current\ yield = \frac{\$120}{\$1,000} = \textbf{12\%}$$

(d) Since the bonds are selling at par, the yield to maturity equals **the coupon rate = 12%**. The student may wish to confirm this by using the approximate yield to maturity formula or the bond valuation formula.

16-2. (a) **Year 2018**

    (b) 110⅞ = **$1,108.75**

    (c) At a **premium**, 102⅞ = **$1,028.75**

    (d) **Aa2**

16-3. (a) The bond was issued at par; therefore, the yield to maturity was equal to the coupon rate, 8%. The rate can be verified by the approximate yield to maturity formulation.

$$AYTM = \frac{interest\ payment + \dfrac{(par\ value - market\ value)}{number\ of\ periods\ till\ maturity}}{.6(market\ price) + .4(par\ value)}$$

$$AYTM = \frac{\$80 + \dfrac{\$1,000 - \$1,000}{20}}{.6(\$1,000) + .4(\$1,000)} = \frac{\$80}{\$1,000} = 8\%$$

    (b) The yield to maturity is **greater** than the coupon rate as it will always be when the bond is selling at a discount (below face value).

    (c)

$$AYTM = \frac{\$80 + \dfrac{\$1,000 - \$820}{10}}{.6(\$820) + .4(\$1,000)} = \frac{\$80 + \$18}{\$892} = \frac{\$98}{\$892} = 10.99\%$$

    (d) **10.99%** (The best estimate of the yield to maturity required on a new bond would be the yield on the outstanding bond. If, however, the riskiness of the firm were increased by the new issue, the required yield might be greater, etc.)

    (e)

$$Current\ yield = \frac{annual\ interest}{current\ price\ of\ bond}$$

$$Current\ yield = \frac{\$80}{\$820} = 9.76\%$$

16-4. (a)

$$Price\ of\ bond\ (BP) = \frac{\$80}{(1.06)} + \ldots + \frac{\$80}{(1.06)^{20}} + \frac{\$1,000}{(1.06)^{20}}$$

$BP = \$80(11.47) + \$1,000(.312)$
$BP = \$917.60 + \$312 = \$1,229.60$

    (b)

$$BP = \frac{\$80}{(1.08)} + \ldots + \frac{\$80}{(1.08)^{20}} + \frac{\$1,000}{(1.08)^{20}}$$

$BP = \$80(9.818) + \$1,000(.215)$
$BP = \$785.44 + \$215 = \$1,000.44$ (bond sells at par; coupon rate = market rate)

(c)

$$BP = \frac{\$80}{(1.10)} + \ldots + \frac{\$80}{(1.10)^{20}} + \frac{\$1,000}{(1.10)^{20}}$$

$BP = \$80(8.514) + \$1,000(.149)$
$BP = \$681.12 + \$149 = \$830.12$

16-5. (a) STEP A--Computation of outflows:

Call premium = .06 x $60,000,000 = $3,600,000
Floatation costs $1,500,000

The call premium will be expensed at the time of the deduction, but the floatation costs will be written off over the life of the bond. The present value of the tax savings resulting from the writeoff of the floatation costs must be computed to determine the net cost of underwriting expenses of the new issue.

$$Annual\ floatation\ expense = \frac{total\ floatation\ expense}{life\ of\ new\ bond}$$

$$Annual\ floatation\ expense = \frac{\$1,500,000}{20} = \$75,000$$

Annual tax savings from writing off floatation expense = $75,000 x .3 = $22,500

Present value of $22,500 tax savings for 20 years

$22,500 x 10.594(n = 20, i = 7%) = $238,365

Net cost of underwriting expense

Actual expenditure	$1,500,000
- PV of future tax savings	238,365
	$1,261,635

STEP B--Computation of inflows:

Annual cost savings in lower interest rates
12% x $60,000,000 = $7,200,000
10% x $60,000,000 = 6,000,000
                    $1,200,000

Aftertax annual cost savings in lower interest rates

$1,200,000 x .7 = $840,000

PV of annual interest savings

$840,000 x 10.594(n = 20, i = 7%) = $8,898,960

Underwriting cost on old issue

$$\text{Underwriting cost per year} = \frac{\$1,000,000}{25} = \$40,000$$

Original amount	$1,000,000
Written off over five years	200,000
	$ 800,000

Present value of future writeoffs

$40,000 x (PV$_{IFA}$, n = 20, i = 7%)
$40,000 x (10.594) = $423,760

Net gain from the underwriting cost on the old issue

Immediate writeoff	$800,000
PV of future writeoff	423,760
Gain in immediate writeoff	$376,240
Tax savings	x .3
	$112,872

STEP C--Net present value

Outflows		Inflows	
Net cost of call premium	$2,520,000	Cost savings in lower interest rates	$8,898,960
Net cost of underwriting expense	1,261,635	Net gain from under-writing cost (old issue)	112,872
	$3,781,635		$9,011,832

Present value of inflows	$9,011,832
Present value of outflows	3,781,635
Net present value	**$5,230,197**

An alternative approach to the bond refunding calculations is also presented:

Cash investment to refund:

$60,000,000	face value of old bond
3,600,000	add the call premium = .06(60,000,000)
$63,600,000	
60,000,000	subtract receipts from sale of new bond
$ 3,600,000	
1,500,000	add floatation expense of new bond
$ 5,100,000	
1,080,000	subtract tax reduction from writing off call premium = .30 x 3,600,000
$ 4,020,000	
240,000	subtract tax reduction from writing off unamortized underwriting cost of old bond
$ 3,780,000	net cash investment required to refund

Annual cash benefits:

$7,200,000	annual interest on old bond = .12 x 60,000,000
6,000,000	annual interest on new bond = .10 x 60,000,000
$1,200,000	annual interest savings

$ 75,000	annual amortization of issue expense on new bond
40,000	annual amortization of issue expense on old bond
$ 35,000	increase in annual amortization of issue expense

	Income	Cash	
Increase in income due to interest savings	$1,200,000	$1,200,000	Increase in cash due to interest savings
Increase in amortization of issue expense	35,000		
Increase in taxable income	$1,165,000		
Taxes (30%)	349,500	349,500	Taxes
		$ 850,500	Annual cash benefits from refunding

Net present value of refunding:

$NPV = \$850,500(PV_{IFA} = 10.594) - \$3,780,000$
$NPV = \$9,010,197 - \$3,780,000 = \mathbf{\$5,230,197}$

Note: The present value of inflows and present value of outflows differ slightly in the alternative calculations. The NPV, however, will always be the same.

(b)   *Outflows*

Call premium = 10% x $60,000,000 = $6,000,000
Net cost of call premium (.66) x $6,000,000 = $3,960,000

Annual floatation costs $= \dfrac{\$2,000,000}{10} = \$200,000$

Annual tax savings from writing off floatation expense = $200,000 x .34 = $68,000
Present value of $68,000 tax savings for 10 years
    $68,000 x 8.111(n = 10, i = 4%) = $551,548

Net cost of underwriting expense	
Actual expenditure	$2,000,000
- PV of future tax savings	551,548
	$1,448,452

Inflows

Annual cost savings in lower interest rates
    7% x $60,000,000 = $4,200,000
    6% x $60,000,000 = 3,600,000
                            $ 600,000

Aftertax annual cost savings in lower interest rates
    $600,000 x .66 = $396,000

PV of annual interest savings
$396,000 x 8.111(n = 10, i = 4%) = $3,211,956

Underwriting cost on old issue

$$\text{Underwriting cost per year} = \frac{\$1,000,000}{25} = \$40,000$$

Original amount	$1,000,000
Written off over 15 years	600,000
	$ 400,000

Present value of future writeoffs
$40,000 x ($PV_{IFA}$, n = 10, i = 4%)
$40,000 x 8.111 = $324,440

Net gain from the underwriting cost on the old issue

Immediate writeoff	$400,000
PV of future writeoff	324,440
Gain in immediate	$ 75,560
writeoff	x .34
	$ 25,690
Tax savings	

Net present value

Outflows		Inflows	
Net cost of call premium	$3,960,000	Cost savings in lower	$3,211,956
Net cost of underwriting	1,448,542	interest rates	
expense	$5,408,452	Net gain from under-	25,690
		writing cost (old issue)	$3,237,646
Present value of inflows	$3,237,646		
Present value of outflows	5,408,452		
Net present value	($2,170,806)		

No, the answer would not be the same. The NPV of refunding is negative.

16-6. *Annual loan payment*

$$A = PV_A / PV_{IFA}$$

$$A = \frac{\$100,000}{2.855} = \$35,026.27$$

Amortization Table

Year	Beginning Balance	Annual Payment	Annual Interest	Payment of Principal	Ending Balance
1	$100,000.00	$35,026.27	$15,000.00	$20,026.27	$79,973.73
2	79,973.73	35,026.27	11,996.06	23,030.21	56,943.52
3	56,943.52	35,026.27	8,541.53	26,484.74	30,458.78
4	30,458.78	35,026.27	4,568.82	30,457.45*	0*

*Principal payment differs slightly from the amount owed because of rounding.

Depreciation Schedule

Year	Rate of Depreciation	Cost of Asset	Annual Depreciation
1	.333	$100,000	$33,300
2	.445	100,000	44,500
3	.148	100,000	14,800
4	.074	100,000	7,400

Aftertax Cost of Operating Leases

Year	Payment	Tax Shield	Aftertax Cost
1	$30,000	$10,200	$19,800
2	30,000	10,200	19,800
3	35,000	11,900	23,100
4	35,000	11,900	23,100

Aftertax Cost of Borrow-Purchase

Year	Payment	Interest	Depreciation	Total Tax Deduction	Tax Shield	Net After-Tax Cost
1	$35,026.27	$15,000.0 0	$33,300	$48,300.00	$16,422.00	$18,604.27
2	35,026.27	11,996.06	44,500	56,496.06	19,208.66	15,817.61
3	35,026.27	8,541.53	14,800	23,341.53	7,936.12	27,090.15
4	35,026.27	4,568.82	7,400	11,968.82	4,069.40	30,956.87

Discount rate = aftertax cost of debt = .15(1 - .34) = .099 = 10%

Net Present Value Comparison

Year	Leasing Aftertax Cost of Leasing	IF at 10%	Present Value	Borrow-Purchase Aftertax Cost of Borrow-Purchase	IF at 10%	Present Value
1	$19,800	.909	$17,998.20	$18,604.17	.909	$16,911.28
2	19,800	.826	16,354.80	15,817.61	.826	13,065.35
3	23,100	.751	17,348.10	27,090.15	.751	20,344.70
4	23,100	.683	15,777.30	30,956.87	.683	21,143.54
			$67,478.40			$71,464.87

Based solely on the present value of costs, the leasing arrangement is the preferable means of acquiring the asset. The choice may be based on other factors, however, since the difference in costs is not large.

Summary: The characteristics of common and preferred stock and the rights pertaining to the ownership of each are considered in this chapter.

I. Common Stock and Common Stockholders [pp. 490-500]

   A. Although management controls the corporation on a daily basis, ultimate control of the firm resides in the hands of the stockholders.

   B. Management has become more sensitive to the growing institutional ownership of common stock. Mutual funds, pension funds, and bank trust accounts are examples of financial institutions that in combination own a large percentage of many leading corporations.

   C. Common stockholders have a **residual claim** on the income stream; the amount remaining after creditors and preferred stockholders have been satisfied belongs to the owners (common stockholders) whether paid in dividends or retained. [p. 490]

   D. A corporation may have several **classes of common stock** that differ in regard to voting rights and claim on the earnings stream. [p. 491]

   E. Owners of common stock have the right to vote on all major issues including election of the board of directors. [pp. 491-494]
       1. **Majority voting**--holders of majority of stock can elect all directors.
       2. In some firms such as Ford Motor Company, different classes of stock are entitled to elect a specified percentage of the board of directors.
       3. **Cumulative voting**--possible for minority stockholders (own less than 50% of stock) to elect some of the directors.
           a. The stockholder can cast one vote for each share of stock owned *times* the number of directors to be elected.
           b. The following formula may be employed to determine the number of shares needed to elect a given number of directors under cumulative voting.

$$\textit{Shares required} = \frac{\textit{number of directors desired x total number of shares outstanding}}{\textit{total number of directors being elected} + 1} + 1$$

   F. The type of voting process has become more important to both stockholders and management because of the threat of takeovers, leveraged buy-outs, and other challenges to management's control of the firm.

   G. The stockholder may have the right to maintain his percentage of ownership, voting power, and claim to earnings through the **preemptive right** provision which requires that existing stockholders be given the first option to purchase new shares.

   H. Financing through rights offerings. [pp. 494-498]
       1. Even if the preemptive right provision is not required, the corporation may finance through a **rights offering**. Rights offerings are especially popular in Europe.
       2. Each stockholder receives one right for each share of stock owned and is allowed to buy new shares of stock at a reduced price (below market value) plus the required number of rights/share.

3. The number of rights required to purchase a new share equals the ratio of shares outstanding to the new shares issued.

$$Number\ of\ rights\ required\ for\ purchase\ 1\ new\ share\ =\ \frac{number\ of\ shares\ outstanding}{number\ of\ shares\ being\ issued}$$

4. Rights have market value since they entitle the holder to purchase shares of stock at less than market price.
    a. Initially, after the rights offering announcement, stock trades **rights-on**. The formula for the value of a right during the rights-on period is:

$$R = \frac{M_0 - S}{N + 1}$$

M_0 = Market value of stock, rights-on
S = Subscription price
N = Number of rights required to purchase a new share of stock

    b. After a certain period, the right no longer trades with the stock but may be bought and sold separately. On the **ex-rights** date, the stock price falls by the theoretical value of a right. The ex-rights value of a right is:

$$R = \frac{M_e - S}{N}$$

M_e = Market value of stock, ex-rights

5. Existing stockholders usually do not have a monetary gain from a rights offering. The gain from purchasing shares at less than market price is eliminated by dilution of previously owned shares.
6. A stockholder has three options when presented with a rights offering.
    a. Exercise the rights; no net gain or loss.
    b. Sell the rights; no net gain or loss.
    c. Allow the rights to lapse; a loss will be incurred due to the dilution of existing shares that is not offset by value of unsold or unexercised rights.
7. Desirable features of rights offerings.
    a. Protects stockholders' voting position and claim on earnings.
    b. Existing stockholders provide a built-in market for new issues; distribution costs are lower.
    c. May create more interest in stock than a straight offering.
    d. Lower **margin requirements**,

I. Poison pills. [p. 498]
    1. A **poison pill** is a rights offering made to existing shareholders of a company with the sole purpose of thwarting an acquisition attempt by another company. The increased number of shares may dilute the ownership percentage of the firm pursuing the takeover.
    2. Some investors feel that a poison pill strategy is contrary to the goal of maximizing the wealth of the owners.

II. **American Depository Receipts (ADR)** [pp. 499-500]

A. ADRs are certificates that have a legal claim on an ownership interest in a foreign company's common stock.
    1. Shares of a foreign company are purchased and placed in a trust in a foreign branch of a U.S. bank.

211

2. The bank receives and can issue depository receipts to the American shareholders of the foreign firm. ADRs allow foreign shares to be traded in the U.S. in a manner similar to domestic stock. ADRs are sometimes called American Depository Shares (ADSs).

B. Advantages of ADRs for the U.S. investor.
1. Annual reports are presented in English according to generally accepted accounting principles.
2. Dividends are paid in dollars and are more easily collected than if actual shares of foreign stock were owned.
3. ADRs are more liquid, less expensive, and easier to trade than actual shares of foreign stock.

C. Disadvantages of ADRs.
1. Although ADRs trade in the U.S. in dollars, they are traded in their own country in their local currency. The investor in ADRs is subject to foreign exchange risk.
2. Foreign companies do not report financial results as often as U.S. companies. Also, there is a lag caused by the translation of the reports into English.

III. Preferred Stock Financing [pp. 500-505]

A. Characteristics of preferred stock:
1. Stipulated dividends must be paid before dividends on common stock but are not guaranteed or required.
2. Dividends are not tax deductible.

B. Preferred stock contributes to capital structure balance by expanding the capital base without diluting common stock or incurring contractual obligations.

C. Primary purchasers of preferred stock are corporate investors, insurance companies and pension funds primarily because 70% of dividend income received by corporations is exempt from taxation whereas interest received is fully taxable.

D. Provisions associated with preferred stock:
1. Cumulative dividends.
2. Conversion feature.
   a. Convertible preferred stock is convertible to common stock at the option of the preferred stockholder. (See Chapter 19 for a thorough discussion of the conversion feature associated with debt.)
   b. Convertible preferreds include a recent innovation--**convertible exchangeable preferreds** that allow the firm to force conversion from convertible preferred stock into convertible debt.
3. Call feature.
4. Participation provision.
5. Floating rate.
   a. Investors purchase floating rate preferreds to minimize risk of price changes and to take advantage of tax benefits.
   b. Price stability makes preferred stock the equivalent of a safe, short-term investment.
6. Dutch auction preferred stock.
   a. Similar to floating rate preferred but is a short-term security.
   b. Preferred stock is issued to bidders willing to accept lowest yield.
   c. Security matures every seven weeks and is reauctioned at a subsequent bidding.
7. Par value.

IV. Key Formulas

A. Shares required to elect a specific number of directors [p. 493]

$$\text{Shares required} = \frac{\text{number of directors desired} \times \text{total number of shares outstanding}}{\text{total number of directors being elected} + 1} + 1$$

B. Number of directors that can be elected [p. 493]

$$\text{Number of directors that can be elected} =$$

$$\frac{(\text{shares owned} - 1) \times (\text{total number of directors being elected} + 1)}{\text{Total number of shares outstanding}}$$

C. Value of a right, rights-on [p. 496]

$$R = \frac{M_0 - S}{N + 1}$$

D. Value of a right, ex-rights [p. 496]

$$R = \frac{M_e - S}{N}$$

TABLE 17-1
FEATURES OF ALTERNATIVE SECURITY ISSUES

		Common Stock	Preferred Stock	Bonds
1.	Ownership and Control of the Firm	Belongs to common stock-holders through voting right and residual claim to income	Limited rights when dividends are missed	Limited rights under default in interest payments
2.	Obligation to Provide Return	None	Must receive payment before common stockholders	Contractual obligation
3.	Claim to Assets in Bankruptcy	Lowest claim of any securityholder	Bondholders and creditors must be satisfied first	Highest claim
4.	Cost of Distribution	Highest	Moderate	Lowest
5.	Risk-Return Trade-Off	Highest risk, highest return (at least in theory)	Moderate risk, moderate return	Lowest risk, moderate return
6.	Tax Status of Payment by Corporation	Not deductible	Not deductible	Tax deductible; cost = interest payment x (1 - tax rate)
7.	Tax Status of Payment to Recipient	70% of dividends to another corporation is tax exempt	Same as common stock	Municipal bond interest is tax exempt

Chapter 17 - Multiple Choice Questions

1. Which type of voting allows minority stockholders to elect some of the directors of a corporation? [p. 492]
    a. Majority
    b. Preferred
    c. Common
    d. Cumulative
    e. Preemptive

2. The number of rights required to purchase one new share in a rights offering is found by: [p 495]
    a. Dividing the subscription price by the ex-rights value of a right.
    b. Dividing the number of shares outstanding by the number of shares to be issued.
    c. Multiplying the subscription price by *N*.
    d. Subtracting the subscription price from the ex-rights price of the stock.
    e. Adding the rights-on right value to the ex-rights right value.

3. A stockholder may be protected against dilution of percentage of ownership by: [p. 494]
    a. Cumulative voting.
    b. A call option.
    c. A participation provision.
    d. A preemptive right.
    e. An ESOP.

4. Which of the following has the lowest claim to assets in bankruptcy? [p. 504]
    a. Common stock
    b. Convertible preferred stock
    c. Preferred stock
    d. Corporate bonds
    e. Convertible exchangeable preferred stock

5. Which of these securities is short term? [p. 503]
    a. Convertible preferred stock
    b. Corporate bonds
    c. Dutch auction preferred stock
    d. Common stock
    e. Municipal bonds

6. The purpose of a "poison pill" rights offering is to: [p. 498]
    a. Thwart a takeover attempt.
    b. Get rid of the current management.
    c. Maximize the wealth of the owners.
    d. Lower margin requirements.
    e. Force conversion of convertible preferred stock.

7. Which of the following statements about a rights offering is incorrect? [pp. 496-497]
    a. A stockholder may exercise rights.
    b. A stockholder will normally be able to buy stock at a price less than the market price.
    c. A stockholder will always have a gain on a rights offering.
    d. A stockholder may sell rights.
    e. A stockholder may allow rights to lapse.

8. Certificates traded in the U.S. that represent a legal claim on an ownership interest in a foreign company's common stock are called: [p. 499]
   a. Foreign trust certificates.
   b. Eurobonds.
   c. Dutch Auction Preferreds.
   d. LIBORs.
   e. ADRs.

9. Theoretically, the price of a share of stock should: [pp. 495-496]
   a. Rise by N x the value one right on the ex-rights date.
   b. Fall by the value of one right on the ex-rights date.
   c. Fall by the value of one right on the rights-on date.
   d. Rise by N x the value of one right on the rights-on date.
   e. Not be affected on the ex-rights date.

10. Which of the following statements is correct? [p. 501]
   a. Preferred stock dividends are tax deductible.
   b. Common stock dividends are tax deductible.
   c. Seventy percent of intercorporate interest is tax exempt.
   d. The cost of distribution is highest for corporate bonds.
   e. Seventy percent of intercorporate dividends are tax exempt to the receiving firm.

Multiple Choice Answer Key - Chapter 17

1. d	2. b	3. d	4. a	5. c
6. a	7. c	8. e	9. b	10. e

Chapter 17 - Problems

17-1. The Lotsa-Luck Gold Mining Company is seeking to raise $10,000,000 through a rights offering. The company presently has 1,000,000 shares of common stock outstanding at a current market price of $25 per share.

(a) How many new shares must be sold via the rights offering if the subscription price is $20?

(b) How many new shares could a stockholder owning 100 shares purchase?

(c) What is the value of one right?

(d) What will be the approximate price of the stock ex-rights?

17-2. Suppose you owned 100 shares of Lotsa Luck Gold Mining stock. Assuming that you have sufficient cash to purchase the number of shares available to you from the rights offering (17-1 above), indicate your position under each of the following circumstances:

(a) You exercise your rights.

(b) You sell your rights.

(c) You neither exercise nor sell your rights.

17-3. The TVG Corporation has not paid dividends on its $3 preferred stock for the previous two years. There are 1,000,000 shares of preferred stock outstanding. How much can the firm pay to common stockholders if it limits dividends to current earnings under each of the following circumstances?

    (a)   Current earnings are $1,000,000.

    (b)   Current earnings are $9,000,000.

    (c)   Current earnings are $12,000,000 and the firm wishes to retain 50% of earnings available to common stockholders.

17-4. The Slip-n-Slide Corporation has experienced several consecutive years of declining profits. D. S. Satisfied and several other stockholders are seeking to replace as many corporate directors as possible. The disgruntled stockholders own 18,001 shares of 72,000 outstanding voting shares.

    (a)   If the company employs the cumulative voting procedure, how many directors can they elect to an 11-member board?

    (b)   How many additional shares must the dissident shareholders acquire to enable them to elect five directors?

Chapter 17 - Solutions

17-1.   (a)

$$\frac{\$10,000,000}{\$20} = 500,000 \text{ new shares}$$

    (b)

$$\frac{1,000,000}{500,000} = 2 \text{ rights required for purchase of one new share}$$

Each stockholder receives one right per share of stock. A holder of 100 shares of stock would receive 100 rights.

$$\frac{number\ of\ rights\ owned}{number\ of\ rights/new\ share} = \frac{100}{2} = 50 \text{ shares can be purchased}$$

    (c)

$$R = \frac{M_0 - S}{N + 1} \qquad\qquad R = \frac{\$25 - \$20}{2 + 1} = \frac{\$5}{3} = \$1.67$$

    (d) $25 - 1.67 = **$23.33**

17-2. (a)

$$\text{number of shares that can be purchased} = \frac{\text{number of shares owned}}{\text{number of rights required for purchase of one share}}$$

$$50 = \frac{100}{2}$$

Cash required to purchase 50 shares = 50 x $20 = $1,000

Position at time of rights offering announcement:

Cash	$1,000
100 shares at $25	2,500
Total value	$3,500

Position if rights are exercised:

Cash	$ -0-
150 shares at $23.33	3,499.50
	$3,499.50 (approximately $3,500)

(b)

100 shares at $23.33	$2,333
Proceeds, sale of 100 rights	167
Cash	1,000
Total	**$3,500**

(c)

100 shares at $23.33	$2,333
Cash	1,000
	$3,333

17-3. (a) *Annual preferred dividends* = $3 x 1,000,000 = $3,000,000
Dividends in arrears = 2 (years) x $3,000,000 = $6,000,000

Preferred dividends due:	Current dividends	$3,000,000
	Pf. dividends in arrears	6,000,000
		$9,000,000

No dividends could be paid to common stockholders.

(b)

Current earnings	$ 9,000,000
Preferred dividends due	9,000,000
Earnings available to common stockholders	$ -0-

(c)

Current earnings	$12,000,000
Preferred dividends due	9,000,000
Earnings available to common stockholders	$ 3,000,000
Payout ratio (.50)	.50
Common stock dividends	**$ 1,500,000**

17-4. (a) *Number of directors that can be elected =*

$$\frac{(\text{shares owned} - 1)(\text{total number of directors being elected} + 1)}{\text{total number of shares outstanding}}$$

Number of directors that can be elected $= \dfrac{(18,001 - 1)(11 + 1)}{72,000} = \textbf{3}$

(b)

Shares required $= \dfrac{\text{number of directors desired} \times \text{total number of shares outstanding}}{\text{total number of directors being elected} + 1} + 1$

Shares required $= \dfrac{5 \times 72,000}{11 + 1} + 1$

Shares required $= \dfrac{360,000}{12} + 1$

Shares required $= 30,001$

Additional shares needed $= 30,001 - 18,001 = \textbf{12,000}$

Summary: The Board of Directors of a corporation must decide what portion of the firm's earnings will be paid to the stockholders. This chapter examines the many factors that influence the dividend policy decision and processes.

I. **The Marginal Principle of Retained Earnings** [pp. 517-520]

    A. **Life cycle growth** and dividends.
        1. The corporate growth rate in sales is a major influence on dividends.
        2. A firm's dividend policy will usually reflect the firm's stage of development.
            a. Stage I--small firm, initial stage of development--no dividends.
            b. Stage II--successful firm, growing demand for products and increasing sales, earnings and assets--stock dividends followed later by cash dividends.
            c. Stage III--cash dividends rise as asset expansion slows and external funds are more readily available--stock dividends and stock splits also common.
            d. Stage IV--the firm reaches maturity and maintains a stable sales growth rate and cash dividends tend to be 35%-50% of earnings.

    B. According to the passive **residual theory of dividends**, earnings should be retained as long as the rate earned is expected to exceed a stockholder's rate of return on the distributed dividend.

    C. The residual dividend theory assumes a lack of preference for dividends by investors.
        1. Much disagreement exists as to investor's preference for dividends or retention of earnings.
        2. Relevance of dividends arguments.
            a. **Resolves uncertainty**.
            b. **Information content**.

II. Corporate Dividend Policy [pp. 519-520]

    A. Growth firms with high rates of return usually pay relatively low dividends.

    B. Mature firms follow a relatively high payout policy.

    C. The average payout of U.S. corporations since WW II has been about 35%-50% of aftertax earnings.

    D. The stable dividend policy followed by U.S. corporations indicates that corporate management feels that stockholders have a preference for dividends.

III. Other Factors Influencing Dividend Policy [pp. 520-523]

    A. Legal rules--most states have enacted laws protecting corporate creditors by forbidding distribution of the firm's permanent capital in the form of dividends.

    B. Cash position--the firm must have cash available regardless of the level of past or current earnings in order to pay dividends.

    C. Access to capital markets--the easier the access to capital markets, the more able the firm is to pay dividends rather than retain earnings.

D. Desire for control.
   1. Small, closely-held firms may limit dividends to avoid restrictive borrowing provisions or the need to sell new stock.
   2. Established firms may feel pressure to pay dividends to avoid stockholders' demand for change of management.

E. Tax position of shareholders.
   1. High tax-bracket stockholders may prefer retention of earnings.
   2. Lower tax-bracket individuals, institutional investors, and corporations receiving dividends prefer higher dividend payout.
   3. Stockholder preferences for dividends or capital gains fosters investor behavior called the **clientele effect**. High tax bracket investors often invest in growth-oriented firms that pay no or low dividends. Low tax bracket investors often purchase stocks with high dividend payouts.

IV. Dividend Payment Procedures [pp. 523-524]

A. Dividends are usually paid quarterly.

B. Three key dividend dates:
   1. **Holder of record date**--the date the corporation examines its books to determine who is entitled to a cash dividend.
   2. **Ex-dividend date**--two business days prior to the holder of record date. If an investor buys a share of stock after the second day prior to the holder of record date, the investor's name would not appear on the firm's books.
   3. **Payment date**--approximate date of mailing of dividend checks.

V. Stock Dividends and Stock Splits [pp. 524-526]

A. **Stock dividends**--an additional distribution of stock shares, typically about 10% of outstanding amount.
   1. An *accounting* transfer is required at fair market from retained earnings. The par value of the stock dividend is transferred to the common stock account, and the remainder (if any) is added to the capital in excess of par account.
   2. Unless total cash dividends increase, the stockholder does not benefit from a stock dividend.
   3. Use:
      a. **Informational content**--retention of earnings for reinvestment.
      b. Camouflage inability to pay cash dividends.

B. **Stock split**--a distribution of stock that increases the total shares outstanding by 20%-25% or more.
   1. Accounting transfer from retained earnings is not required. Par value of stock is reduced, and the number of shares increases proportionately.
   2. Benefits to stockholders, if any, are difficult to identify.
   3. Primary purpose is to lower stock price into a more popular trading range.

VI. **Repurchase of Stock** [pp. 527-530]

A. Alternative to payment of dividends.
   1. Often used when firm has excess cash and inadequate investment opportunities.
   2. With the exception of a lower capital gains tax, the stockholder would be as well off with a cash dividend.

B. Other reasons for repurchase.

1. Management may deem that stock is selling at a very low price and is the best investment available.
2. Used for stock options or as part of a tender offer in a merger or acquisition.
3. To reduce the possibility of being "taken over."

VII. **Dividend Reinvestment Plans** [pp. 530-531]

A. Plans provide investors with an opportunity to buy additional shares of stock with the cash dividend paid by the company.

B. Types of plans:
1. The company sells treasury stock or authorized but unissued shares. The stock is often sold at a discount since no investment banking or underwriting fees have to be paid. This plan provides a cash flow to the company.
2. The company's transfer agent buys shares of stock in the market for the stockholder. This plan does not provide a cash flow to the firm but is a service to the stockholder.

C. Plans usually allow stockholders to supplement dividends with cash payments up to $1,000 per month in order to increase purchase of stock.

Chapter 18 - Multiple Choice Questions

1. One of the arguments for the relevancy of dividends is the: [p. 519]
   a. Resolution of uncertainty.
   b. Residual theory of dividends.
   c. Tax deductibility of dividends.
   d. Management entrenchment.
   e. NYSE requirements.

2. A firm that follows a residual dividend policy will probably have: [pp. 518-520]
   a. High dividends per share.
   b. Low dividends per share.
   c. Widely fluctuating dividends per share.
   d. Stable dividends per share.
   e. A high payout ratio.

3. Corporate creditors are protected against distribution of a firm's capital by: [p. 521]
   a. The cash position of the firm.
   b. The SEC.
   c. Legal rules.
   d. The NYSE.
   e. Dividend reinvestment plans.

4. The date on which a stockholder must be listed on the firm's books as the owner in order to receive declared dividends is the: [p. 524]
   a. Holder of record date.
   b. Payment date.
   c. Ex-dividend date.
   d. Dividend declaration date.
   e. Legal date.

5. Growth firms with high rates of return usually have: [pp. 517-518]
   a. High dividends.
   b. A high payout rate.
   c. A low retention rate.
   d. A high retention rate.
   e. A high proportion of stockholders who prefer dividends.

6. Which of the following requires an accounting transfer at fair market value from retained earnings? [pp. 524-525]
   a. Stock split
   b. Repurchase of stock
   c. Dividend reinvestment plans
   d. Stock dividend
   e. Declaration of a cash dividend

7. Stockholder preference for dividends or capital gains often leads to: [p. 523]
   a. A residual dividend policy.
   b. A clientele effect.
   c. Stock dividends.
   d. A repurchase of stock.
   e. High taxes.

8. Which of the following statements about U.S. corporations is correct? [p. 520]
   a. Dividends are more volatile than corporate earnings.
   b. There is no relationship between corporate earnings and dividends.
   c. All stock exchange listed firms must distribute at least 10% of earnings.
   d. The Tax Reform Act of 1986 encouraged firms to retain earnings.
   e. Corporate earnings are more volatile than dividends.

9. A firm with excess cash and inadequate investment opportunities may elect to: [p. 527]
   a. Declare a stock dividend.
   b. Split its stock.
   c. Reduce its cash dividends.
   d. Repurchase stock.
   e. Retain all earnings.

10. The payout ratio of U.S. corporations in the post-WW II era has been approximately: [p. 529]
    a. 10%-20%.
    b. 25%-30%.
    c. 35%-50%.
    d. 50%-60%.
    e. 60%-70%.

Multiple Choice Answer Key - Chapter 18

1. a	2. c	3. c	4. a	5. d
6. d	7. b	8. e	9. d	10. c

Chapter 18 - Problems

18-1. The stock of Jennifer Plummer Dance Academy is currently trading at $25 per share. The firm's dividend yield is 10%.

  (a) If the firm distributes 40% of its earnings, what are the earnings per share?

  (b) What is the firm's P/E ratio?

18-2. The Watkins Corporation has current aftertax earnings of $6,000,000.

  (a) If the firm follows a 60% payout policy, what amount of earnings will it retain?

  (b) How much will it retain under a residual dividend policy if it has the following acceptable investment opportunities: (1) $0; (2) $4,000,000; (3) $8,000,000.

18-3. The Bungling Brothers Circus Company recently experienced a 2-for-1 stock split. Its partial balance sheet after the split is presented below.

After

Common stock (12,000,000 shares at $1 par)	$12,000,000
Capital in excess of par	4,000,000
Retained earnings	10,000,000
	$26,000,000

  (a) Reproduce Bungling's partial balance sheet that existed before the stock split.

  (b) If the partial balance sheet above is the result of a 20% stock dividend, determine the pre stock dividend balance sheet. The price of Bungling's stock was $3 when the new stock was issued.

18-4.

D.I.V. CORPORATION
Balance Sheet

Cash	$ 2,000,000	Current liabilities	$18,000,000
Accounts receivable	10,000,000	Long-term debt	15,000,000
Inventory	25,000,000	Common stock	19,000,000
Plant & equipment	40,000,000	Retained earnings	25,000,000
	$77,000,000		$77,000,000

  (a) How much can D.I.V. Corporation legally pay in dividends?

  (b) What is the probable maximum dividend the firm can pay if it seeks to maintain a minimum cash balance of $1,000,000 and other asset balances at present levels?

  (c) Assume that D.I.V. is a rapidly growing firm that faces severe difficulty in raising needed capital. If substantial additional credit sales have been approved, is the passing (not paying) of dividends likely or unlikely?

18-5. You own 900 shares of Magfin Corporation which recently announced a 3-for-1 stock split. At the time of the announcement, the firm's stock price of $60 per share represented a P/E ratio of 20. The firm follows a 50% payout dividend policy.

(a) What was the market value of your stock holdings when the stock split was announced?

(b) Assuming that the $60 price has not impeded trading of the stock, what will be the likely price per share of your stock after the split?

(c) Compute the earnings per share before and after the stock split.

(d) Compute the dividends per share before and after the stock split.

(e) If the $60 stock price has retarded trading of the stock, are you likely to benefit from the split?

18-6. Rising Star Corporation plans to enlarge its capacity during the coming period. The increase in capacity will require $40,000,000 in additional assets. The firm anticipates net income of $20,000,000 and follows a 60% dividend payout policy. If Rising Star desires to maintain its debt/assets ratio of 40%, how much external equity and debt financing will be required?

Chapter 18 - Solutions

18-1. (a)

$$Dividend\ yield = \frac{dividend}{stock\ price} = .10$$

$$Dividend = \$25 \times .10 = \$2.50$$

$$Payout\ ratio = .4 = \frac{dividends\ per\ share}{earnings\ per\ share}$$

$$Payout\ ratio = .4 = \frac{\$2.50}{EPS}$$

$$EPS = \frac{\$2.50}{.4} = \mathbf{\$6.25}$$

(b)

$$P/E\ ratio = \frac{\$25.00}{\$6.25} = \mathbf{4}$$

18-2. (a) *Retention ratio* = 1 - payout rate
Retention ratio = 1 - .60 = .40

Retained earnings = .40 x $6,000,000 = **$2,400,000**

(b) (1) **None. All earnings will be distributed.**
     (2) *Retained earnings* = $6,000,000 - $4,000,000 = **$2,000,000**

(c) **All earnings will be retained.**

18-3. (a)

Before 2-for-1 Split

Common stock (6,000,000 shares at $2 par)	$12,000,000
Capital in excess of par	4,000,000
Retained earnings	10,000,000
	$26,000,000

(b)

Before 20% Stock Dividend

Common stock (10,000,000 shares at $1 par)	$10,000,000
Capital in excess of par	-0-
Retained earnings	16,000,000
	$26,000,000

Calculations:

$$\textit{Number of previously existing shares} = \frac{12,000,000}{1.2} = 10,000,000$$

$$\textit{Total par value of original stock} = \frac{\$12,000,000}{1.2} = \$10,000,000$$

$$\textit{Par value/share of original stock} = \frac{\$10,000,000}{10,000,000} = \$1$$

Change in capital in excess of par:

(new shares)(market price) - (new shares)(par value)
(2,000,000 x $3) - (2,000,000 x $1)
$6,000,000 - $2,000,000 = $4,000,000

Change in retained earnings = number of new shares x market value/share
Change in retained earnings = 2,000,000 x $3 = $6,000,000

18-4. (a) **$25,000,000**

(b) **$1,000,000**

(c) **Very likely**

18-5. (a) 900 x $60 = **$54,000**

(b) Likely price = $60/3 = **$20/share**

(c)   Before split: P/E = 20 = $60/E   E = **$3**

After split (assuming P/E remains at 20)
P/E = 20 = $20/E   E = **$1**

(d)   Assuming 50% payout

Dividend/share = (.5)(E) = (.5)($3) = **$1.50 before**
Dividend/share = (.5)($1) = **.50 after**

(e)   **Yes**

18-6.

$20,000,000	net income
.6	payout ratio
$12,000,000	dividends

$40,000,000	financing required
8,000,000	internal equity financing (earnings retention)
$32,000,000	**external financing** required

$40,000,000	
.4	
$16,000,000	**debt financing required** to maintain debt/assets ratio = .4

$32,000,000	external financing required
-16,000,000	debt financing
$16,000,000	**external equity financing needed**

Chapter 19

Summary: In this chapter the characteristics and uses of convertibles and warrants as issued securities are explained.

I. Convertible Securities [pp. 541-548]

    A. A convertible is a fixed income security, bond, or preferred stock that can be converted at the option of the holder into common stock. (The chapter focuses on convertible bonds.)

    B. Convertible terminology:
        1. **Conversion ratio**--number of shares of common stock into which the security may be converted.
        2. **Conversion price**--face value of bond divided by the conversion ratio.
        3. **Conversion value**--conversion ratio times the market price per share of common stock.
        4. **Conversion premium**--market value of convertible bond minus the larger of conversion value or pure bond value.
        5. **Pure bond value**--the value of the convertible bond as a straight bond; the present value of the annual interest payments and maturity payment discounted at the market rate of interest.

    C. Value of a convertible bond.
        1. At issue, investors pay a conversion premium, and the price of the convertible exceeds both the pure bond value and the conversion value.
        2. If the market price of the common stock exceeds the conversion price, the market value of the bond will rise above its par value to the conversion value or higher.
        3. The convertible bond's value is limited on the downside by its pure bond value.

    D. Disadvantages to the investor.
        1. All downside risk is not eliminated. When the conversion value is very high, the investor is subject to much downward price movement.
        2. The pure bond value will fall if interest rates rise.
        3. Interest rates on convertibles are less than on nonconvertible straight bonds of the same risk.
        4. Convertibles are usually subject to a call provision.

    E. Advantages to the corporation.
        1. Lower interest rate than a straight bond.
        2. May be only means of gaining access to the capital market.
        3. Enables the sale of stock at higher-than-market price.

    F. **Forcing conversion**.
        1. Conversion may be forced by calling the convertible when the conversion value exceeds the call price.
        2. Conversion is encouraged by a "step-up" provision in the conversion price.

    G. Accounting considerations.

        1. Prior to 1969 the possible dilution effect of convertible securities on earnings per share was not required to be reflected in financial reports.
        2. Currently, the accounting profession applies the concept of **basic earnings per share** and **diluted earnings per share**.
            a. Basic earnings per share is not adjusted for convertible securities.

b. Diluted earnings per share adjusts for all potential dilution from the issuance of any new share of stock arising from convertible bonds, convertible preferred stock, warrants, or any other options outstanding.

$$\text{Diluted earnings per share} = \frac{\text{adjusted earnings after taxes}}{\text{shares outstanding} + \text{all convertible securities}}$$

II. Warrants [pp. 549-553]

A. A **warrant** is an option to buy a stated number of shares of stock at a specified price over a given period.
1. Sweetens a debt issue.
2. Usually detachable.
3. Speculative; value dependent on market movement of stock.

B. Value of a warrant.
1. Applying this formula, the intrinsic value of a warrant may be found:

   Intrinsic value of warrant = [market value of common stock - exercise price of warrant] x number shares each warrant entitles holder to purchase

   $I = (M - E) \times N$

2. The actual price of the warrant may substantially exceed the intrinsic value due to the speculative nature of warrants. The amount above the intrinsic value is a speculative premium, S.

   $S = W - I$

   where W = warrant price
   I = intrinsic value of warrant

C. Use of warrants for corporate financing.
1. Enhances a debt issue.
2. Add-on in a merger or acquisition.
3. Cannot be forced with a call, but the exercise price is sometimes "stepped-up."
4. Equity base expands when warrants are exercised but the underlying debt remains.

D. Potential dilution of earnings per share upon exercise of warrants must be disclosed in financial reports.

III. Derivative Securities

A. Value is derived from an underlying security.

B. Options give the owner the right but not the obligation to buy or sell an underlying security at a set price for a given time period.
1. Call option: an option to buy. Standardized call options on the Chicago Board Options Exchange (CBOE) guarantee that the seller of the option will sell the option holder 100 shares of the associated stock at the specified price if the option is exercised within the stated time period.
2. Put option: an option to sell. A standardized put option on the CBOE is the same as the call except the seller of the option guarantees a purchase of 100 shares at the specified price.

C. Futures: contracts to buy or sell an asset (commodities, etc.) in the future for a specified price.

IV. Key Formulas

A. Diluted earnings per share [p. 548]

$$Diluted\ EPS = \frac{adjusted\ earnings\ after\ taxes}{shares\ outstanding\ +\ all\ convertible\ securities}$$

B. Intrinsic value of a warrant [p. 550]

$$I = (M - E)\ x\ N$$

C. Speculative premium on a warrant [p. 550]

$$S = W - I$$

Chapter 19 - Multiple Choice Questions

1. The difference between the price of a warrant and the warrant's intrinsic value is the: [p. 550]
    a. Exercise price.
    b. Conversion premium.
    c. Speculative premium.
    d. Pure bond value.
    e. Conversion ratio.

2. The floor value of a convertible bond is the: [p. 542]
    a. Conversion premium.
    b. Conversion value.
    c. Conversion price.
    d. Market price of common stock x conversion ratio.
    e. Pure bond value.

3. The pure bond value of a convertible bond will _____ when interest rates fall and the conversion value will _____ when the underlying stock price increases. [pp. 541-543]
    a. Rise, fall
    b. Fall, rise
    c. Fall, fall
    d. Rise, rise
    e. Not change, rise

4. The Templeton Company recently issued convertible bonds. The conversion price is $50 and its common stock is currently selling for $45 per share. The conversion ratio and conversion value of the bonds are: [p. 541]
    a. 50 and $1,000.
    b. 20 and $900.
    c. 20 and $1,000.
    d. 20 and $45.
    e. 50 and $900.

5. Which of the following statements about convertible bonds and warrants are correct? [Chpt. 19]
   a. A firm receives cash when warrants are exercised and when bonds are converted.
   b. A firm's equity base is increased when warrants are exercised and bonds are converted.
   c. Conversion may be forced when the call price exceeds the conversion value.
   d. Warrants normally sell below intrinsic value.
   e. The conversion option is usually detachable from a convertible bond.

6. Which of the following statements about the downside risk of a convertible bond is true? [p. 544]
   a. The conversion option eliminates downside risk.
   b. Downside risk is usually greatest at the time of issue of the convertible.
   c. Downside risk is greatest when the conversion value is high.
   d. Downside risk is greatest when the conversion value is below the pure bond value.
   e. Downside risk is greatest when the market price of a convertible is below its pure bond value.

7. A convertible bond: [p. 541]
   a. Is convertible at the option of the bond owner.
   b. Is convertible at the option of the bond issuer.
   c. Is automatically converted when the conversion price is stepped up.
   d. Has no value when the market price of the underlying stock is less than the conversion price.
   e. Usually has a higher coupon rate than a pure bond of equal risk.

8. Which of the following describes a difference in warrants and convertible bonds? [pp. 549-552]
   a. Warrants sweeten an issue.
   b. The conversion option is always exercised.
   c. Debt is eliminated when convertibles are converted but remains when warrants are exercised.
   d. The pure bond value falls when interest rates rise on a bond with warrants attached but not on convertible bonds.
   e. Warrants are callable.

9. Refer to Table 19-1 in the text. Which of the following is correct? [p. 553]
   a. Sepracor B bonds have no downside risk.
   b. Double-Click BB- bonds are priced primarily as convertible bonds.
   c. Xerox AA bonds will probably be converted voluntarily.
   d. If the call premium is 5%, conversion of Ken-McGee BB+ bonds could be forced.
   e. All of the above

10. A warrant is selling for $5. The warrant will allow a holder to purchase one share of stock for $60. The current price of the stock is $60. The intrinsic value and speculative premium of this warrant are: [p. 561]
   a. $60 and $60.
   b. $0 and $0.
   c. $60 and $5.
   d. $0 and $5.
   e. $5 and $0.

Multiple Choice Answer Key - Chapter 19

1. c	2. e	3. d	4. b	5. b
6. c	7. a	8. c	9. d	10. d

Chapter 19 - Problems

19-1. Blackwell Lumber Company has an outstanding convertible bond that is currently quoted at $900 in the bond market. The bond has a coupon rate of 9% and matures in 15 years. The conversion price is $50, and the common stock is currently selling at $40.

(a) How many shares of stock can the convertible bondholders obtain by converting?

(b) Why is the bond selling for an amount larger than its conversion value?

(c) If the stock price has not changed since the bond was first issued and the pure bond value was $750, what was the conversion premium at the issue date if the bonds were sold at their $1,000 face value?

(d) If the stock rises to $60 per share, what will be the approximate price of the bond?

19-2. Roemer Engineering has warrants outstanding that entitle the holder to purchase one new share of common stock for $23. The stock is currently selling for $38. The warrant is quoted at $20.

(a) What is the intrinsic value of the warrant?

(b) How much is the speculative premium on the warrant?

(c) As the warrant nears maturity, will the speculative premium increase or decrease?

(d) Suppose you bought a share of the firm's common stock at $38. If the stock price rises to $57, what would be your percentage gain? If you had bought a warrant for its intrinsic value instead, what would be your percentage gain?

(e) If the price of the stock were $19, what would be the intrinsic value of the warrant? Will the warrant sell at this price?

19-3. Flintstone, Inc., has a convertible bond outstanding bearing a coupon rate of 10%. The bond which matures in 10 years is convertible into 20 shares of common stock. The common stock is presently selling at $40 per share.

(a) If the current interest rate on bonds of the same risk class is 12%, what will be the pure bond value of this bond?

(b) What is the conversion price?

(c) What will be the price of the bond under the condition stated above?

(d) Assuming a call price of 110, would Flintstone be able to force conversion when the stock was selling for $52?

19-4. The JMA Corporation produced net income of $10,000,000 during the past year. The firm has 3,000,000 shares of common stock outstanding. JMA also has a $25,000,000 issue of convertible bonds outstanding which pays 8% interest annually. The firm is in the 34% tax bracket. The conversion price of the $1,000 convertible bonds is $40.

(a) Compute the basic earnings per share for the firm.

(b) Compute the diluted earnings per share for the firm.

Chapter 19 - Solutions

19-1. (a)

$$Conversion\ ratio = \frac{face\ value\ of\ bond}{conversion\ price}$$

$$Conversion\ ratio = \frac{\$1,000}{\$50} = 20$$

(b) Conversion value = price/share of stock x conversion ratio
Conversion value = $40 x 20 = $800

The bond is selling above conversion value because **the convertible bond's value as a pure bond is greater than its conversion value**.

(c) Conversion premium = market value of bond - conversion value of bond
Conversion premium = $1,000 - $800 = **$200**

(d) The price of the bond will rise above $1,000 as the stock price rises above the conversion price. If the stock price rises to $60, the bond will sell at approximately **$1,200** = 20 x $60

19-2. (a) Intrinsic value of a warrant = [market value of common stock - exercise price of warrant] x number of shares warrant entitles holder to purchase

Intrinsic value of a warrant = [$38 - $23] x 1 = **$15**

(b) Speculative premium of warrant = market price of warrant - intrinsic value of warrant
Speculative premium = $20 - $15 = **$5**

(c) **Decrease**

(d) Buy stock.

$$Percentage\ gain = \frac{57 - 38}{38} = \frac{19}{38} = 50\%$$

Buy warrant.

Intrinsic value of warrant after stock price rises:

Intrinsic value of warrant = (57 - 23) x 1 = 34

$$Percentage\ gain = \frac{34 - 15}{15} = \frac{19}{15} = \textbf{127\%}$$

(e) *Intrinsic value of warrant* = ($19 - $23) x 1 = **-$4**

No. The warrant cannot sell below zero. A price of -$4 would mean that the holder would pay $4 for someone to take the warrant--an unlikely occurrence!

19-3. (a) *Bond price = present value of interest stream + present value of lump-sum payment*
Bond price = $A \times PV_{IFA}(n = 10, i = 12\%) + FV \times PV_{IF}(n = 10th, i = 12\%)$
Bond price = 100(5.65) + 1,000(.322)
BP = $565 + $322
BP = **$887**

(b)

$$Conversion\ price = \frac{face\ value\ of\ bond}{conversion\ ratio}$$

$$Conversion\ price = \frac{\$1,000}{20} = \textbf{\$50}$$

(c) *Conversion value* = 20 x $40 = $800
Price of bond will be **$887**. The pure bond value is greater than the conversion value.

(d) *Conversion value* = 20 x $52 = $1,040
No, convertible bondholders would probably accept the call.

19-4. (a)

$$Basic\ earnings\ per\ share = \frac{earnings\ after\ tax}{shares\ of\ common\ stock}$$

$$Basic\ EPS = \frac{\$10,000,000}{3,000,000} = \textbf{\$3.33}$$

(b)

$$Diluted\ EPS = \frac{adjusted\ earnings\ after\ taxes}{shares\ outstanding + all\ convertible\ securities}$$

Interest savings = (1 - .34) ($25,000,000 x .08) = $1,320,000

Adjusted earnings after taxes = current net income + interest savings

$$\text{Conversion ratio} = \frac{\$1,000}{\$40} = 25 \text{ shares}$$

$$\text{Total new shares} = \frac{\$25,000,000}{\$1,000} \times 25 = 625,000$$

$$\text{Diluted EPS} = \frac{\$10,000,000 + \$1,320,000}{3,000,000 + 625,000} = \frac{\$11,320,000}{3,625,000} = \textbf{\$3.12}$$

Chapter 20

External Growth through Mergers

Summary: This chapter focuses on the significant financial and management variables influencing the merger decision including the price to pay, the accounting implications, the stock market effect and the motivation of the participating parties.

I. Motives and Characteristics of Recent Merger Movements [pp. 567-568]

    A. The impetus for mergers in the mid-1990s and early 2000s has been low interest rates, rising stock prices, changing regulation, intense competition, evolving technology, and other factors as firms position themselves for the 21st century.

    B. Major players in the recent merger movement have been communication giants (America Online and Time Warner) financial institutions and insurance companies (Travelers, Inc. and Citicorp), and oil giants (Exxon and Mobil). Other major merger areas included telecommunications, healthcare, aerospace, food processing, and entertainment industries.

II. Motives for Business Combinations [pp. 569-572]

    A. Business combinations may be either **mergers** or **consolidations**.
        1. Merger: A combination of two or more companies in which the resulting firm maintains the identity of the acquiring company.
        2. Consolidation: Two or more companies are combined to form an entirely new entity.

    B. Financial motives.
        1. Risk reduction as a result of the **portfolio effect**.
            a. Lower required rate of return by investors.
            b. Higher value of the firm.
        2. Improved financing posture.
            a. Greater access to financial markets to raise debt and equity capital.
            b. Attract more prestigious investment bankers to handle financing.
            c. Strengthen cash position and/or improve debt/equity ratio.
        3. Obtain a **tax loss carryforward**.

    C. Nonfinancial motives.
        1. Expand management and marketing capabilities.
        2. Acquire new products.
        3. **Synergism**: 2 + 2 = 5.

    D. Motivation of selling stockholders.
        1. Desire to receive acquiring firm's stock which may have greater acceptability in the market.
        2. Provides opportunity to diversify their holdings.
        3. Gain on sale of stock at an attractive price.
        4. Attractive post-merger management contracts as well as directorships.
        5. Bias against smaller businesses.

III. Terms of Exchange [pp. 572-575]

    A. Cash purchases.

1. Capital budgeting decision: Net present value of purchase of going concern = present value of cash inflows including anticipated synergistic benefits minus cash outlays including adjustment for tax shield benefit from any tax loss carryforward.
2. Some firms were purchased for cash in the last two decades at a price below the replacement cost of their assets.

B. Stock for stock exchange.
   1. Emphasizes the impact of the merger on earnings per share.
   2. If the P/E ratio of the acquiring firm is greater than the P/E ratio of the acquired firm, there will be an immediate increase in earnings per share.
   3. Stockholders of the acquired firm are usually more concerned with market value exchanged than earnings, dividends, or book value exchanged.

C. In addition to the immediate impact on earnings per share, the acquiring firm must be concerned with the long-run impact of the merger on market value.
   1. An acquired firm may have a low P/E ratio because its future rate of growth is expected to be low. In the long run, the acquisition may reduce the acquiring firm's earnings per share and its market value.
   2. The acquisition of a firm with a higher P/E ratio causes an immediate reduction in earnings per share. In the long run, however, the higher growth rate of the acquired firm may cause earnings per share, and the market value of the acquiring company to be greater than if the merger did not take place.

D. Determinants of earnings per share impact of a merger.
   1. Exchange ratio.
   2. Relative growth rates.
   3. Relative sizes of the firms.

E. Portfolio effect.
   1. If the risk assessment of the acquiring firm is decreased by a merger, its market value will rise even if the earnings per share remain constant.
   2. Two types of risk reduction may be accomplished by a merger.
      a. Business risk reduction may result from acquiring a firm that is influenced by an opposite set of factors in the business cycle.
      b. Financial risk reduction may result from a lower use of debt in the postmerger financial structure of the acquiring firm.

IV. Accounting Considerations in Mergers and Acquisitions [pp. 575-576]

A. A merger prior to December 2000 was treated as either a **pooling of interests** or a **purchase of assets** on the books of the acquiring firm.

B. Criteria for pooling of interests treatment.
   1. The acquiring firm issues only common stock, with rights identical to its old outstanding voting stock in exchange for substantially all the voting stock of the acquired company.
   2. The acquired firm's stockholders maintain an ownership position within the surviving firm.
   3. The merged firm does not intend to dispose of a significant portion of the assets of the combined companies within two years.
   4. The combination is effected in a single transaction.

C. Purchase of assets
   1. Necessary when the tender offer is in cash, bonds, preferred stock, or common stock with restricted rights.

2. Any excess of purchase price over book value is recorded as **goodwill** and written off over a maximum period of 40 years.

D. Pooling of interests versus purchase of assets.
    1. The nondeductibility of goodwill expense for tax purposes was a disadvantage of the purchase of assets because reported income is reduced without any tax relief.
    2. Under the plan adopted by the Financial Accounting Standards Board on December 6, 2000, firms will no longer use pooling of interests. Purchase of assets will be used regardless of circumstances. Also goodwill may now remain on the books of the acquiring firm and does not have to be written off against future earnings.

V. Negotiated Versus Tender Offers [pp. 576-577]

A. Friendly versus unfriendly mergers.
    1. Most mergers are friendly, and the terms are negotiated by the officers and directors of the involved companies.
    2. Less friendly offers, **takeover tender offers** have occurred more frequently, and many proposed mergers have been opposed by the management of candidate firms.

B. Unfriendly takeover attempts have resulted in additions to the Wall Street vocabulary.
    1. **Saturday Night Special**--a surprise offer made right before the market closes for the weekend.
    2. **White Knight**--a third firm that management of the target firm calls upon to help avoid the initial, unwanted tender offer.
    3. **Leveraged takeover**--the acquiring firm negotiates a loan based on the target company's assets (particularly a target company with large cash balances).

C. Actions by target companies to avoid unwanted takeovers.
    1. White Knight arrangements.
    2. Moving corporate offices to states with protective provisions against takeovers.
    3. Buying up company's own stock to reduce amount available for takeover.
    4. Encouraging employees to buy stock under corporate pension plan.
    5. Increasing dividends to keep stockholders happy.
    6. Staggering election of members of the board of directors.
    7. Buying other firms to increase size.
    8. Avoiding large cash balances which encourage leveraged takeover attempts.
    9. Poison pills (discussed in Chapter 17).

VI. Premium Offers and Stock Price Movements [pp. 577-579]

A. Typically, the average premium paid over market value in mergers or acquisitions is 40% to 60%. Much of the price movement often occurs before the public announcement of the merger offer.

B. Substantial profits can be made by buying the stock of merger candidates. The strategy is risky, however, because the merger may be called off. If an investor purchases stock after the price has risen, substantial losses may be incurred if the potential merger is not consumated.

C. **Two-step buyout**.
    1. The acquiring firm attempts to gain control by offering a very high cash price for 51% of the outstanding shares of the target firm. Simultaneously, a second lower price is announced that will be paid, either in cash, stock, or bonds at a subsequent point in time.

2. The procedure provides a strong incentive for stockholders of the target firm to quickly react to the offer. Also, the two-step buyout enables the acquiring firm to pay a lower total price than if a single offer is made.
3. The SEC is keeping a close watch on the two-step buyout because of fears that the less sophisticated stockholders may be at a disadvantage when competing against arbitrageurs and institutional investors.

Chapter 20 - Multiple Choice Questions

1. A surprise takeover offer made immediately before the market closes for the weekend is called a: [p. 576]
   a. White Knight.
   b. Saturday Night Special.
   c. Leveraged takeover.
   d. Poison pill.
   e. Pooling of interests.

2. A business combination of two or more firms resulting in a new entity is a(n): [p. 569]
   a. Merger.
   b. Acquisition.
   c. Synergism.
   d. Consolidation.
   e. Purchase of assets.

3. Prior to December 2000, which of the following often required goodwill to be written off over a period of time? (Choose the best answer.) [pp. 575-576]
   a. Merger
   b. Acquisition
   c. Purchase of assets
   d. Pooling of interests
   e. Consolidation

4. An acquisition attempt in which an acquiring firm announces an offer for shares to be followed later by a lower offer is called a(n): [p. 578]
   a. Two-step buyout.
   b. Holding company.
   c. Pooling of interests.
   d. Goodwill offer.
   e. Saturday Night Special.

5. Which of the following discourages takeover attempts: [p. 577]
   a. Large cash balances of target firms
   b. Business risk reduction
   c. Financial risk reduction
   d. Increasing dividends of target firm
   e. Synergism

6. Which of the following is a financial motive for business combination? [pp. 569-570]
   a. Expansion of marketing capabilities
   b. Acquisition of new products
   c. Attract prestigious investment bankers
   d. 2 + 2 = 5
   e. Obtain a corporate jet

7. Which of the following is probably the most important nonfinancial motive for a merger? [p. 571]
   a. Acquisition of new products
   b. Synergism
   c. Portfolio effect
   d. Expansion of management capabilities
   e. Tickets to the Super Bowl

8. The acquisition of a company that has a lower P/E ratio will: [p. 574]
   a. Not affect the current earnings per share of the acquiring firm.
   b. Raise the current earnings per share of the acquiring firm.
   c. Lower the current earnings per share of the acquiring firm.
   d. May raise or lower the current earnings per share of the acquiring firm.
   e. Raise the current earnings per share of the acquired firm.

9. Which of the following combination of companies constituted the largest merger in the last decade? [p. 568]
   a. Nations Bank/Bank America
   b. AT&T/MediaOne Group
   c. Pfizer/Warner Lambert
   d. Exxon/Mobil
   e. America Online/Time Warner

10. The typical premium paid over market value in mergers is: [p. 577]
    a. 5% - 10%.
    b. 20% - 25%.
    c. 40% - 60%.
    d. 80% - 90%.
    e. Over 100%.

Multiple Choice Answer Key - Chapter 20

| 1. b | 2. d | 3. c | 4. a | 5. d |
| 6. c | 7. b | 8. b | 9. e | 10. c |

Chapter 20 - Problems

20-1. Gibraltar is considering the acquisition of Roller Coaster Corporation. Although Roller Coaster is expected to have a bright future, it has recently experienced large financial losses and has an operating loss carryforward of $2,000,000. Gibraltar's taxable earnings have varied only slightly in recent years and are expected to be $800,000; $815,000; and $825,000 for the next three years if the proposed acquisition does not take place. Gibraltar has a 34% tax rate.

   (a) What will Gibraltar's taxes be for the next three years if the proposed acquisition is accomplished (assume Roller Coaster operations break even during this period)?

   (b) What will be the tax savings to Gibraltar from the acquisition?

   (c) If Gibraltar has a cost of capital of 14%, what would be the value of the tax savings available from the acquisition?

   (d) Rework (a) under the assumption that Roller Coaster operations will generate $500,000 per year in taxable income.

20-2. The Cain Corporation can expand by acquiring Abel Corporation for $1,500,000 cash. The Cain Corporation would be able to lower its taxes as a result of Abel's $500,000 tax loss carryforward. Cain officials think that Abel would contribute $200,000 aftertax cash flow per year for a period of 10 years. Cain is expected to have $250,000 per year in taxable income if the merger is not consumated. Cain is in a 40% tax bracket and its cost of capital is 12%. Should Cain acquire Abel for $1,500,000?

20-3. The management of the Block Corporation are considering a cash purchase of Hirt Corporation for $3,000,000. Hirt has a $300,000 tax loss carryforward that could be used immediately. The expected cash inflows and synergistic benefits to be derived from the purchase of Hirt are:

Years	1-5	6-10	11-15
Cash inflow	$450,000	$300,000	$150,000
Synergistic benefits	30,000	25,000	10,000

Block has a cost of capital of 10% and a 34% tax rate. Should Block acquire the Hirt Corporation?

20-4. Officials of the North Corporation and the South Corporation have been negotiating the terms of a merger of the two firms. The financial information for the prospective merging firms is as follows:

	North	South
Total earnings	$ 500,000	$ 700,000
# shares of stock outstanding	200,000	350,000
Earnings per share	$ 2.50	$ 2.00
Price-earnings ratio	10	13
Market price per share	$ 25.00	$ 26.00

(a) If one share of South Corporation is traded for one share of North Corporation, what will postmerger earnings per share be? (Assuming earnings remain the same.)

(b) If South Corporation pays a 20% premium over market value of North Corporation, how many shares will be issued?

(c) With a 20% premium, what will postmerger earnings per share be?

(d) Suppose a 10% synergistic increase in total earnings is effected by the merger. What will postmerger earnings per share be if a 20% premium is paid?

20-5. Apple Corporation has agreed to a 40% premium over market value exchange of stock with Orange Corporation. The financial information for the two firms is as follows:

	Orange Corp.	Apple Corp.
Total earnings	$8,000,000	$20,000,000
# of shares of stock outstanding	2,000,000	8,000.000
Earnings per share	$4.00	$2.50
Price-earnings ratio	12	8
Market price per share	$48.00	$20.00
Projected annual growth rate for next 10 years	14%	4%

(a) Compute postmerger earnings per share.

(b) Compute the postmerger growth rate for the combined firms for the next 10 years.

(c) Project no-merger and postmerger earnings per share for Apple Corporation for the next 10 years.

(d) Compare the premerger and postmerger position of a shareholder in Orange Corporation. Assume that the postmerger P/E ratio is 10 and the shareholder owns 100 shares prior to the merger.

(e) Compare the with-merger and without-merger position of a stockholder in Apple Corporation at the end of years 1 and 10. Assume that the stockholder owns 100 shares and the postmerger P/E ratio is 10 and the premerger P/E ratio is 8.

Chapter 20 - Solutions

20-1. (a)   *Gibraltar's Taxes with Acquisition*

	Year 1	Year 2	Year 3
Beforetax earnings	$800,000	$815,000	$ 825,000
Tax loss carryforward	800,000	815,000	385,000
Taxable income	$ 0	$ 0	$440,000
Taxes (34%)	$ 0	$ 0	$149,600

(b)   *Gibraltar's Taxes Without Acquisition*

	Year 1	Year 2	Year 3
Beforetax earnings	$800,000	$815,000	$825,000
Taxes (34%)	$272,000	$277,100	$280,500

Tax Savings from Acquisition

	Year 1	Year 2	Year 3
Taxes without acquisition	$272,000	$277,100	$280,500
Taxes with acquisition	0	0	149,600
Tax savings	$272,000	$277,100	$130,900

*Total tax savings = $272,000 + $277,100 + $130,900 = **$680,000***

Total tax savings can also be found in the following manner:

Tax loss carry forward x tax rate

$2,000,000 x .34 = **$680,000**

As will be shown in (*c*), the **value** of the tax savings, however, differs from the amount of the tax savings.

(c) *Value of tax savings = $272,000($PV_{IF}$, n = 1, i = 14%) + $277,100($PV_{IF}$, n = 2, i = 14%)*
        + $130,900($PV_{IF}$, n = 3, i = 14%)

Value of tax savings = $272,000(.877) + $277,100(.769) + $130,900(.675)

*Value of tax savings = $238,544 + $213,090 + $88,358 = **$539,992***

(d)   *Gibraltar's Taxes with Acquisition and $500,000 Profit/Year from RC*

	Year 1	Year 2	Year 3
Beforetax earnings	$1,300,000	$1,315,000	$1,325,000
Tax loss carryforward	1,300,000	700,000	0
Taxable income	$ 0	$ 615,000	$1,325,000
Taxes	$ 0	$ 209,100	$ 450,500

20-2. Tax savings from tax loss carryforward of $500,000 ($250,000 in each of first two years since Cain has $250,000 taxable income annually).

Year 1	Year 2
$250,000	$250,000
.4	.4
$100,000	$100,000

Value of Abel Corporation to Cain Corporation

Value of Abel = $200,000($PV_{IFA}$, n = 10, i = 12%) + $100,000($PV_{IFA}$, n = 2, i = 12%)

Value of Abel = $200,000(5.650) + $100,000(1.690)

*Value of Abel = $1,130,000 + $169,000 = **$1,299,000***

The value of Abel Corporation to Cain Corporation is $1,299,000 and **should not be purchased for $1,500,000**.

20-3.   *Cash Outflow*

Purchase price	$3,000,000
Less tax shield from tax loss carryforward	204,000
(.34 x $600,000)	
Net cash outflow	$2,796,000

	Cash Inflows		
	Years 1-5	Years 6-10	Years 11-15
Cash inflow	$450,000	$300,000	$150,000
Synergistic benefits	30,000	25,000	10,000
Total cash inflow	$480,000	$325,000	$160,000

Present value of inflows = $480,000(PV$_{IFA}$, n = 5, i = 10%) + $325,000(PV$_{IFA}$, n = 10 - 5, i = 10%) + $160,000(PV$_{IFA}$, n = 15 - 10, i = 10%)

Present value of inflows = $480,000(3.791) + $325,000(6.145 - 3.791) + $160,000(7.606 -6.145)

Present value of inflows = $1,819,680 + $765,050 + $233,760 = $2,818,490

Net present value = $2,818,490 - $2,796,000 = **$22,490**

Block Corporation should acquire the Hirt Corporation.

20-4. (a) Postmerger earnings per share

Total earnings = $500,000 + $700,000 = $1,200,000

Number of shares outstanding = 200,000 + 350,000 = 550,000

$$New\ EPS = \frac{\$1,200,000}{550,000} = \$2.18\ (rounded)$$

(b) If a 20% premium is paid, shareholders of North Corporation would receive [$25 + $25(.20)] = $30 worth of South Corporation stock for each share of stock held.

Total value of stock paid to North Corporation shareholders will be
200,000 x $30 = $6,000,000.

Number of shares issued = $6,000,000/$26 = **230,769** (rounded)

(c) Postmerger earnings per share with a 20% premium will be:

Postmerger EPS = $1,200,000/580,769 = **$2.07** (rounded)

(d) Postmerger earnings with a 10% synergistic increase in total earnings will be:

Postmerger earnings = $1,200,000 + $1,200,000(.10) = $1,320,000

Postmerger EPS with a 10% synergistic effect and a 20% premium equals $1,320,000/580,769 = **$2.27** (rounded).

20-5. (a) Number of shares issued

Value paid per share of Orange = $48 + $48(.4) = $67.20

Total value paid = $67.20(2,000,000) = $134,400,000

Number of shares issued = $134,400,000/$20.00 = 6,720,000

Postmerger earnings per share

$28,000,000/14,720,000 = **$1.90** (rounded)

(b) Postmerger growth rate

8/28(14%) + 20/28(4%) = **6.86%** (rounded)

(c)

Expected Earnings Per Share for Apple Corporation with and without Merger

	Without Merger			With Merger		
Year	Beginning EPS	Growth Rate	Expected EPS	Beginning EPS	Growth Rate	Expected EPS
1	$2.50	4%	$2.60	$1.90	6.86%	$2.03
2	2.60	4	2.70	2.03	6.86	2.17
3	2.70	4	2.81	2.17	6.86	2.32
4	2.81	4	2.92	2.32	6.86	2.48
5	2.92	4	3.04	2.48	6.86	2.65
6	3.04	4	3.16	2.65	6.86	2.83
7	3.16	4	3.29	2.83	6.86	3.02
8	3.29	4	3.42	3.02	6.86	3.23
9	3.42	4	3.56	3.23	6.86	3.45
10	3.56	4	3.70	3.45	6.86	3.69

(d) Value of premerger shares = $48 x 100 = **$4,800**

Total premerger earnings = $4 x 100 = **$400**

Number of postmerger shares per premerger share $= \dfrac{\$48 + \$48(.4)}{\$20} = 3.36$

Total number of postmerger shares = 100 x 3.36 = 336

Price of postmerger shares = 10 x $1.90 = $19.00

Value of postmerger shares = 336 x $19 = **$6,384**

Amount of postmerger earnings = 336 x $1.90 = **$638.40**

(e)

			Without Merger			
Year	EPS	Number of Shares	Total Earnings	P/E Ratio	Price Per Share	Market Value of Stock
1	$2.60	100	**$260**	8	$20.80	**$2,080**
10	3.70	100	**370**	8	29.60	**2,960**

			With Merger			
Year	EPS	Number of Shares	Total Earnings	P/E Ratio	Price Per Share	Market Value of Stock
1	$2.03	100	**$203**	10	$20.30	**$2,030**
10	3.69	100	**369**	10	36.90	**3,690**

Summary: This chapter deals with the international dimensions of corporate finance and provides a basis for understanding the complexities of international financial decisions.

I.   Introduction [pp. 586-587]

    A.   The world economy is becoming increasingly integrated and nations are dependent on one another for many valuable and scarce resources.

    B.   It is impossible for any country to isolate itself from the international developments in an integrated world economy.

    C.   The typical corporation is becoming more global in focus and many U.S. firms derive the majority of their sales and profits from foreign markets.

    D.   International business operations are complex and risky and require special understanding.

II. The **Multinational Corporation (MNC)** [pp. 588-589]

    A.   Basic forms of a MNC.
        1.   **Exporter**--exportation to foreign markets of domestically produced products.
        2.   **Licensing agreement**--granting of a license to an independent local (in the foreign country) firm to use the "exporting" firm's technology.
        3.   **Joint venture**--cooperative business operation with a firm (or firms) in the foreign country.
        4.   **Fully owned foreign subsidiary**.

    B.   International environment versus domestic environment.
        1.   More risky--in addition to normal business risks, the MNC is faced with **foreign exchange risk** and **political risk**. The portfolio risk of the parent company, however, may be reduced if foreign and domestic operations are not highly correlated.
        2.   Often more profitable.
        3.   More complex--the laws, customs, and economic environment of the host country may vary in many respects.
            a.   Rates of inflation.
            b.   Tax rules.
            c.   Structure and operation of financial institutions.
            d.   Financial policies and practices.
            e.   Work habits and wages of laborers.

III. **Foreign Exchange Rates** [pp. 597-605]

    A.   To facilitate international trade, currencies must be exchanged. For example, an exporter will usually desire payment in the currency of his home country. The importer must swap his domestic currency for the currency desired by the exporter in order to pay his bill.

    B.   Factors affecting exchange rates:
        1.   Supply of and demand for the currencies of the various countries.
        2.   The degree of central bank intervention.
        3.   Inflation rate differentials (**Purchasing Power Parity Theory**).

4. Interest rate differentials (**Interest Rate Parity Theory**).
5. **Balance of payments**.
6. Government policies.
7. Other factors:
    a. Capital market movements.
    b. Changes in supply of and demand for the products and services of individual countries.
    c. Labor disputes.

C. Many variables affect currency exchange rates. The importance of each variable or set of variables will change as economic and political conditions change throughout the world.

D. Spot rates, forward rates, and cross rates.
1. **Spot rate**--the exchange rate between currencies with *immediate* delivery.
2. **Forward rate**--the rate of exchange between currencies when delivery will occur in the *future*.
3. **Cross rate**--the exchange rate between currencies such as French francs and British pounds based on their exchange rate with another currency such as U.S. dollars.

E. Foreign exchange risk--the possibility of experiencing a drop in revenue or an increase in cost in an international transaction due to a change in foreign exchange rates.
1. There are two types of foreign exchange risk exposure.
    a. Accounting or **translation exposure**--depends upon accounting rules established by the parent company's government. Under SFAS 52, all foreign currency denominated assets and liabilities are converted at the rate of exchange in effect on the date of balance sheet preparation.
    b. **Transaction exposure**--in the U.S., foreign exchange gains and losses are reflected in the income statement for the current period--this increases the volatility of earnings per share.
2. There are three strategies used to minimize transaction exposure.
    a. Hedging in the forward exchange market--the recipient (seller) of foreign currency in an international transaction sells a **forward contract** to assure the amount that will be received in domestic currency.
    b. Hedging in the money market--the recipient borrows foreign currency in the amount to be received and then immediately converts to domestic currency. When the receivable is collected, the loan is paid off.
    c. Hedging in the currency futures market--**futures contracts** in foreign currencies began trading in the International Monetary Market (IMM) of the Chicago Mercantile Exchange on May 16, 1972, and on the London International Financial Futures Exchange (LIFFE) in September 1982.

IV. Foreign Investment Decisions [pp. 598-601]

A. Reasons for U.S. firms to invest in foreign countries:
1. Fear of import tariffs (in foreign countries).
2. Lower production costs particularly with regards to labor costs.
3. Ease of entry because of advanced American technology.
4. Tax advantages.
5. Strategic considerations--competition.
6. International diversification.

B. Foreign firms are expanding their investment in the United States.
1. Foreign investments in the United States provide employment for millions of people.
2. Reasons for foreign expansion in U.S.:
    a. International diversification.
    b. Strategic considerations.

> c. Increasing labor costs.
> d. Saturated markets.
> e. Shortage of land for development.
> f. Large market in U.S.
> g. Labor restrictions overseas.
> h. Access to advanced technology.
> i. Political stability.

C. Analysis of political risk.
> 1. The structure of the foreign government and/or those in control may change many times during the lengthy period necessary to recover an investment. "Unfriendly" changes may result in:
> > a. Foreign exchange restriction.
> > b. Foreign ownership limitations.
> > c. Blockage of **repatriation of earnings**.
> > d. Expropriation of the foreign subsidiary's assets.
> 2. Safeguards against political risk.
> > a. A thorough investigation of the country's political stability prior to investment.
> > b. Joint ventures with local (foreign) companies.
> > c. Joint ventures with multiple companies representing multiple countries.
> > d. Insurance through the federal government agency, **Overseas Private Investment Corporation (OPIC)** or private insurance companies.

V. Financing International Business Operations [pp. 601-608]

A. **Letters of credit**--in order to reduce the risk of nonpayment, an exporter may require an importer to furnish a letter of credit. The letter of credit is normally issued by the importers bank and guarantees payment to the exporter upon delivery of the merchandise if the specified conditions are met.

B. Export credit insurance--a private association of 60 U.S. insurance firms, the **Foreign Credit Insurance Association (FCIA)**, may provide insurance against nonpayment of foreign customers.

C. Funding of transactions.
> 1. **Eximbank (Export-Import Bank)**--facilitates the financing of U.S. exports through several programs.
> 2. Loans from the parent company or sister affiliate.
> > a. **Parallel loans**--an arrangement where two parent firms in different countries each make a loan to the affiliate of the other parent. The procedure eliminates foreign exchange risk.
> > b. **Fronting loans**--loans from a parent firm to a foreign subsidiary via a bank located in the foreign country.
> 3. **Eurodollar loans**--loans from foreign banks that are denominated in dollars.
> > a. There are many participants in the Eurodollar market from throughout the world particularly the U.S., Canada, Western Europe, and Japan.
> > b. Lower borrowing costs and the absence of compensating balance requirements are significant incentives for U.S. firms.
> > c. The lending rate is based on the **London Interbank Offered Rate (LIBOR)**.
> > d. Lending in the Eurodollar market is almost exclusively done by commercial banks. Large Eurocurrency loans are frequently syndicated and managed by a lead bank.
> 4. **Eurobond market**--long-term funds may be secured by issuing Eurobonds. These bonds are sold throughout the world but are denominated primarily in U.S. dollars and deutsche marks.

a. Disclosure requirements are less stringent than required by the SEC on domestic issues.
b. Registration costs are lower than in U.S.
c. Some tax advantages exist.
d. Caution must be exercised because of the exposure to foreign exchange risk.

5. International equity--selling common stock to residents of a foreign country provides financing and also reduces political risk.
a. Multinational firms list their shares on major stock exchanges around the world. Half the stocks listed on the Amsterdam stock exchange are foreign.
b. Marketing securities internationally requires firms to adjust their procedures. For example, commercial banks have a dominant role in the securities business throughout Europe.

6. **International Finance Corporation (IFC)**--the IFC was established in 1956 and is a unit of the World Bank. Its objective is to promote economic development in the 119-member countries of the World Bank.
a. A multinational firm may be able to raise equity capital by selling partial ownership to the IFC.
b. The IFC decides to participate in the venture on the basis of profitability and the potential benefit to the host country.
c. Once the venture is well established, the IFC frees up its capital by selling its ownership interest.

VI. Unsettled Issues in International Finance [p. 608]

A. The complexity of the multinational business environment generates questions for which there are no easy answers.
1. Should a foreign affiliate design a capital structure similar to that of the parent firm or one that fits the acceptable pattern of the host country?
2. Who should determine the dividend policy of a foreign affiliate--the affiliate management or the parent management?

B. Successful participation in the international business environment requires cohesive, coordinated financial management.

Chapter 21 - Multiple Choice Questions

1. The _____ is the exchange rate between currencies with immediate delivery. [p. 593]
   a. Cross rate
   b. Transaction rate
   c. Spot rate
   d. Forward rate
   e. LIBOR

2. Which of the following may provide insurance against nonpayment by foreign customers? [p. 603]
   a. OPIC
   b. IFC
   c. IMM
   d. FCIA
   e. FASB

3. Which of the following is a loan from a parent firm to a foreign subsidiary via a bank located in the foreign country? [p. 604]
    a. Parallel loan
    b. Letter of credit
    c. IFC loan
    d. Fronting loan
    e. LIBOR loan

4. The most widely used currencies in the Eurobond market are: [p. 606]
    a. U.S. dollars and British pounds.
    b. Deutsche marks and British pounds.
    c. Italian lira and Japanese yen.
    d. Russian rubles and Japanese yen.
    e. U.S. dollars and Deutsche marks.

5. In order to reduce the risk of nonpayment, an exporter may require an importer to: [p. 603]
    a. Furnish a letter of credit.
    b. Obtain a parallel loan.
    c. Repatriate earnings.
    d. Pay with foreign currency.
    e. Expropriate assets.

6. Foreign exchange risk exposure that is associated with existing accounting rules is called: [p. 596]
    a. Transaction exposure.
    b. Translation exposure.
    c. Economic exposure.
    d. Political risk.
    e. Repatriation risk.

7. Which of the following is most useful in reducing political risk? [p. 601]
    a. A forward contract
    b. A futures contract
    c. A joint venture with a foreign company
    d. Hedging in the money market
    e. Exchanging currency in the spot market

8. Which of the following statements concerning international business is correct? [Chpt. 21]
    a. Currency exchange rates tend to vary inversely with their respective purchasing powers.
    b. The relationship between interest rate differentials and exchange rates is called the purchasing power parity theory.
    c. The balance of payments is the difference in a countries exports and imports.
    d. United Nations' member countries are prohibited from intervening in the foreign exchange market.
    e. Currencies always sell forward at a discount from the spot rate.

9. Which of the following statements about international business is correct? [p. 602]
    a. International business espionage is growing rapidly.
    b. Many former intelligence agents currently pursue corporate business secrets instead of national security information.
    c. A stolen laptop computer of a Fortune 500 executive will bring a high price from many foreign companies.
    d. U.S. businessmen tend to be naive and unprepared to deal with international business espionage.
    e. All of the above statements are correct.

10. The rate on Eurodollar loans is usually based on the: [p. 605]
   a. Forward rate.
   b. Cross rate.
   c. London Interbank Offered Rate.
   d. Spot rate.
   e. Interest rate parity theory.

Multiple Choice Answer Key - Chapter 21

1. c	2. d	3. d	4. e	5. a
6. b	7. c	8. a	9. e	10. c

Chapter 21 - Problems

21-1. Referring to Table 21-2 in the text, compute the amount of each of the following currencies that could be bought with $5,000 on October 19, 2000.

   (a) Austrian schillings

   (b) British pounds

   (c) Japanese yen

   (d) Indian rupees

21-2. (a) Which of the currencies in *21-1* above weakened relative to the U.S. dollar from October 7, 1998 to October 19, 2000? Which strengthened?

   (b) What was the percentage change in the value of each of the currencies?

21-3. Stacy Johnson is planning a trip to Europe. A local bank sells German deutsche marks for $.63 (asking price).

   (a) What is the exchange rate expressed in marks?

   (b) How many marks will Stacy be able to buy for $1,000?

   (c) The banks' bid price (what they pay for marks) is $.60. If Stacy charges all of his German purchases on credit cards and brings all of the marks (from *b*) home, how much will the bank pay for the marks in U.S. dollars?

21-4. If *The Wall Street Journal* reports the following exchange rates for the British pound:

Spot	$1.5523
30-day forward	$1.5483
90-day forward	$1.5462
180-day forward	$1.5456

(a) Is the British pound selling forward at a premium or at a discount?

(b) What is the 180-day forward premium (or discount)?

(c) If you exchanged 1,000,000 British pounds in the spot market, how many U.S. dollars would you receive?

(d) If you executed a 180-day forward contract to exchange 1,000,000 British pounds for U.S. dollars, how many dollars would you receive in 180 days.?

21-5. Courtney Walker has forecasted that the Swiss franc will rise in value relative to the U.S. dollar over the next 360 days. The Swiss franc is currently being exchanged in the spot market for .71 U.S. dollars per franc.

(a) If Courtney converts $1,000 to francs and deposits the francs in a Swiss bank earning 6% interest annually, how many francs will she have at the end of the year?

(b) If the exchange rate of Swiss francs increases to .75 dollars per franc, how many dollars will Courtney have after she exchanges?

(c) What rate of return will she earn?

(d) If Courtney's forecast proves to be incorrect and the exchange rate at the time she exchanges is .69 dollars per franc, what will her rate of return be?

21-6. Suppose the spot exchange rates of the French franc and the Dutch guilder are $.2030 and $.6194, respectively. On the same date, the cross rate between the French franc and the Canadian dollar is 3.6347 (francs to Cdn $).

(a) What is the rate of exchange (cross rate) of French francs to Dutch guilders?

(b) What is the U.S. dollar value of the Canadian dollar?

21-7. Sgt. Anderson is considering visiting Germany where he served in the military. He recalls that the exchange rate in 1970 was $.25/DM. He does not have access to current exchange rates, but he knows that the price indices for the U.S. and Germany relative to 1970 are 432 and 180, respectively. Using the purchasing power parity theory, provide Sgt. Anderson with an estimate of the current exchange rate.

21-8. The Jonah Corporation is evaluating a joint venture with a Belgian firm (Whale, Inc.). Jonah would be required to contribute 100,000,000 Belgian francs to the construction of a plant in Belgium. The current exchange rate of U.S. dollars/Belgian franc is $.0288. Jonah's estimated aftertax (Belgian and U.S.) cash flows from the project are 40,000,000 Belgian francs per year for five years. Jonah's required rate of return on international projects is 16%.

(a) Assuming that the exchange rate remains constant over the five years, should Jonah enter into the joint venture? Use the NPV method to make your determination.

(b) Assuming that the aftertax cash flows are repatriated each year and the following exchange rates are expected, should Jonah participate in the joint venture.

Year	Exchange Rate
1	.030
2	.032
3	.028
4	.024
5	.021

Chapter 21 - Solutions

21-1. (a)

$$Austrian\ schillings = \frac{\$5,000}{\$.0613} = \mathbf{81,566.0685}$$

(b)

$$British\ pounds = \frac{\$5,000}{\$1.4405} = \mathbf{3,471.0170}$$

(c)

$$Japanese\ yen = \frac{\$5,000}{\$.0092} = \mathbf{543,478.2609}$$

(d)

$$Indian\ rupees = \frac{\$5,000}{\$.0216} = \mathbf{231,481.4815}$$

21-2. (a) The Japanese yen strengthened relative to the dollar. The others weakened.

(b)

$$\%\ change\ of\ the\ Austrian\ schilling = \frac{.0613 - .0871}{.0871} = \mathbf{-29.62\%}$$

$$\%\ change\ of\ the\ British\ pound = \frac{1.4405 - 1.6852}{1.6852} = \mathbf{-14.52\%}$$

$$\%\ change\ of\ the\ Japanese\ yen = \frac{.0092 - .0075}{.0075} = \mathbf{22.67\%}$$

$$\%\ change\ of\ the\ Indian\ rupee = \frac{.0216 - .0236}{.0236} = \mathbf{-8.47\%}$$

21-3. (a)

$$Exchange\ rate = \frac{\$1}{\$.63} = \textbf{1.5873 } \textit{\textbf{marks}}$$

(b) *Marks purchased with $1,000 = 1,000 × 1.5873 =* **1,587.30**

(c) *Dollars received = 1,587.30 × $.60 =* **$952.38**

21-4. (a) At a discount.

(b)

$$Forward\ discount = \frac{1.5456 - 1.5523}{1.5523} \times \frac{12}{6} \times 100 = \textbf{-.863\% } \textit{\textbf{(discount)}}$$

(c) *$ received = 1,000,000 × $1.5523 =* **$1,552,300**

(d) *$ received = 1,000,000 × $1.5456 =* **$1,545,600**

21-5. (a)

$$Swiss\ francs\ deposited = \frac{\$1,000}{\$.71} = \textbf{1408.45}$$

$$Interest\ earned = .06 \times 1408.45 = \textbf{84.51}$$

$$Total\ francs = 1408.45 + 84.51 = \textbf{1492.96}$$

(b) *Dollars received at time of exchange = 1492.96 × .75 =* **$1,119.72**

(c)

$$Rate\ of\ return = \frac{\$119.72}{\$1,000} = \textbf{11.97\%}$$

(d) *$ received at time of exchange = 1492.96 × .69 = $1,030.14*

$$Rate\ of\ return = \frac{\$30.14}{\$1,000} = \textbf{3.01\%}$$

Note that half of Courtney's 6% return on the Swiss franc deposit was eroded by the unexpected drop in the value of the Swiss franc.

21-6. (a)

$$Rates\ of\ exchange\ of\ French\ francs\ into\ Dutch\ guilders = \frac{\$.6194}{\$.2030} = \textbf{3.0512}$$

254

(b)

U.S. dollar value of Canadian dollar = X

$$\frac{X}{\$.2030} = 3.6347$$

$X = 3.6347 \times \$.2030 = \textbf{\$.7378}$

21-7.

$$\textit{Comparative rate of inflation} = \frac{432}{180} = 2.4$$

$\$/DM(NOW) = \$.25/DM \times 2.4 = \textbf{\$.60}$

21-8. (a) *Initial investment* = 100,000,000 × .0288 = $2,880,000

Annual aftertax cash flow in $ = 40,000,000 × .0288 = $1,152,000

$NPV = \$1,152,000 \times PV_{IFA}(n = 5, i = 16\%) - \$2,880,000$
$NPV = \$1,152,000 \times 3.274 - \$2,880,000$
$NPV = \$3,771,648 - \$2,880,000 = \textbf{\$891,648}$

On the basis of the expected net present value, Jonah should enter into the joint venture

(b) **Annual Cash Flow in U.S. Dollars**

Year	Exchange Rate	Belgian Francs	U.S. Dollars
1	.030	40,000,000	$1,200,000
2	.032	40,000,000	1,280,000
3	.028	40,000,000	1,120,000
4	.024	40,000,000	960,000
5	.021	40,000,000	840,000

$NPV = \$1,200,000(.862) + \$1,280,000(.743) + \$1,120,000(.641) + \$960,000(.552)$
$\quad + \$840,000(.476) - \$2,880,000$

$NPV = \$1,034,400 + \$951,040 + \$717,920 + \$529,920 + \$399,840 - \$2,880,000$

$NPV = \$3,633,120 - \$2,880,000 = \textbf{\$753,120}$

The joint venture is acceptable even with the declining exchange rate in the latter years. If the exchange rates declined earlier, however, the situation could change significantly.